B 2009

WRESTLING'S
GREATEST MOMENTS

WRESTLING'S
GREATEST MOMENTS

MIKE RICKARD

ECW Press

Published by ECW Press
2120 Queen Street East, Suite 200
Toronto, Ontario, Canada M4E 1E2
416.694.3348 / info@ecwpress.com

LIBRARY AND ARCHIVES CANADA CATALOGUING IN PUBLICATION

Rickard, Mike
Wrestling's greatest moments / Mike Rickard.

ISBN 978-1-55022-841-0

1. Wrestling — History. I. Title.

GV1195.R53 2008   796.812   C2008-902418-4

Editor: Michael Holmes
Cover Photos: Matt Balk
Typesetting: Gail Nina
Printing: Printcrafters

This book is set in Adobe Garamond and Trajan

PRINTED AND BOUND IN CANADA

ECW PRESS
ecwpress.com

TABLE OF CONTENTS

Acknowledgments VII

Introduction IX

CHAPTER ONE: THE GREATEST MOMENTS 1

CHAPTER TWO: THE SUPERCARDS 35

CHAPTER THREE: THE TERRITORIES (1977–1983) 47

CHAPTER FOUR: TELEVISION 71

CHAPTER FIVE: THE ROCK AND WRESTLING ERA (1984–1989) 82

CHAPTER SIX: THE MATCHES 109

CHAPTER SEVEN: THE BEATDOWNS 118

CHAPTER EIGHT: THE TURNS 137

CHAPTER NINE: WE CAN'T HAVE ANYTHING NICE AROUND HERE!
(CELEBRATIONS GONE WRONG) 154

CHAPTER TEN: THE INDUSTRY STAGGERS (1990–1994) 159

CHAPTER ELEVEN: THE PIER SIX BRAWLS 172

CHAPTER TWELVE: THE MONDAY NIGHT WAR (1995–2001) 177

CHAPTER THIRTEEN: HE'S NOT SUPPOSED TO BE HERE! 193

CHAPTER FOURTEEN: CONTEMPORARY (2001–PRESENT) 201

ACKNOWLEDGMENTS

Success has a thousand fathers, and failure is an orphan. . . .

I've always wondered why so many writers have phonebook size acknowledgments, now I know. This book would never have happened without the help of many, chief among them Derek "The Dean" Burgan and Sir James Guttman. Derek got me started writing about wrestling for his site Gumgod.com and James encouraged me to write for World Wrestling Insanity. Both are great guys, and both represent the new generation of wrestling journalists — people who respect the sport but aren't afraid to question. Thanks also go out to Stu Saks from *Pro Wrestling Illustrated* for giving me a shot as well.

Special thanks to my editor Michael Holmes who was nothing short of amazing in helping to make this happen. His guidance and encouragement helped keep this project on track and helped me keep my sanity. Thanks also to Mallory Mahling who read the book back when it was still just a manuscript. Thanks to David Dale for proofreading and offering some much needed constructive criticism. I'd also like to thank the legions of fans online that filled me in on angles I hadn't had the chance to see.

During the last year, I've had a lot of encouragement from friends and family. Thanks to my parents, my brother Dave and his family, Laura, Tabby, Mighty Mel, Chris, and everyone else who asked, "How's the book coming?" and rallied me to make it the best it could be.

Of course, none of this would have happened without my grandmother; she got me hooked on wrestling and believed in me when not too many other people did. This book is for her and the generations of fans who have enjoyed the sport of kings.

And, last but not least, thanks to the men and women who have given so much to make professional wrestling one of the greatest forms of entertainment in the world.

INTRODUCTION

Hey! Gotta gotta pay back!! (The big payback)
Revenge!! I'm mad (the big payback)
Got to get back! Need some get back!! Pay Back! (The big payback)
That's it!! Payback!!! Revenge!!!
I'm mad!!

—"The Payback," James Brown

At its heart, professional wrestling is about two men (or women) settling their differences through violence. There is no problem that can't be settled by pinning someone's shoulders to the mat or beating a foe senseless within the confines of the squared circle. This formula has sustained over the sport for its 100-plus year history and continues to do so today.

In the beginning, ticket sales were the lifeblood of the wrestling business. While "putting asses in the seats" might not be recognized as a classic business model, it sums up the foundation of any successful wrestling promotion. With the advent of television and pay-per-view, ticket sales to live events, while still important, were no longer the only way for a promoter to bring in money. Nevertheless, promotional angles are still what draw in the fans, whether they're buying a ticket, ordering a pay-per-view, or watching television.

What makes a promotional angle (hereafter referred to simply as an "angle") great? For the purposes of this book, I've considered their originality, impact on future generations, and box-office success. Not all great angles have led to big bucks at the box office, but they've been memorable nonetheless. Even when a storyline is executed perfectly, all sorts of external factors can affect its success. At the same time, some historic angles were seen by a relatively small audience, but were just as important as those seen widely today: the proof is in the fact that their quality was recognized and later copied by others.

So sit back and let's revisit some of wrestling's most memorable moments from the last thirty years.

CHAPTER 1

THE GREATEST MOMENTS

All the world's a stage,
And all the men and women merely players:
They have their exits and their entrances;
And one man in his time plays many parts . . .
—*As You Like It,* **William Shakespeare**

When the principles play their parts well, professional wrestling is a thing of beauty, as much an art form as anything else seen on stage, television, or in the cinema. Professional wrestling elicits strong emotions, whether it's hatred for a heinous act committed by a heel (wrestling slang for villain) or delight in a babyface (the wrestler playing the hero)'s hard-fought victory. That, combined with the amazing displays of athletic ability makes professional wrestling unique. Whether it's called performance art, soap opera, or sports entertainment, wrestling is a complicated art form that has entertained people from all walks of life for generations.

In *The Seven Basic Plots: Why We Tell Stories*, Christopher Booker posits that all of the world's narratives can be broken down into any one of seven categories (such as overcoming the monster, rags to riches, and the journey/quest). While this may be true, storytellers have had no problem keeping things interesting. By the 1980s, film critics proclaimed the western dead, only to see a resurgence in the genre with movies like *Silverado, Young Guns, Tombstone,* and *Unforgiven.* People weren't tired of westerns; they were just tired of the bad westerns Hollywood had been producing for so long.

With wrestling, it's easy to see that there are classic storylines, angles exploited time and time again — the quest for a championship, revenge for being wronged, and the friend-turned-enemy (or the enemy-turned-friend) are just some of the most obvious. Anyone who has watched wrestling for a while has seen the same stories played out time after time, but they can still be entertained — as long as each new story is told well. That's the secret of good storytelling and it's the secret of good promotion. The same fans who watched Paul Orndorff turn on his friend Hulk Hogan could be entertained years later when Shawn Michaels turned on his partner Marty Jannetty. The story was essentially the same, but it was just as fun to watch because of how it was told.

While what goes on inside the ring is important, the story behind the match is just as crucial. Before a wrestling card or program can take place, the stories and angles that establish the motivation for the confrontations in the squared circle have to be put in place. Two wrestlers can put on an excellent in-ring exhibition but, with few exceptions, the best matches are the ones with compelling storylines driving them. A match does not have to be a five-star classic to succeed. Some of the weakest matches in terms of workrate or technical prowess have been considered classics because of the buildup behind them. Consider the showdown between Andre the Giant and Hulk Hogan at *WrestleMania III.* While the match itself was nothing special in terms of the action (nor was it, as it was billed at the time, their first meeting), the buildup was so strong the WWF sold out the Pontiac Silverdome and made millions off pay-per-view buys. The story of Hogan defending his WWF belt against his former friend and mentor, the undefeated Andre the Giant, became the stuff of legend.

What follows are the very best wrestling stories from the last thirty years. Every one changed the industry and the people involved and around them. These angles took wrestlers to new levels of fame and in some way transformed the industry.

1. WRESTLEMANIA

> *When there was not enough whale oil or coal oil,*
> *there were not enough lamps to go around.*
> *Some said that what was needed was social engineering,*
> *to move more people to the lamplight available.*
> *What was really needed was one Edison.*
> **—R. Buckminster Fuller**

Inspired by the success of a rival, Jim Crockett Promotions (JCP), and its big wrestling show *Starrcade,* and driven by his dream of transforming the World Wrestling Federation (WWF) from a regional promotion into a national one, Vince McMahon met with advisors in the fall of 1984. Under discussion were plans for a show he hoped would make *Starrcade* look like the high school gymnasium cards the WWF ran in small venues for fundraisers. *Starrcade* had brought in over half a million dollars of additional revenue by airing on closed circuit television in arenas across three states. McMahon was going to outdo JCP by broadcasting his show across the country, and in the process establish the WWF as a national brand.

> While he's often referred to as Vince McMahon Jr., the WWE chairman's full name is Vincent Kennedy McMahon, while his father was named Vincent Jesse McMahon. For convenience sake, Vincent K. McMahon is referred to as Vince McMahon while his father is referred to as Vince McMahon Sr.
>
> Pay-per-view technology had been around since the 1970s, but it was not really commonplace until the mid 1980s. Until then, wrestling "pay-per-views" typically referred to those fans watching events broadcast on closed circuit television at remote locations.

McMahon's advisors were not as confident; and in reality, they had every right to be worried. The last time someone had attempted a national wrestling show it had failed miserably — and not coincidentally that promoter's name was also Vince McMahon. To make matters worse, McMahon's failure was a case of lightning striking twice. His first venture into pay-per-view (as closed circuit events were known before technological advances made the home viewing of pay-per-view commonplace) was a disastrous showing of stuntman Evel Knievel's ill-fated attempt to cross Snake River Canyon. Undeterred by the Knievel fiasco, McMahon tried a second run at a closed circuit promotion by airing the much maligned boxer vs. wrestler matchup involving Muhammad Ali and Antonio Inoki. Like the Knievel event, this too failed.

Still, this time around, McMahon had every reason to believe that a wrestling pay-per-view would work. Not only did he have one of the hottest acts (Hulk Hogan) but he had worked hard to get the WWF broadcast into homes across the United States. McMahon had established a national presence via weekend syndication of WWF programming, along with a weekly show, *Tuesday Night Titans*, which aired across the country on the fledgling USA Network. The last piece of the puzzle fell into place when McMahon entered into a partnership that catapulted the WWF into the national spotlight: a venture with singer Cyndi Lauper.

Lauper, a rising pop star, first became involved with the WWF thanks to the machinations of her manager/boyfriend David Wolff. Wolff, a wrestling fan, initially recruited WWF manager Captain Lou Albano to participate in the music video for "Girls Just Want To Have Fun." The success of the video (in part due to the crossover audience garnered by Albano's appearance) caused the two to realize the sky was the limit when it came to a partnership with the WWF. Wolff met with McMahon and proposed a match between a wrestler managed by Lauper and a wrestler managed by Albano. It didn't take long for McMahon to set up an angle where Albano claimed the lion's share of success for "Girls Just Want To Have Fun" and insulted Lauper and women in general. An enraged Lauper then challenged Albano to a battle by proxy, selecting Wendi Richter to represent her against Albano's wrestler, WWF legendary women's champ the Fabulous Moolah. Thus was born *The Brawl To Settle It All*, where Lauper's charge battled Albano's in Madison Square Garden and MTV aired the clash to record ratings.

The success of *The Brawl To Settle It All* demonstrated just how big wrestling could be with the right mainstream publicity. But McMahon understood publicity was just one part of the equation. In order to build *WrestleMania* up as a must-see show, the WWF kingpin knew he had to have a red-hot angle. Drawing upon the success of *The Brawl To Settle It All*, McMahon staged an angle around an awards ceremony in Madison Square Garden, once again involving Lauper and Captain Lou. The event was supposed to honor the duo's fundraising work for research into multiple sclerosis and featured a presentation by TV and radio personality Dick Clark. In true wrestling fashion, the celebration broke down thanks to the unwanted arrival of "Rowdy" Roddy Piper, the WWF's number one heel. Piper took Albano's award and smashed it over the Captain's head, knocking him senseless. The carnage continued as Piper powerslammed Lauper's manager David Wolff and kicked Lauper in the head. Only the timely arrival of Hulk Hogan saved Lauper and her friends from further punishment. Happy to capitalize on the ratings of *The Brawl To Settle It All*, MTV vee-jays reported on the incident in Madison Square Garden, treating it as the equivalent of the Japanese attack on Pearl Harbor.

The angle generated tremendous publicity for Lauper, and more importantly, for McMahon's WWF. It couldn't have come at a better time either, as the WWF was then facing the very real possibility that *WrestleMania* was going to be a failure. As discussed in the book *Sex, Lies, and Headlocks,* ticket sales for *WrestleMania* had been so slow that there wasn't enough money to cover the cost of renting the 200 theaters scheduled to carry the pay-per-view. McMahon purchased the services of Bozell and Jacobs, a New York public relations firm in his bid to save the event, but that was just part of his strategy. . . . The WWF was putting all of its eggs in one basket with *WrestleMania*, and it couldn't afford anything less than a complete success.

Bozell and Jacobs' efforts helped, but the success of the MTV angle was the catalyst that drove *WrestleMania* into high gear. After the ratings brought in by *The Brawl To Settle It All*, MTV eagerly agreed to air *The War To Settle The Score,* a sequel of sorts involving WWF champion Hulk Hogan battling Roddy Piper to avenge the honor of Cyndi Lauper. The hour-long special aired live, and while the actual match didn't begin until late in the program, viewers were enthralled by the larger than life theatrics of the wrestlers (including an unforgettable interview by Piper in which he mocked rock and roll music and said MTV stood for "music to vomit by").

> Legend has it that rival promoters contemplated hiring notorious tough guy Bruiser Brody to attack Mr. T before the main event. No one has ever said how the promoters would have had anything to gain, given that the tickets to the show would already have been bought.

The short match was nothing special until the referee was inadvertently knocked out and Piper's partners in crime, "Cowboy" Bob Orton and Paul "Mr. Wonderful" Orndorff, arrived on the scene. Lauper raced to the Hulkster's rescue but the fans knew she was nothing more than a guppy facing off against three sharks. Fortunately for Lauper and Hogan, television tough-guy Mr. T was also in the audience, and he quickly made his way toward the ring to help the Hulkster. While T got beat down for his efforts, he gave Hogan enough time to recover and rally against Piper and his allies.

The War To Settle The Score outdid *The Brawl To Settle It All* in the ratings, and the mainstream publicity for the WWF was just as impressive. Before long, the buzz began to build; it was like the chain reaction of a nuclear explosion, each event feeding off the previous one and growing stronger. An appearance on Richard Belzer's Lifetime television show *Hot Properties* saw Hogan knock the host out with a headlock, earning additional publicity for the Hulkster as well as a lawsuit from Belzer for injuries sustained during the headlock demonstration (rumor has it that Belzer purchased a lavish farmhouse in France with the proceeds of his settlement and named it Chez Hogan). But unquestionably, the *piece de resistance* in the WWF's *WrestleMania* publicity campaign was Hulk Hogan and Mr. T guest-hosting NBC's *Saturday Night Live* the night before the big show.

Thanks to these high profile appearances, people swarmed to see *WrestleMania*. Just weeks before the show, WWF officials had considered canceling some of the closed circuit venues to cut their losses, but virtually overnight defeat had turned to victory. *WrestleMania* became a resounding success and it completed the transformation of the WWF from a northeastern territory promotion to a national juggernaut.

But still, the road to *WrestleMania* was not without potholes. The WWF faced challenges from both outside and from within. Foremost were the grumblings of certain wrestlers: that Mr. T was unworthy of a main event spot. "Dr. D" David Schultz, in particular took umbrage with T being featured at the top of the card. Stories vary, but Schultz reportedly tried to attack Mr. T before the show, either to knock T out of the event or to create such a buzz for himself that he would take Paul Orndorff's spot as Piper's tag team partner.

Mr. T himself proved troublesome. The bad blood between Piper and T wasn't limited to the squared circle. Behind the scenes, it seemed as if Mr. T and Piper couldn't wait for *WrestleMania* to lock horns. Things got off to a bad start during a press conference at Rockefeller Center when Piper squeezed Mr. T's head and commented that it felt soft. Unbeknownst to Piper, that was a big no-no as far as T was concerned. This led to a second press conference at Rockefeller Center —

and this time the TV star tackled Piper off a stage and security had to be called in to separate the two.

The problems with Mr. T continued right up to the day of the big event. Two hours before the show, Mr. T was nowhere to be found. When he finally showed up, his celebrity entourage was barred from entering Madison Square Garden; this caused T to threaten to walk out. Fortunately, cooler heads prevailed and everything was smoothed over.

The main event saw Hulk Hogan and Mr. T defeat the team of "Rowdy" Roddy Piper and Paul Orndorff after interference from Piper's bodyguard "Cowboy" Bob Orton backfired. Despite the bad blood, Piper and the star of *The A-Team* wrestled the match without trouble (T and Piper would meet in a boxing match the following year at *WrestleMania 2*). Mr. T carried his weight in the ring, despite concerns about his lack of experience, and the main event was well received.

WrestleMania also saw the return of fan favorite Tito Santana (Santana's real-life knee injury was incorporated into a storyline that saw him suffer an injury at the hands of the much-hated Greg "The Hammer" Valentine); the shocking defeat of the U.S. Express (Barry Windham and Mike Rotunda) at the hands of the foreign villains Nikolai Volkoff and the Iron Sheik; a wild brawl between Greg Valentine and the Junkyard Dog; the impressive debut of King Kong Bundy; and the career-saving victory of Andre the Giant over arch-rival "Big" John Studd (Andre had put his career up against Studd in a special match that could only be won by body-slamming your opponent). The card also saw rising women's wrestling star Wendi Richter (accompanied by Cyndi Lauper) regain the WWF woman's championship from Leilani Kai; a win for newcomer Ricky Steamboat (defeating Matt Borne); and a bout between Brutus Beefcake and David Sammartino that ended in a no-contest.

The show also featured a number of other celebrity appearances, from guest ring announcer (legendary New York Yankees manager) Billy Martin, to guest timekeeper Liberace. *WrestleMania* was an eclectic combination of showbiz and wrestling and it would herald the arrival of "the Rock and Wrestling Era," a period dominated by the WWF. While other promotions differed in their style of wrestling, the WWF's larger than life characters featured in short matches would become the product the public thought of as wrestling.

Professional wrestling was now a mainstream phenomenon. While the Rock and Wrestling Era might be called a passing fad, wrestling enjoyed a popularity that enticed new, more casual fans to the sport. It also led television networks to the industry once more, with NBC eventually airing *Saturday Night's Main Event.*

The larger audience meant additional revenue from ticket and merchandise sales. *WrestleMania* also demonstrated that pay-per-view was no flash in the pan. It would quickly become a major source of revenue for promoters, and over time, one of the biggest sources of income. Wrestling was no longer limited by how many seats an arena or stadium held: the industry had been transformed.

What the wrestling world needed was a Vince McMahon.

2. GENESIS OF THE HORSEMEN (THE ANDERSONS BREAK DUSTY'S ANKLE)

> *The heart is deceitful above all things,*
> *and desperately wicked: who can know it?*
> **—Jeremiah 17:9**

In 1985, Nikita Koloff set out to win the world heavyweight championship from "Nature Boy" Ric Flair. The two met throughout the summer, including a much-hyped match at the first ever *Great American Bash*. In September of that year, Nikita challenged Flair in a cage, and once more, he was unsuccessful. Never one to let sportsmanship get in the way of his ambition, Nikita (aided by his uncle Ivan Koloff) attacked Flair after the match.

Back in the 1970s, Flair had been established as the cousin of Gene and Ole Anderson, the infamous heel team known as the Minnesota Wrecking Crew. Interestingly, Flair had wanted to debut as a relative of his idol Dusty Rhodes, but Rhodes convinced him to make a name on his own rather than on his coattails.

While Flair was a full-fledged heel at the time, the fans couldn't help but cheer the American born and bred superstar as he defended the NWA title against the hated Russian (it didn't hurt that Flair was wrestling for his hometown promotion, JCP, where fans loved him ever since a babyface turn in the late 1970s). A hated villain throughout most of the NWA's territories, he rarely heard boos during matches for Jim Crockett Promotions, and perhaps Dusty Rhodes shared the fans' opinion, or maybe was just acting out of common decency. . . . Whatever his motives, the American Dream came to Flair's rescue, saving him from the brutal double-team and what could have been a career ending injury. The Russians soon bailed out of the cage, leaving Dusty alone with his longtime rival.

The fans cheered, no doubt happy Dusty had chased off the Ruskies, but there was probably more in their minds than gratitude. Could it be that Flair would form some kind of alliance with Rhodes? Ever since he arrived in JCP, Rhodes had earned the adulation of the fans and a partnership with Flair would be a dream team in more ways than one. Fans soon had their answer when Flair's "cousins," Ole and Arn Anderson, rushed into the cage and confronted Dusty. On September 29, 1985, Ric Flair proved that no good deed goes unpunished and set events in motion that would lead to the formation of one of the greatest factions in wrestling, the Four Horsemen.

With the Russians out of the picture, Rhodes extended his hand to Flair. Rather than take it in friendship, Flair snubbed the American Dream and walked to the door as the Andersons attacked. As the NWA world champion, Flair had to pick his battles. So it wasn't really a bad choice to leave Rhodes on his own. But Flair stopped when he reached the cage door. . . . Had he changed his mind about saving his rival? Fans quickly discovered that was the furthest thing from Flair's mind. Instead, the Nature Boy locked the door, leaving Rhodes at the mercy of three of the most dangerous men in professional wrestling. Inside this locked cell, the three men began to pummel Dusty with hands and fists, leaving him a crumpled heap on the mat apron.

The brutal beating was only beginning. The three wrestlers, all graduates of the Minnesota Wrecking Crew School of mayhem, targeted Dusty's ankle and worked it over mercilessly. Since his arrival in the mid-Atlantic area, the American Dream had been a thorn in the side of the Andersons and a constant threat to Flair's NWA championship. Now, he would pay.

The grim silence of the gathered throng turned to cheers when they saw some familiar faces appear at ringside. Rhodes' friends rushed out of the dressing room like the proverbial cavalry charge. But getting to the ring was one thing; getting into it was another. The Andersons and Flair fought off Dusty's would-be rescuers, using the cage as a fortress to repel Rhodes' saviors. Wrestlers scaled the walls, only to be knocked off by Flair and the Andersons. After what must have seemed like forever for Rhodes fans, an enraged Magnum T.A. finally broke through the cage door and made his way in. Unfortunately, by the time Rhodes' friends could make the save, Dusty's ankle had been shattered.

As Flair and the Andersons bailed, Magnum T.A. and the Rock 'n' Roll Express gathered around their fallen friend. David Crockett, one of the JCP announcers (and brother to promoter Jim Crockett) rushed in to check on

Rhodes. It was clear to everyone that Dusty was badly hurt. Ricky Morton held on to Rhodes as the American Dream's face showed the incredible pain he was suffering. Further complicating the situation was the fact Rhodes was still trapped in a cage. No one could get him out until the structure was taken down. After several minutes, a ring crew was able to take off one of the four walls surrounding the ring, as well as the adjacent ring ropes, giving medical personnel the chance to get Rhodes to a hospital.

The fallout from the attack was tremendous. Dusty would be stripped of his NWA television title because his ankle injury prevented him from making his mandatory title defense. (For years, most promotions followed the rule that a champion had to defend his title every thirty days or forfeit the belt.) Ric Flair had made it clear he didn't need the fans' cheers, nor would he court them. Flair was world heavyweight champion — and all he needed was the ten pounds of gold he wore around his waist.

The event has often been called the birth of the Four Horsemen (although the Horsemen would not officially become a group until the arrival of its fourth member, Tully Blanchard), with the Andersons becoming Flair's de facto bodyguards. Wrestling historians, however, generally consider the true formation of the Horsemen as having taken place the night Arn Anderson, Ric Flair, Ole Anderson, and Tully Blanchard gathered for interviews and Arn Anderson famously remarked, "The only time this much havoc had been wreaked by this few a number of people, you need to go all the way back to the Four Horsemen of the Apocalypse!"

The formation of the Horsemen ushered in an era that changed the way people looked at wrestlers. While the Horsemen were by no means the first heels to draw cheers from the fans, they were so over (popular) with fans that JCP gave them with their own line of merchandise (including, of all things, Four Horsemen vitamins). Over time, people began cheering whoever they liked, regardless of whether they were babyfaces or heels. Initially, this caused problems for promoters who were slow to adjust their product to meet the changing times. But eventually, it would lead rise of wrestling's greatest antihero, "Stone Cold" Steve Austin, and the ultimate evolution of the Horsemen: the New World Order.

3. AUSTIN 3:16 SAYS I JUST KICKED YOUR ASS

After Pearl Harbor was bombed on December 7, 1941, American morale needed a major boost. With sizable portion of its Pacific fleet resting in Davy Jones' locker, things looked bleak for the U.S. in its war against the Imperial Japanese Navy. During the early months of 1942, things worsened as the Japanese military scored victory after victory in the Pacific theater. Then on April 18, 1942, U.S. Air Force Colonel James Doolittle led a surprise aerial raid, bombing the Japanese mainland. Although the attack did minimal damage to Japanese property, it gave America a much needed morale boost and showed the Japanese government that the United States was not going to roll over and die. Although there would be a long fight ahead, this seemingly insignificant event signaled the beginning of the end of the war with Japan.

In 1996 another seemingly insignificant event provided a much-needed morale boost for a company on the losing end of a corporate war. At the 1996 *King of the Ring* (KOTR) pay-per-view, Steve Austin discarded the albatross of his "Ringmaster" character by developing a catchphrase that would personify the redneck badass that was "Stone Cold" Steve Austin. An off the cuff remark would resonate with fans, and within a year Stone Cold would be the hottest commodity in all of professional wrestling.

In the spring of 1996, World Championship Wrestling delivered a bombshell to the WWF by signing away two of its top stars, Scott Hall and Kevin Nash. The men eventually appeared on WCW *Monday Night Nitro* and launched what appeared to be a WWF invasion. At the June 16 *Great American Bash* pay-per-view, Hall and Nash brutalized WCW announcer Eric Bischoff and challenged WCW to a match that would spawn the New World Order (nWo). As the WCW storyline heated up, the WWF quickly became yesterday's news as fans tuned in to *Nitro* to watch the saga of the nWo unfold.

Stung by the loss of Hall and Nash (just two of many top stars who eventually left for WCW), the WWF was in desperate need of someone new to excite the fans. They got that and so much more when "Stone Cold" Steve Austin defeated Jake "The Snake" Roberts to win the KOTR tournament. While Austin's victory itself was relatively inconsequential, the promo he cut afterwards gave the WWF what it needed most — a controversial wrestler the fans would pay to see.

Interestingly, Austin was not originally slated to win the KOTR. Hunter Hearst Helmsley was supposed to go over, until an emotional lapse in judgment nearly sank his career. Earlier that year, when Scott Hall and Kevin Nash wrestled their last WWF match in Madison Square Garden, Helmsley joined Shawn Michaels in bidding them goodbye by breaking *kayfabe* (wrestling terminology for the code of secrecy wrestlers used to adhere to regarding the fact that the sport is "worked") to celebrate with them in the ring (Helmsley was a heel at the time while Hall was a babyface). While the Internet and the rise of wrestling dirtsheets had twigged fans to the fact all four men were close friends outside of the ring, Vince McMahon was furious at the blatant onstage disregard for kayfabe. WWF officials sanctioned Helmsley by changing his planned tournament win into an embarrassing first-round elimination at the hands of Jake Roberts.

Roberts' showing at the *King of the Ring* marked the zenith of his remarkable WWF comeback. Years of substance abuse had taken their toll on the Snake's career, sending him into obscurity in small promotions. In 1996, however, Jake returned to the WWF, proclaiming that he had turned his life over to Christ and rid himself of the personal demons that had prematurely ended his career. The always-charismatic Roberts cut heart-wrenching promos where he talked about his battles with substance abuse and how he was determined to salvage his once-illustrious reputation. After defeating Hunter Hearst Helmsley and Justin Bradshaw, Jake advanced to the tournament semifinals.

Mirroring Roberts' bid for redemption, Austin was equally determined to make a name for him by winning the tournament. Like Roberts, Austin had arrived in the WWF in January 1996, but despite a strong push, his character had misfired. While Vince McMahon had felt Austin would thrive being managed by "The Million Dollar Man" Ted DiBiase, and defending a pseudo-championship title known as the Million-Dollar Belt, Austin's Ringmaster character had flopped. Fate intervened when DiBiase left the WWF to join WCW. With the Million Dollar Man out of the picture, Austin was able to discard the Ringmaster gimmick for something closer to home — namely a redneck, beer-drinking badass who did whatever the hell he pleased and said whatever was on his mind.

With Helmsley out early, Austin worked his way into the finals, where he squared off against the veteran Roberts. Austin took the battle to Roberts, concentrating on the injured ribs Roberts had sustained in his semifinal bout. Although Roberts had beaten Big Van Vader by disqualification, he didn't look like a winner during the brutal post-match attack delivered to him by the 400-plus-pound sore loser. The final itself was almost no match at all, with Austin beating Roberts senseless, stomping him into the mat and working away at his injured ribs. When Austin began to tear the protective tape off of Roberts' ribs, WWF president Gorilla Monsoon halted the contest to see if Roberts was able to continue.

Roberts' body may have been beaten but his spirit hadn't been crushed. Roberts told Monsoon he wasn't prepared to surrender and he went after Austin, taking advantage of the breather offered by Monsoon's intervention. Caught off guard, Austin found himself reeling from Roberts' offense. Roberts gave the crowd the signal that he was ready to deliver his famous finisher, the DDT.

Unfortunately for Roberts, that brief pause was all Austin needed to counter Jake's attempted coup de grace. Austin drove his head into Roberts' ribs and quickly floored his opponent. After delivering more punishment, Austin effortlessly set Roberts up for the Stone Cold Stunner, and a three-count later, Austin was declared the winner and the new King of the Ring.

Although Austin's victory was impressive, it was nothing compared to what happened next. Walking to the podium, where a kingly robe, crown, and throne awaited the victor, Austin was greeted by announcer Dok Hendrix. Austin wasted no time in cutting one of the greatest promos in wrestling history: "The first thing I want to be done is to get that piece of crap out of my ring. Don't just get him out of the ring; get him out of the WWF. Because I proved, son, without a shadow of a doubt, you ain't got what it takes anymore. You sit there and you thump your Bible and you say your prayers and it didn't get you anywhere. Talk about your Psalms, talk about John 3:16 — Austin 3:16 says I just whipped your ass."

Stone Cold's words were the equivalent of throwing gasoline onto a fire. Austin's career seemed to take off overnight thanks to Austin 3:16. Although "Stone Cold" was a heel, the promo helped transform him into an anti-hero, and it soon spearheaded the WWF's more adult-oriented marketing strategy, an approach that would become known as "WWF Attitude." Austin 3:16 T-shirts began popping up everywhere as his popularity grew. Within a year, he would win the WWF championship, and although nothing would change about Austin's anti-authority character, he would go from one of the most hated men in wrestling to one of the most popular.

Equally important was the fact that this promo made fans notice the WWF again. While the battle with WCW was just beginning (in July of 1996 the nWo would form and take WCW to unprecedented success), the WWF had finally demonstrated it had something fresh to offer. In time, Austin would help lead the WWF to victory over WCW in the Monday Night War.

4. OH WHAT A RUSH! THE ROAD WARRIORS WIN THE NATIONAL TAG TEAM TITLES

The passion for destruction is also a creative passion.
—**Mikhail Bakunin**

If necessity is the mother of invention, then wrestling fans owe necessity quite a lot. The team known as the Road Warriors, comprised of two young men known as Hawk and Animal, came into being after Georgia Championship Wrestling (GCW) booker Ole Anderson needed a new duo to take the place of one dissolved after legal problems led to the firing of one of its members. Anderson's search would lead him to two rookies, Michael Hegstrand and Joseph Laurinaitis.

Hegstrand and Laurinaitis grew up together in Minnesota before a move prevented them from attending the same school. After graduating high school, the two ran into each other at a local gym and renewed their friendship. Both were avid bodybuilders and earned money bouncing rowdy patrons from nearby biker bars. Their passion for bodybuilding and their fondness for a good scrap led them to consider careers as professional wrestlers. Both men attended Ed Sharkey's school, where they learned the basics of professional wrestling. They each embarked on a singles career, with Hegstrand wrestling in western Canada and Laurinaitis moving to Georgia.

After some thought, Anderson chose Hegstrand and Laurinaitis to form his new team, christening them Hawk and Animal. Prior to their alliance, Anderson had toyed with the idea of pairing them against each other on separate teams. After changing their look from that of bikers to characters from Mel Gibson's post apocalyptic action film *The Road Warrior* (Ole took the suggestion of fellow promoter Bill Watts to add face paint to their punk look and the Roadies' trademark image was born), Hawk and Animal quickly became the top team in Georgia.

It was as obvious to Anderson as anyone else that the new tag team was as green as grass, but to his credit he knew how to book them succesfully. The Road Warriors wrestled what were essentially extremely short squash matches. Their opponents were lucky to get in any offense, let alone survive. The formula quickly paid off: fans were awed.

With the help of former wrestler "Precious" Paul Ellering (the Warriors' on-camera manager would also become their behind-the-scenes business advisor), Hawk and Animal soon began to capitalize on their growing popularity. Unlike traditional wrestling managers, who only worked in front of the camera, Ellering actually helped the Road Warriors with their bookings and financial investments. The partnership would prove to be lucrative for all three men.

With the Road Warriors as his centerpiece, Ellering assembled a heel stable known as the Legion of Doom which also included Jake "The Snake" Roberts, King Kong Bundy, and the Spoiler. The Road Warriors captured their first gold when they won a tournament to become the national tag team champions. Their first title loss soon followed, to the team of Buzz and Brett Sawyer, but they regained the belts when Buzz was fired. Over time, the Legion of Doom lost most of its members and the Warriors eventually ended up feuding with King Kong

Bundy and the Masked Superstar over the national tag team titles. After the Masked Superstar left Georgia, another tournament was held and the Warriors defeated the Junkyard Dog and Sweet Brown Sugar in the finals to win the national tag team titles a third time. After dropping the belts to Ron Garvin and Jerry Oates, Hawk and Animal left for the American Wrestling Association (AWA).

The mystique of the Road Warriors soon spread. Their popularity made them a fixture in wrestling magazines, and thanks to the national exposure of GCW, much of the world had the opportunity to see them dominate. When the Road Warriors wrestled, they rarely lost, no matter who the opponent was. The Warriors benefited from established wrestlers giving them the rub — and the time Jerry "The King" Lawler allowed them to kick out of his piledriver is just one example. Lawler recalls facing Hawk and Animal with Austin Idol at the Mid-South Coliseum: in order to help the Road Warriors get over, Lawler agreed to let them no-sell his piledriver, a move which, up to that point, Memphis-area fans regarded as a match-ender.

The Road Warriors arrival on the scene couldn't have been timed any better. They took off just before Vince McMahon's national expansion sparked an industry-wide boom. McMahon's assault on companies like the AWA and the NWA made for fat paychecks for wrestlers who could sell tickets. AWA promoter Verne Gagne was delighted to sign the Warriors after losing Hulk Hogan and many of his other top stars to the WWF. The Warriors were just as eager to sign with the AWA, especially when they realized the Georgia territory was in financial trouble. For Hawk and Animal, it was a chance to work with many of the wrestlers they had grown up idolizing, men like Dick the Bruiser, the Crusher, and Baron Von Raschke. Quickly, however, the hero worship was tempered by the reality of their situation. While Hawk and Animal were supposed to be heels, they were often cheered by fans who appreciated their brutal style and cool look and entrance music (Black Sabbath's "Iron Man") — they contrasted sharply with the AWA's roster of older stars (Crusher, Dick the Bruiser, and Verne Gagne), wrestlers who were anything but hip.

It didn't take the Warriors' long to wrest the AWA tag team titles from the champions, Baron von Raschke and the Crusher. Their popularity continued to soar as they tore through all the competition the AWA had to offer, as well as regularly besting everyone in Memphis's Championship Wrestling Association (CWA). During this time, Hawk and Animal notched impressive victories over Lawler and Idol, the Fabulous Ones, King Kong Bundy and "Ravishing" Rick Rude, and Larry and Curt Hennig.

While the Warriors were clearly a success in the AWA, not everyone there appreciated their presence. Some of the territory's more established teams resented the Road Warriors' quick success, perhaps feeling Hawk and Animal had not paid their dues. Another possible reason for the discontent was the Roadies habit of not selling (allowing their opponents to get in offense and look strong) for other teams. Things began to change a bit after AWA tough guys Larry Hennig and Crusher Blackwell worked a match against the Road Warriors and similarly refused to sell a move. . . . But despite the resentment of some of their peers, the Road Warriors remained the top act in the AWA, holding the belts for over a year.

After the Warriors defied promoter Verne Gagne by refusing to job (lose) to the Fabulous Ones, they began exploring their options in other promotions. Given their success in the industry, it didn't take long for them to find work. The team had become wrestling's free agents, working in both in Japan and the NWA. Still, before leaving the AWA, the Road Warriors agreed to drop the belts to the team of Jimmy Garvin and "Mr. Electricity" Steve Regal.

The success of the Road Warriors and Hulk Hogan led to an influx of body-builders into the ranks of professional wrestlers. Many promoters would try to recreate the Road Warriors phenomenon, but no one was able to match them. The appeal of Hawk and Animal was about more than just their look or the way they were booked to win. Both men had an ineffable quality, a mystique that none of their imitators was ever able to match.

In many ways, the Road Warriors were to tag team wrestling what Hulk Hogan was to singles competition. Tag teams enjoyed a renaissance during the 1980s, leading many fans to consider the period as the second golden age of tag team wrestling. The Road Warriors would remain a hot commodity throughout their careers: Hawk and Animal would go on to become the first team to win the world tag team championship in all three of the national promotions of the time (AWA, NWA, and WWF), a feat which was never duplicated. After splitting up in the early 1990s, the Road Warriors reunited in 1996 and continued working together until Hawk's death in 2003.

5. THE BIRTH OF THE NWO

Wrestling has seen more than its fair share of all-star factions: the Four Horsemen, the Bobby Heenan Family, the Dangerous Alliance, and Evolution are just of few of the most memorable. All of these groups have been successful, but none were as big or as influential as the collection of wrestlers who eventually made up the New World Order (nWo). Just as the success of Hulkamania led the

WWF to national glory during the 1980s, the nWo's popularity led to the seeming-invincibility of WCW during the Monday Night War.

> Wrestling fans weren't the only ones wondering who the third member of the nWo was; even wrestlers were curious. Chris Jericho recalls meeting with Eric Bischoff about working for WCW and quizzing him on the mystery man: "During our lunch, I asked him like a mark, 'So, who's the third member going to be?' He looked at me with a smirk and said, 'If I told you, I'd have to kill you.'"

During the summer of 1996, wrestling fans around the world had just one question — who would join Scott Hall and Kevin Nash as the third member of the Outsiders? At WCW's *Bash at the Beach* pay-per-view, fans learned the identity of the mystery man: the revelation changed the course of wrestling and nearly put the WWF out of business. That night, Hulk Hogan turned his back on his fans, joining a group that would soon become known as the New World Order.

At the time, the Monday Night War was escalating. Eric Bischoff had recently signed Diesel and Razor Ramon out from under Vince McMahon's nose. The signings were important, but what Bischoff did with Nash and Hall was even more important. He used their addition to the WCW roster to create the hottest angle of the year and to catapult WCW to unprecedented success.

The buildup to the match had been masterfully executed. First, Scott Hall appeared on an episode of *Nitro* with a promise that he wasn't there alone. When Nash finally arrived, a confrontation erupted between the two former WWF stars and some of WCW's top names. Drastically outnumbered, the Outsiders (as Hall and Nash were then called) wisely employed guerilla tactics. No one knew where or when they would strike, but when the Outsiders did, someone from WCW got hurt. After weeks of attacking the stars of WCW, the Outsiders were issued a challenge: they would square off against WCW's top three wrestlers. At the 1996 *Great American Bash* pay-per-view, WCW announcer Eric Bischoff asked whether the Outsiders were going to accept WCW's challenge. Nash and Hall said yes, but not before power-bombing Bischoff through the stage.

At *Bash at the Beach,* the mood could only be described as ominous. Throughout the show, announcers Tony Schiavone, Bobby "The Brain" Heenan, and "The American Dream" Dusty Rhodes speculated on who the third Outsider might be while talking about the importance of the match. WCW had assembled

Sting, Lex Luger, and "Macho Man" Randy Savage to defend its honor against Hall, Nash and a mystery partner. The main event was aptly named "The Hostile Takeover" — and it became a battle for the very future of wcw. Hall and Nash had made it clear that they were after more than championship gold, they were after the company itself.

Things became more and more tense as the card progressed to the main event. The Outsiders were locked in their dressing room but no one reported seeing anyone but Hall and Nash in the building. Then when the match began, only Hall and Nash entered the ring. Where was the third man? Announcer "Mean" Gene arrived and asked the Outsiders that very question. After Scott Hall called him "Scheme Gene" (referring to a wwf skit which had parodied wcw's overuse of former wwf stars), he told him the third man *was* already in the building. Then Kevin Nash boldly claimed that they didn't need anyone else to take on wcw's champions.

When Sting, Luger, and Savage finally emerged, Tony Schiavone was more than happy to see wcw with a three-on-two advantage. Unfortunately, it wouldn't last long. Early on in the contest, Sting delivered his patented stinger splash to Kevin Nash but accidentally knocked Luger off of the mat apron and onto the unforgiving concrete outside the ring. Luger was quickly taken backstage on a stretcher. "The Hostile Takeover" had become a traditional tag battle, but Team wcw would be at a disadvantage if the Outsiders' third man made an appearance.

Both teams seemed evenly matched but it didn't take Hall and Nash long to seperate Sting from the Macho Man. The two former wwf superstars delivered a tremendous beating to the Stinger and things looked gloomy for wcw. Finally, Sting capitalized on a mistake by the Outsiders and reached the Savage for the hot tag. Savage came in and lived up to his name by cleaning house. Soon, Nash and Hall were reeling as the Macho Man delivered flying axe handles to both. When things got too hot, Nash delivered a low blow that instantly immobilized Savage. With that, the Outsiders had regained the upper hand!

Or had they? The fans' sudden cheers could only mean one thing — someone was coming to wcw's rescue. And it wasn't just anyone; it was *Hulk Hogan*. The Hulkster had been absent, filming a movie, but he'd clearly returned in the nick of time. Just as he had done so many times before, Hogan charged the ring, ripped off his shirt and prepared to deliver some justice, Hulkamania style. Nash and Hall backed off as Hogan approached his old friend Randy Savage.

And then it happened, the moment that shook wcw to its very foundation. Hogan delivered his famous leg drop — to Randy Savage! "Hollywood" Hulk

Hogan was the third man the Outsiders had promised to unleash at *Bash at the Beach*. Fans immediately started booing and littering the ring with garbage as Hall and Nash congratulated Hogan on his turn. Hogan bounced off the ring ropes and delivered yet another leg drop to the Macho Man — a smirking Hall made a contemptuous three count, ending the debacle.

After the match, Sting and a referee helped the Macho Man limp back to the dressing room. Once more, "Mean" Gene Okerlund tried to get to the bottom of things. Okerlund had known Hogan for most of his storied career, something the announcer brought up as soon as he got the wrestling legend on microphone. Hogan quickly made it clear why he had betrayed both the company and his fans — he'd had spent the last two years doing all the right things, only to be disrespected by fickle fans. Now, the Hulkamaniacs could stick it. Hogan described Hall and Nash as the new blood of professional wrestling and told Okerlund that together they represented the New World Order. Hulk ended the tirade by twisting his usual catchphrase and asking the fans, "Whatcha gonna do when the new world organization runs wild on you?" As the show ended, announcer Tony Schiavone made his famous call: "Hulk Hogan you can go to hell — straight to hell!"

> Bobby Heenan's "But whose side is he on?" has been blown out of proportion over the years, with so-called insiders claiming he almost ruined the surprise of Hogan's turn. The reality was that *none* of the announcers (including Heenan) knew Hogan was turning heel. For years, Heenan had badmouthed Hogan whenever he was on the air (as part of Heenan playing his role as a heel) so his comments were just par for the course.

With the birth of the nWo it was like wcw could do no wrong. The excellent buildup to the match, the suspense over who the third man would be (the rumor mill suggested that the Outsiders' partner could be anyone from Bret Hart to other current wcw stars such as Lex Luger), and the freshness of the angle itself made for exciting viewing. Fans were so surprised by Hogan's turn that they ignored one of the biggest screwups in wrestling history when Bobby Heenan questioned Hogan's allegiance as he came out for what looked like a save.

Fueled by the success of the angle, wcw entered an unprecedented period of growth and popularity. *Nitro* enjoyed record ratings, while house show and pay-per-view business exploded. wcw went from a money-losing venture to a highly profitable division of Ted Turner's empire. For a while it seemed all but inevitable that wcw was going to run the wwf out of business.

One of the most prevalent clichés used by wrestling announcers is the one about a wrestler "going to the well once too often." And such was ultimately the case with the nWo. As successful as the angle was, wcw began overusing it. At first, the faction was so popular wcw decided to launch an nWo themed pay-per-view entitled *Souled Out*. But the pay-per-view was not well received. Then, when wcw experimented with an all-nWo edition of *Nitro,* the ratings sunk.

Despite the warning signs, wcw continued to overexpose and then dilute the nWo with the addition of more and more members. The once "elite" group soon seemed to feature more names than a phone book. Worse, some of the wrestlers weren't exactly the cream of the crop. It wasn't long before fans stopped wondering who was a member, but who wasn't.

An often-overlooked reason for the nWo's demise was that their opponents never got any payback. The public tired of seeing wcw stars beat up week after week while their tormentors never seemed to receive their commupence. The nWo's biggest stars were definitely over, but there were still plenty of wcw fans, people who wanted to see the stars of the home team, Lex Luger, Sting, the Four Horsemen, and others, get their pound of flesh. After months of abuse at the hands of the nWo, wcw's stars looked helpless — and their fans stopped caring.

After several failed attempts to recapture their original mystique, wcw finally realized there was nothing left in the tank and the nWo faded away. After the demise of wcw, Vince McMahon decided to revive the faction in wwe by bringing back the original threesome. The return of the nWo was met with much enthusiasm but not as much as the wwe fans had for the returning Hulk Hogan, who had been absent for almost ten years. As a result, wwe was forced to turn Hogan face and the nWo lost a lot of its steam. When Scott Hall was eventually released due to substance abuse problems (better known in wrestling slang as "personal demons"), the original nWo was left with just one member. New blood was once again recruited, but after Kevin Nash suffered an injury that would put him out of action for several months, Vince McMahon abandoned the whole angle.

Although the nWo died a slow, awkward death, the initial impact of the angle was astounding. The faction sustained wcw for two years before fans tired of it. Had the company managed to build new stars while it was riding high with the nWo, it might still be in business.

6. HULK HOGAN WINS THE WWF CHAMPIONSHIP!

Whatcha gonna do when Hulkamania runs wild on you?
—Hulk Hogan

HOW HOGAN BECAME HULK HOGAN

During a promotional appearance on a morning talk show, Hogan was introduced after Lou Ferrigno (a bodybuilder who played the title character on TV's *The Incredible Hulk*). The show's host was astounded at Hogan's size and remarked that he was bigger than the Hulk. When Hogan replied "That's because I'm the real Hulk," his colleagues began calling him Hulk and the nickname stuck.

If *WrestleMania* was the last step in the WWF's journey from regional promotion to national powerhouse, then Hulk Hogan's win over the Iron Sheik for the WWF championship was the first. Hogan's title reign would be the first salvo in Vince McMahon's ambitious plan to transform the wrestling industry.

Born Terry Bollea, the man who would become Hulk Hogan admired the wrestlers he watched at the Tampa Sportatorium as a teenager. Bollea also enjoyed playing bass guitar, and his gigs as a rock musician band allowed him to meet many of the grapplers he admired in the bars he played. When Jack and Jerry Brisco suggested he try his hand at wrestling, Hogan hooked up with Hiro Matsuda for training. Matusda promptly broke Hogan's ankle. (Back when the worked nature of professional wrestling was still in doubt, wrestlers routinely went out of their way to discourage wannabes to protect the tough-guy image of their sport). Undeterred, Hogan returned to Matsuda's tutelage after his ankle had healed, and Matsuda began training him in earnest.

For the next several years, Bollea worked in the territories using names like Sterling Golden and Terry Boulder; he even worked under a mask as the Super Destroyer. Bollea's size and charisma made him stand out but the demands of life on the road soon got to him. When homesickness got the better of him, Bollea decided to hang up his tights. But after a conversation with Terry Funk, Bollea got in touch with Vince McMahon Sr., the owner of the World Wide Wrestling Federation (the WWWF would be renamed the World Wrestling Federation in

1979). McMahon Sr. had heard good things about Hogan's work and had asked Funk to put Bollea in touch.

Fascinated by the man's size and charisma, McMahon Sr. persuaded Bollea to come to work for his promotion. He gave him the surname Hogan, reportedly because he wanted a wrestler who could appeal to the Irish-Americans in his promotion's fanbase. Managed by "Classy" Freddie Blassie, Hogan became a top star, working main event programs, including a long-running feud with Andre the Giant.

The Hulk's blossoming career hit a snag when he was asked to appear in Sylvester Stallone's *Rocky III*. The film role was a huge plum but it turned into a nightmare when Vince McMahon Sr. gave him an ultimatum: forget about acting or you'll never work for the WWF again. (He refused to allow Hogan to miss wrestling dates to participate in the film.) Hogan made the choice: he appeared in the film as "Thunderlips," a professional wrestler working an exhibition bout with the legendary Rocky. The role added luster to Hogan's already rising star and after *Rocky III* was released (and following an appearance on *The Tonight Show*), Hogan quickly found work in the American Wrestling Association.

Hogan entered the AWA as a heel, but the adoration of fans forced promoter Verne Gagne to turn him babyface. This was the real beginning of the phenomenon known as Hulkamania. While Gagne recognized Hogan's incredible drawing power, he felt uncomfortable with the idea of Hogan carrying the AWA world heavyweight championship. As a result, he put Hogan in bouts against AWA champion Nick Bockwinkel, but then came up with ever-more convoluted ways to end their matches in a way that kept the belt on the champ without Hulk actually losing the match.

Meanwhile, new WWF owner Vince McMahon (who had purchased the company from his father Vince McMahon Sr.) was envisioning taking the WWF to new heights. While he had a popular champion with Bob Backlund, he believed he needed someone with more charisma. McMahon searched the rosters of wrestling promoters everywhere before deciding to go after Hogan. Frustrated by his experience in the AWA and lured by Vince McMahon's promise of fame and fortune, Hogan left Gagne's promotion for a tour of Japan — and he never came back.

In order to put Hogan on top, McMahon had to get the belt off of Backlund. Babyface vs. babyface matchups were practically unheard of in the WWF (the Bruno Sammartino vs. Pedro Morales match from 1972 being a rare exception) of those days, so McMahon put the much-hated Iron Sheik over Backlund in controversial fashion. McMahon painted the champion in a sympathetic light by having the Iron Sheik sneak attack and injure him prior to defending the title. As a result, Backlund went into the match with a shoulder injury. The Iron Sheik capitalized on Backlund's weakened state and ultimately seized the laurels when he put Backlund in the camel clutch, a move that placed enormous pressure on an opponent's neck, shoulders, and back.

With Backlund locked in the camel clutch in the center of the ring, victory seemed all but certain for the Iron Sheik. No one in the WWF had escaped from the finishing move and it seemed unlikely that an injured Backlund would be the first to do so. But Backlund defiantly refused to give up as the Sheik continued to apply the hold. Outside the ring, Backlund's manager Arnold Skaaland watched with concern as his wrestler refused to quit. Realizing the power of the hold as well as his client's stubbornness, Skaaland became concerned that Backlund might suffer a career-ending injury. With no other course of action available, he threw in the towel, ending both the match and Backlund's title reign.

The Iron Sheik was now the WWF champ, but under WWF rules, he would have to give the former titleholder a return bout. Back then, the rules involving titles were sacrosanct to fans. So, Vince McMahon had to come up with a way to insert Hulk Hogan into the title picture. He devised an angle where Backlund's shoulder was reinjured, and then Backlund passed his title shot to the Hulkster. Hogan had already won over the WWF fans, and thanks to Backlund's generosity they had no problem with the Hulkster getting a title shot, despite his short tenure in the Federation.

The night of January 23, 1984, saw the Iron Sheik make his first title defense — against Hulk Hogan in Madison Square Garden. The fans in attendance went nuts as Hulk was introduced as the challenger. Wasting no time, Hogan attacked the champ from behind, making it clear he would do whatever was necessary to take the belt from the much-hated Iron Sheik. Hogan pounded the villain with clotheslines and knee drops, battering the champ as the fans cheered on.

A miscalculation saw the Iron Sheik launch a counteroffensive. After Hogan missed a charge, the Iron Sheik began laying into him with a series of kicks. These were no ordinary kicks, however — thanks to the custom-made boots the Sheik wore in all of his matches. Rumor was that the Iron Sheik loaded his boots with lead. . . . The many wrestlers who had fallen to his footwork would say this was fact. Realizing his challenger was not someone to toy with, the champion worked over Hogan's back, clearly softening him up for the camel clutch.

With Hogan softened up, the Iron Sheik placed the Hulkster in his signature hold. The fans gasped as Hogan found himself trapped in the champion's much-feared finisher. To their delight, however, Hogan used his incredible strength to power his way out. Hulk picked the Iron Sheik up and drove himself backward into the corner of the ring. Since the Iron Sheik was still holding on to Hogan, he absorbed all the punishment. Suddenly the tide had turned in Hulk's favor!

In mere seconds, Hogan regrouped and launched himself off the ring ropes, delivering a thunderous leg drop. A quick three-count later, Hogan was crowned the new WWF champion. Madison Square Garden erupted into chants of "Hogan, Hogan . . ." as the Hulkster basked.

For years to come Hulk Hogan would be the foundation of Vince McMahon's WWF, the sun around which everything else revolved.

7. I'M FROM HOLLYWOOD MR. LAWLER (ANDY KAUFMAN WRESTLES JERRY LAWLER)

A celebrity is one who is known to many persons he is glad he doesn't know.
—Lord Byron

As history has shown, celebrities and wrestling are rarely a good match. For every celebrity who has made a positive contribution to the business (Mike Tyson) there are a dozen others who have done nothing but waste the fans' time and money (David Arquette, Jay Leno, Mary Hart, Susan Saint-James, among others). Despite the theatrical aspect of wrestling, celebrities rarely do anything to justify their appearance in or near the squared circle.

But if ever a celebrity was the perfect fit for the mat game, it was Andy Kaufman. Kaufman built his reputation as a comedian who blurred the line between fantasy and reality. He delighted in pulling a con, often leaving fans and colleagues alike scratching their heads, wondering if they'd been had. A perfect example was Tony Clifton, the obnoxious lounge singer who opened for Kaufman's comedy shows. Rumors that the two didn't get along were confirmed when Clifton complained during an interview that Kaufman was getting rich off him. When Clifton was asked by Kaufman to guest star on the sitcom *Taxi*, Clifton stormed off of the set, infuriating Kaufman's co-stars. As outrageous as these antics were, they paled in comparison to the fact that the singer and the comic were usually the same person. Andy Kaufman was a master of the swerve.

During the early 1980s, Kaufman began challenging women to wrestle, offering a thousand dollar prize awaiting the first woman who pinned him. After winning his first few bouts, Kaufman declared himself the inter-gender champion of the world and began defending his title across the United States. His antics scored him more publicity including a feature in *Playboy*, but that was just the beginning. Before long, Kaufman would climb into the ring with a professional wrestler and learn just how real the business was (at least, that's the way it *seemed* at the time).

Andy Kaufman was introduced to Jerry "the King" Lawler by *Pro Wrestling Illustrated* editor Bill Apter. Kaufman had approached Apter about putting him in touch with Vince McMahon Sr. to work his inter-gender angle, but McMahon declined, feeling uncomfortable about putting an actor in the ring. Apter then suggested Memphis, a hot territory where his good friend Lawler starred. Kaufman and the King quickly went to work on devising an angle that would eventually capture the nation's attention.

A story began circulating: Lawler, the co-owner of Memphis Championship Wrestling Association (CWA) did not appreciate Kaufman's approach to the sport, believing he was degrading professional wrestling's already questionable reputation. Never one to shun publicity, Kaufman added fuel to the fire by sending CWA videotaped promos insulting the people of Memphis. After inciting the fans this way, Kaufman finally traveled to Memphis to defend his "Inter-Gender" belt.

Just as he had done previously, Kaufman invited the women of Memphis to try to pin him. Each challenger had three minutes to win a cash prize of $1,000. After he'd polished off his first three challengers, a Memphis woman by the name of Foxy squared off against the television star. Foxy was game and skilled, and looked to be a real challenge, but in the end Kaufman was once more victorious.

Impressed by the turnout generated by Kaufman's appearance, Lawler successfully lobbied for a rematch. The King told the fans that he'd agreed to train Foxy and would be in her corner for the return bout. To show the fans how confident he was, Kaufman added a stipulation to the match: he'd marry Foxy if he lost!

The angle turned out to be a huge success, with the Kaufman/Foxy rematch selling out the Mid-South Coliseum. Despite another strong effort, Foxy lost. Kaufman, never a gracious winner, humiliated her after the match, rubbing her face in the mat apron. Jerry Lawler came to her rescue and pulled Kaufman off. Kaufman, outraged, antagonized Lawler until the King finally shoved him to the apron. Kaufman grabbed the house microphone and told Lawler that he only wrestled women. And that he was going to sue Lawler for attacking him.

When Lawler next appeared on the CWA's *Championship Wrestling* television program he told fans about Kaufman's legal threats, but the look on his face made it clear that he wasn't taking a lawsuit seriously. What he did take seriously, however, was the way Kaufman was mocking the sport he loved. Kaufman was living in a fantasy world — so Lawler challenged Kaufman to a match with the hope of giving him a reality check.

On April 5, 1982, another capacity Memphis Coliseum crowd watched Kaufman battle Lawler in the main event. For the first few minutes of the match Kaufman stalled by running in and out of the ring, taunting the King but refusing to lock up. These tactics quickly wore thin, both with the fans and with Lawler. The Memphis legend grabbed the microphone and asked Kaufman if he was there to wrestle or to make an ass out of himself? The fans howled with delight.

Despite the fans' taunts, Kaufman was still reluctant. Lawler offered to let Kaufman put him in a headlock, the wrestling equivalent of a free shot. After some hesitation, Kaufman took the offer and clamped on a headlock. Quickly, he realized the mistake he'd made. Lawler suplexed the comedian effortlessly. The fans cheered as Lawler stood next to Kaufman's seemingly lifeless body. Lawler then signalled that the end was at hand and forested up a piledriver. Referee Jerry Calhoun warned Lawler not to execute the move (piledrivers were banned in Memphis and resulted in an automatic disqualification), but Lawler ignored him.

After piledriving Kaufman once, Lawler asked the fans if they wanted more. Naturally, they urged the King to piledrive Kaufman again. Playing to the crowd, Lawler lifted Kaufman up and hit his piledriver for a second time. Ring announcer Lance Russell announced that Lawler had been disqualified, but in the fans' eyes, Kaufman was the real loser.

True to form, Kaufman refused to get up from the mat, telling Lawler and Mid-South officials he would need an ambulance called in. Kaufman was going to milk the piledrivers for everything he could, despite Lawler earnestly pleading with him to get up. Lawler told the prone Kaufman it would cost $500 to pay for an ambulance. When Kaufman finally offered to pick up the tab, Lawler gave in.

After the match, the Inter-Gender Champion spent three days in hospital, selling a neck injury. In traction, Kaufman told reporters that while he once had doubts about the nature of wrestling, his injury was proof of just how real it was. Kaufman was so convincing he actually fooled the hospital staff into thinking he had compressed vertebrae. For Lawler's part, his "attack" on Kaufman earned him accolades from peers around the country, including a telegram from Houston promoter Paul Boesch commending him for defending the business.

Legendary wrestling manager Jimmy "The Mouth of the South" Hart, who eventually worked with Kaufman in Memphis, recalls Andy's dedication to the sport: "Andy was great. I believe he loved and respected professional wrestling very much — that he loved it as much as being on *Saturday Night Live*. He loved to entertain. From the time he arrived in a building he played it up. Everything he did, he gave his all. He didn't mind taking bumps and getting bruised for a pop — in that way, he was just one of the boys. He earned our respect; he became a wrestler."

Lawler's "assault" and Kaufman's "injury" made headlines across the United States. Kaufman and Lawler parlayed the national attention into an appearance on *Late Night with David Letterman*. Lawler defended his actions, telling Letterman that Kaufman insulted his sport. Kaufman began a profanity-laced tirade at Lawler after "the King" slapped Kaufman and knocked him out of his seat. Naturally, the appearance garnered even more publicity.

The angle was so convincing that for the next fifteen years, most of the world believed Kaufman had been legitimately hurt. At a time when most territorial promotions were at best regional, Lawler garnered national attention thanks to a well-built storyline.

8. DICK MURDOCH SPOILS DIBIASE'S TITLE SHOT

> *It is in the character of very few men to honor*
> *without envy a friend who has prospered.*
> **—Aeschylus**

When Dante ranked the seven deadly sins, he put pride at the top of the list. Had he been privy to the goings-on in the world of professional wrestling, he might have chosen envy. Many grapplers have turned on a friend at the sight of them winning a championship — sometimes at just the thought of it. One of the best examples is the time Dick Murdoch tried to end the career of Ted DiBiase.

Back when wrestling promotions carved the country into small regional territories, appearances by the world champion were as scarce as common sense is on WWE television today. When the champ did arrive, local wrestlers would fight tooth and nail for the opportunity to face him. For Ted DiBiase, however, the chance to wrestle for wrestling's most coveted prize nearly cost him his career.

Bill Watts' Mid-South promotion had earned its reputation as one of the toughest in the country. Watts, a former star himself, assembled some of the baddest names in the game, men like "Hacksaw" Jim Duggan, Jake "The Snake" Roberts, Steve "Dr. Death" Williams, and Dick Murdoch. He prided himself on booking Mid-South light on pretty boys and heavy on brawlers and shooters. Mid-South featured a "realistic" style, and Watts liked to believe he had the fiercest roster in the National Wrestling Alliance.

Not surprisingly, the chance to wrestle Ric Flair for the NWA world heavyweight championship did not come easy. As was often the case, the area's champion was the de facto number-one contender. Butch Reed held the North American heavyweight championship in Mid-South, and was named as Flair's opponent. When Reed faced off against Flair in a non-title match and defeated the champion, the Nature Boy was livid.

But Flair wasn't the only one who was angry. Dick Murdoch was bothered with Reed's status as the number-one contender, and he took out his frustration by beating Butch senseless. With Reed now out of the title hunt a new number-one contender had to be named. To Murdoch's chagrin, the next week, Ted DiBiase, a much-hated (but respected) heel who held the North American championship on four different occasions, was tapped for the honor.

A week later, Ric Flair (whose name was misspelled "Rick") appeared on Mid-South television to defend his world championship against DiBiase. Before the match, however, DiBiase was confronted by Murdoch — a former mentor — and told to step aside. Murdoch argued that it had been him who had trained DiBiase and taken out Reed, and that while his former protégé was a great wrestler, he was no Dick Murdoch. DiBiase countered by saying that no one had held the area's title as often as he had, and called Murdoch yesterday's news. Stung, Murdoch punched DiBiase, but the new number-one contender struck back, clearing the ring of the would-be challenger — but turning his back on Ric Flair. . . .

The always-opportunistic world champ wasted no time and delivered a knee to DiBiase's back, hurling him through the ropes and into the waiting hands of Dick Murdoch. Murdoch promptly launched DiBiase's head into an unforgiving ring post. DiBiase hit the concrete floor, hard. When he turned over, the camera captured the grisly sight: blood covered DiBiase's face and body.

While Murdoch walked away from the slaughter, referees tended to DiBiase. Ted's tag team partner Steve Williams also appeared to check on the condition of his friend. A cocky Ric Flair told the fans at ringside that DiBiase had blown his opportunity. He'd had his mind somewhere else when he should have been taking care of business. Then, butchering the English language just as badly as Murdoch had butchered DiBiase, ring announcer Boyd Pierce confirmed the Nature Boy's message: "I don't guess there will be a title match . . ."

But as I said, Mid-South wrestlers were notoriously tenacious. During the break, DiBiase had doctors apply a pressure bandage to his head and demanded he be allowed to wrestle. Then "Cowboy" Bill Watts appeared and told the fans that despite his injuries, DiBiase was going to get his title shot. Watts also warned that the match would not be for the squeamish. . . . (A cynic might point out that such warnings might also ensure fans stay tuned.)

When order was finally restored, DiBiase returned to the ring, his head heavily bandaged. Flair attacked immediately, trying to reopen his wounds, chopping away and sending him through the ropes. DiBiase had lost so much blood he was clearly off his game, but he fought with the heart of a champion, giving Flair everything he had. Fans chanted DiBiase's name, but Flair capitalized on the challenger's injury, punching and tearing at the bandage until once more the blood began to flow. As the match neared its conclusion, both wrestlers were covered in DiBiase's blood.

Like Flair, DiBiase was a master of the figure-four leglock, a painful submission hold. When the opportunity finally came, DiBiase locked it in on, hoping to submit the world champion. Flair, however, was close enough to the ring ropes to force the hold to be broken. Realizing his mistake, DiBiase went to apply the move again, this time in the center of the ring, but as he did, Flair kicked the challenger, once again knocking him out of the ring. Exhausted and almost incapacitated by the loss of so much blood, DiBiase lay outside the ring as the referee counted him out. And Ric Flair raised his own hand in victory.

Outside the ring, DiBiase drifted in and out of consciousness. The match was over but further punishment awaited. Murdoch reappeared and the announcers wondered whether he'd congratulate his former pupil on a hard-fought match. Naturally, consolation was the furthest thing from Murdoch's mind: he beat the bloody man silly, capping things off by delivering a brainbuster to DiBiase on the concrete floor.

Ted DiBiase won the admiration of fans that day, displaying tremendous heart in his bid for the NWA world heavyweight championship. At the same time, Dick Murdoch earned the fans' hatred for his loathsome display of envy. While DiBiase's title bid was unsuccessful, the match made him look stronger than ever and set the stage for his transformation from heel to babyface. The angle was a classic example of how to use a championship to promote a program between two wrestlers while maintaining the prestige of the championship belt.

9. FREEBIRDS/VON ERICH FEUD

> *Friday night they'll be dressed to kill*
> *Down at Dino's bar and grill*
> *The drink will flow and blood will spill*
> *And if the boys want to fight, you'd better let them*
> **—"The Boys Are Back in Town," Thin Lizzy**

For months, it seemed like Kerry Von Erich had the number of NWA champion "Nature Boy" Ric Flair. To the fans of World Class Championship Wrestling (WCCW), it was only a matter of time before Von Erich brought the illustrious prize home to Texas. But Flair wasn't going down easily. Time after time, he'd elude defeat by employing underhanded tactics, including getting himself disqualified.

The son of Fritz Von Erich, Kerry was just one of three boys who had already followed in their father's footsteps (eventually five of Fritz's sons would step into the squared circle). It didn't take the Von Erichs long to achieve rock star status in Texas with their father pushing them as the top babyfaces in the promotion he co-founded in the 1970s.

Flair's dirty tricks had not gone unnoticed by NWA officials, however, and after so many narrow escapes, Flair was ordered to defend his title in a steel cage — with a special referee appointed to police the bout for good measure. Texans were delighted at the news — and downright ecstatic when they learned they could vote for the special referee. It wasn't long before Michael Hayes was named ref, with Terry "Bam Bam" Gordy being appointed as a special ringside enforcer.

Hayes and Gordy were two members of a trio collectively known as the Fabulous Freebirds. They were ahead of their time, because the concept of three-man tag teams, outside of Mexico, was still novel. The Freebirds began working together in Bill Watts' Mid-South Wrestling, establishing themselves as one of the hottest acts in wrestling. With veteran wrestler Buddy Roberts at their side, Hayes and Gordy were in demand across the southern territories. The Freebirds came to World Class just looking to work a few matches. (At the time, WCCW wasn't doing great business.) Once there, though, Hayes and his comrades saw a potential money-making scenario with the Von Erich family.

The Freebirds debuted as babyfaces — the story was that David Von Erich had befriended them while in Georgia Championship Wrestling. Brother Kerry now had the chance to wrest the belt from Flair, and it would be the Freebirds who'd prevent Flair's usual chicanery. With an even playing field, Von Erich had no doubts he'd win. Unfortunately, his friend Michael Hayes — no stranger to rule-breaking, and a man more than savvy to many of the same tactics employed by Flair — wasn't going to pass up an opportunity to push the odds even further in Von Erich's favor. The cage match was a rugged battle. Flair's experience as champion was obvious, but Von Erich's desire for the belt was just as apparent. It looked like either man might prevail until Hayes got into Flair's face and took a swing at the NWA kingpin. With Flair down, Von Erich had a golden opportunity to score a pinfall. But Von Erich's sense of decency wouldn't allow him to become champ this way. To the disgust of Hayes, Von Erich gave Flair time to recuperate.

The Freebird had seen enough. He had given his young comrade a chance to win the belt and he'd thrown it away. When Hayes began to exit the ring, Kerry turned to confront him. Of course Ric Flair took his shot, kneeing Von Erich in the back. Kerry then crashed into Hayes, and spilled from the ring. Enraged, Michael Hayes assumed the worst. Then the angry Freebird slammed the cage door, on both Kerry and the Von Erichs' world championship hopes.

With a faceful of steel, Kerry Von Erich quickly discovered that honor does not come cheap, and the price he paid was the NWA title.

Hayes' attack turned the Freebirds from heroes to heels in a heartbeat. While the fans had fallen in love with the Freebirds, no one was more beloved than the Von Erichs, and no one could stand against them and hope to have the fans' support. Hayes, of course, had no problem with this, and he told Texas he could get by without its support.

The feud took World Class Championship Wrestling to unprecedented heights. Business exploded as the Freebirds waged war against the entire Von Erich family (patriarch Fritz even came out of retirement to battle the Freebirds at the *David Von Erich Memorial Parade of Champions*).

10. LARRY ZBYSZKO TURNS HEEL ON BRUNO SAMMARTINO

Like future champions Hulk Hogan and John Cena, Bruno Sammartino would get over with the fans through a combination of charisma, power, and an unbelievable physique rather than technical wrestling skills.

The age-old story of the student turning on their teacher has often been explored in wrestling, but never with the intensity of the feud that sprung from Larry Zbyszko betraying his mentor "The Living Legend" Bruno Sammartino. Their program would both reinvigorate an ailing WWWF box office and establish Zbyszko as one of the sport's most hated heels.

For nearly two decades, Bruno Sammartino *was* the WWWF. From 1963 to 1971, Sammartino reigned supreme as both the WWWF champion and the promotion's top draw. He sold out the WWWF's crown jewel Madison Square Garden so often (anywhere from 45 to nearly 200 times, depending on who you believe) that there were reportedly talks between the NWA and WWWF about Sammartino uniting both promotions' world belts. After dropping the title to Ivan Koloff in 1971, Sammartino took time off to rest and recuperate from numerous injuries. A marked decline in business led to the WWWF luring Sammartino out of retirement and putting the world title back around his waist. By 1977, after dropping the belt to "Superstar" Billy Graham, Sammartino had finally settled into semi-retirement, though he maintained an on-air presence as a WWWF color commentator.

Larry Zbyszko grew up idolizing Sammartino, and he certainly wasn't alone. The champion was wildly popular in the Northeast. Wrestling lore has it that on the night Sammartino lost to Koloff, the fans were so shocked that there was dead silence when the Russian was announced as the new champ.

Sammartino's in-ring heroics made many want to emulate him, but only one young man had the audacity to crash into Sammartino's home. After discovering where Sammartino lived, a teenage Larry Whistler went to the star's house and boldly invited himself in. It was an entrance truly worthy of the squared circle: Sammartino was relaxing in his backyard when Larry jumped through some hedges and said hello to his idol. Over time, the future Larry Zbyszko made several more appearances. Many would have been annoyed, to say the least, but Zbyszko grew on Sammartino, and before long, the WWWF champion had taken the youngster under his wing. First though, he made Zbyszko promise to get an education, warning him that wrestling held no guarantee of success.

Zbyszko became Sammartino's protégé, a relationship that clearly paved the way for his success. In an online interview, he talked about how much Sammartino's support had meant: "You know, to be Bruno's protégé was an honor. Everybody from the promoters to the top guys . . . at the time, to the older guys . . . everybody was very nice to me. Everybody opened their arms to welcome me to the business, and [they] would tell me things that they wouldn't tell everybody else. How to make money . . . psychology. I had the best array of teachers in the business. I have an education that no one else in this business has . . . because they opened up to me as 'Bruno's protégé.' It was all politics, and he was the man."

Sammartino soon spent part of his time away from the ring training Zbyszko. And the young man quickly became a rising star, achieving some success as co-holder of the WWWF tag team championship. (He and Tony Garea had defeated the Lumberjacks in the finals of a tournament organized to crown new tag team champions when Chief Jay Strongbow and Billy White Wolf were forced to vacate the belts after Wolf suffered a career-ending injury at the hands of Ken

Patera.) Still, despite this success, Zbyszko began to feel that his career would always be eclipsed by Bruon's very large shadow. And eventually that shadow began to consume Zbyszko's very soul.

Behind the scenes, WWWF officials were clamouring for Sammartino to return to the ring and give the business a shot in the arm. An astute Zbyszko realized that whoever worked with Bruno would have it made, and he wisely positioned himself to take that spot. After speaking with his mentor, the two worked out a program that would see Sammartino return to face his protégé.

It went like this: things began to simmer when Sammartino was scheduled to interview Zbyszko after a match, only to have his student walk right past him. When the situation repeated itself the following week, fans knew something was definitely up. Finally, Zbyszko let go with a heartfelt challenge. . . .

Things came to a head with Bruno finally agreeing to meet his protégé in an exhibition. His one proviso? It would have to be a strictly scientific competition. When they finally met, the two traded holds but it was crystal clear that despite his progress training under Sammartino, Zbyszko was still the student, with much to learn. As the younger man was outclassed in the ring, he grew more and more embarrassed. And finally, he exploded in anger. The result was a brutal wooden chair assault that left Sammartino bloody and lying in the ring. Just like that, Zbyszko had become public enemy number one.

Their next encounter saw the two clash in Madison Square Garden, with an enraged Sammartino clearly intent on destroying Zbyszko. Sammartino's rage got him a measure of revenge, but Zbyszko would have the last laugh when Bruno was disqualified. The rematch would be a lead-in to a cage match, with Bruno picking up where he had left off. "The Living Legend" proceeded to beat the man he called "the Judas of Judases," until Zbyszko took a powder and walked away from the ring.

Zbyszko's cowardice made the cage inevitable. Their final confrontation epitomized the rationale behind cage matches at the time — a babyface would finally get a heel opponent in a situation where there was no escape. Zbyszko would finally get what was coming to him.

Bruno wasted no time. True to form, Sammartino punched and kicked his former protégé as the fans cheered him on. Surrounded by a cage, Zbyszko would have to incapacitate his mentor if he hoped to escape. The fans ate up every second of Bruno's triumph — until the unthinkable happened and Bruno went down. With his mentor beating him to within an inch of his life, a desperate Zbyszko struck a low blow. Nowadays, low blows have become so commonplace that they're little more than a transition move, but in 1980, they were the

Zbyszko and Sammartino

wrestling equivalent of pulling a handgun. The crowd literally rioted. As Zbyszko recalls, "That did it, the fans started running through the outfield trying to reach the cage. Police officers and security guards were tackling them. It looked like a football game had broken out."

Sammartino found himself in the fight of his life, but in the end, he rallied and once he regained the upper hand. His fate sealed, Zbyszko was torn apart. The beating continued until Bruno was satisfied and he walked out of the ring.

The feud made Zbyszko's career. Not long after, he left the WWWF and worked for promotions such as GCW and spending much of the 1980s in the AWA until the promotion folded. Afterwards, he worked in WCW both as a wrestler and later, a color commentator on *Monday Night Nitro.*

Sammartino continued making occasional forays into the ring, but most of his time was spent as a color commentator. Eventually, Sammartino left Vince McMahon's WWF, disgusted with scandals and with the company's drastic move away from a style of wrestling he truly believed in.

CHAPTER 2

THE SUPERCARDS

Nothing succeeds like success.
—Alexandre Dumas

Wrestling as media giant? Few people could have imagined the many sources of income the WWE has created for itself. Whether it's providing content for cell phones, merchandise sales, magazine subscriptions, on demand television, or pay-per-view, the WWE seems to have its hands in just about everything. Consider the WWE's 2007 second quarter profit report, which broke down profits from items other than ticket and PPV sales:

Rights fees. . . . . $23.9 million
Home video sales . . . . $14.8 million
WWE magazine . . . . $3.7 million
WWE 24/7 . . . . $1.3 million
WWE.com. $4.6 million

Like many forms of entertainment, professional wrestling has evolved into a sophisticated business with many sources of revenue. Whether it's a local independent selling T-shirts and DVDs or the global empire known as the WWE (which fills its coffers through everything from merchandise to its own cable television channel), promoters have learned to how to draw income from almost everything associated with the business.

Given all of the ways a promoter can make money today, it's hard to imagine a time when wrestling's revenue was limited to ticket sales at live events. In the old days even TV revenues were minimal, as most promoters had to pay just to get their shows on the air. Not that long ago, "putting asses in the seats" was the bread and butter of the business.

Like any wise business owner, old school wrestling promoters were always looking to expand their profits. Unfortunately, their options were limited by the technology of the time. Until the introduction of closed-circuit television, even if a promoter ran a wrestling show every night of the week, profits were capped by an arena's size.

Running shows in large venues was not without risk. The bigger the building; the bigger the potential profit — and the bigger the potential loss. Renting a stadium could be disastrous if a promoter couldn't fill the building. And in outdoor arenas, the weather was a constant problem. Acts of nature could postpone shows, and while rain checks might be issued, scheduling commitments often made it difficult to rebook star performers. The promoters who took the chance knew that there had to be something very special about a show if they hoped to fill a stadium. A supershow had to be a must-see event, drawing in not only the core audience but also more casual fans. To do this, promoters often brought in big name stars from other territories and featured matches that were the climax to hot angles.

Bill Watts' booking of the New Orleans Superdome is a good example of how supercards should be promoted. Watts' shows starred some of the biggest names in wrestling, and featured payoffs to his territory's biggest feuds. One such extravaganza climaxed with a dog collar match between Michael Hayes and the Junkyard Dog. Thousands upon thousands jammed the Superdome to see the much-anticipated bout, making it one of the greatest box office successes of its time.

As pay-per-view became more common, supercards continued, but they evolved from big shows built around filling a stadium to ones geared toward garnering pay-per-view buys. With pay-per-view quickly becoming the biggest source of revenue, promoters had less incentive to schedule stadium house shows. There was no need to risk half-empty buildings if a million fans were buying the show at home. In recent years, however, the WWE has revisited the idea of big stadium shows, booking *WrestleMania* in some of North America's largest venues.

SHOWDOWN AT SHEA

In the 1970s, fans of the World Wide Wrestling Federation bore witness to an event that was wrestling's equivalent of the Olympics. Like the Olympics, the spectacle would occur once every four years and would feature some of the greatest athletes from around the world. It became known as the *Showdown at Shea*, and it would create wrestling memories that would last a lifetime.

While Madison Square Garden has always been associated with the World Wrestling Federation (the arena is known as "the Mecca of professional wrestling"), it was far too small to house the blockbuster World Wide Wrestling Federation promoter Vince McMahon Sr. had in mind. McMahon had proven that he could sell out the Garden on a regular basis; with the right event, he believed he could also fill the much larger Shea Stadium.

Best known as the home of the New York Mets, Shea Stadium has hosted some of the biggest events in New York history, including legendary concerts by the Beatles, an appearance by Pope John Paul II, and the reenactment of the marriage of Marvel comics icon Spider-Man to his girlfriend Mary Jane Watson. To WWF fans, it would be remembered for the three legendary shows that took place there.

The first *Showdown at Shea* featured a main event between Bruno Sammartino and WWWF champion Pedro Morales. The two men were undoubtedly the most beloved stars in the promotion, leading fans to wonder why two good friends were now fighting one another. No one knew for sure. There was the possibility of a hidden grudge; or maybe it was just a matter of pride, with the former titleholder needing to know if he was better than the current. Whatever the true reason, the match was staged when Morales and Sammartino, wrestling as a tag team, were both blinded by a handful of salt thrown by the villainous Professor Tanaka. Unable to distinguish friend from foe, the two accidentally brawled with each other. Fortunately, by the time they faced off on September 1, 1972, their friendship had been repaired. Fans at Shea were treated to a masterful seventy-five-minute draw between the equals.

The second *Showdown at Shea* would see another Sammartino main event, this time pitting Bruno against Stan Hansen. The supercard also featured the infamous match between Muhammed Ali and Japanese wrestler Antonio Inoki that was being broadcast via closed circuit. The wwwf was just one of several promotions that ran a live show the around much-hyped boxer/wrestler bout. The second *Showdown* reportedly drew 32,000 fans, nearly 10,000 more than the first.

The third and final Shea supercard proved even more successful. Once again, the wwwf called upon Sammartino to fill the seats, this time putting Bruno in a steel cage with his former protégé, Larry Zbyszko. The 1980 *Showdown* featured several other big matches, including a heel Hulk Hogan taking on Andre the Giant. Andre had sworn revenge on Hogan after receiving a bloody beatdown at his hands on wwwf television. Eight years later, the two would main-event one of the biggest wrestling shows in history. On this occasion, however, Hogan vs. Andre was just one of the many preliminaries leading to the main event. The match saw Andre score a pinfall victory, only to receive a brutal post-match beating.

Another special bout featured the dream team of Pedro Morales and champion Bob Backlund taking on the Wild Samoans for the wwwf tag team belts in a two out of three falls affair. The Samoans had terrorized the wwwf's tag ranks but they met their match when they faced Morales and Backlund. The babyfaces proved their superiority by beating the Samoans in two straight falls. Their title reign would be short-lived, however, as wwwf rules stated a champion could only hold one belt at a time, forcing Backlund to surrender the belt so he could keep the more prestigious wwwf heavyweight title. (The Samoans would regain the title in a subsequent tournament.)

The third Shea supercard would set an outdoor attendance record for professional wrestling, with 36,295 reportedly in attendance. But it would also be the last *Showdown*. Whether it was the changing nature of the business, Vince McMahon taking over his father's company, or something else entirely, Shea Stadium would not host another New York supercard.

THE REAL GRANDADDY OF THEM ALL

Despite Vince McMahon dubbing *WrestleMania* the "granddaddy of them all," longtime wrestling fans know that the honor really belongs to Jim Crockett Promotions' (JCP) *Starrcade*. While that supercard wasn't wrestling's most widely broadcast closed-circuit show, it was the one that really demonstrated how lucrative pay-per-view could be. The success of *Starrcade* not only led to future, similarly named mega-events, it inspired Vince McMahon to run *WrestleMania* on closed-circuit television for a nationwide audience.

Before pay-per-views and cable television, house shows were where wrestlers ultimately settled their differences. Television was just a means of hooking people into storylines. Holiday events like JCP's Thanksgiving shows or WCCW's annual Christmas card were hyped by promoters as the ultimate house show — the place where long-running feuds ended and babyfaces got their final revenge on their heel opponents. The 1983 *Starrcade* event was no exception. But because the card was available via closed-circuit television, fans elsewhere were able to see the sold-out show.

Wrestling had already embraced CC TV. When Madison Square Garden was sold out, fans could pay to watch the show from the Felt Forum (now known as the Theater at Madison Square Garden). And as I've already mentioned, the Ali vs. Inoki match had been widely broadcast to allow individual wrestling promoters to build a live event around the fascinating boxer/wrestler battle. What was different about *Starrcade* was that the entire event would be broadcast to several cities in the JCP territory.

The card was main-evented by NWA champion Harley Race facing Ric Flair in a steel cage. Christened "A Flair for the Gold," the story behind the match was that former NWA champion Flair would finally get Race in a place where no one could help him. (Race had previously put a $25,000 bounty on Flair, and this had led to Dick Slater and Bob Orton Jr. nearly ending his career.)

The pay-per-view was a bold move. At the time, Crockett was already engulfed in the war with arch-rival Vince McMahon's WWF. McMahon was more than willing to sabotage his competition at every opportunity and he flew Harley Race north just days before the show, offering him $250,000 if he jumped to the WWF. Race refused, and JCP's show went on as planned. Had he taken McMahon's offer, there is no telling what would have happened to *Starrcade*.

Instead, the supercard was a tremendous success. And *Starrcade* forced promoters to reconsider the way they did business. Roughly 45,000 watched the show in person or on closed circuit. Soon, the rise of cable made promoters realize they could offer supershows to fans in numbers previously unimaginable. And as more and more homes became wired to watch cable, pay-per-view took over the wrestling business.

As far as the actual wrestling goes, with special referee Gene Kiniski looking on, despite a fierce defense by Race, Flair prevailed after hitting a high cross-body block off the top rope. After the match, Rufus R. Jones, Ricky Steamboat, and Angelo "King Kong" Mosca ran into the ring to congratulate him on his victory. Flair then cut an emotional promo, thanking the fans for their support.

Besides its main event, *Starrcade* is probably best remembered for the brutal dog collar match between Greg "The Hammer" Valentine and "Rowdy" Roddy Piper. (The men were connected by a long steel chain.) This match was signed after Valentine had injured Piper during a battle over the United States heavyweight championship. Piper would defeat Valentine by pinfall, earning him a modicum of revenge.

DAVID VON ERICH MEMORIAL PARADE OF CHAMPIONS

The *David Von Erich Memorial Parade of Champions* represents the zenith of World Class Championship Wrestling's popularity. The supercard had an unbelievable turnout and featured a who's who of the mat world. The bittersweet nature of the card was transcended when hometown hero Kerry Von Erich finally captured the NWA world championship from Ric Flair.

The saying "everything is bigger in Texas" definitely fit Fritz Von Erich's WCCW. The promotion was run like a small territory, but its scope and impact made it seem more like a national venture. Offering some of the biggest names in the industry, it boasted state of the art production values, and was syndicated around the world. WCCW offered a stark contrast to the World Wrestling Federation. While Fritz Von Erich was certainly in wrestling to make money, he followed no apparent blueprint toward national success.

With memories of the Freebirds/Von Erich feud still igniting the popular imagination, WCCW was riding a wave of success. Then, tragedy struck. On February 10, 1984, David Von Erich was found dead in Japan. Before his untimely death, David was rumored to be in line to win the NWA title: he'd had earned the reputation as a draw in WCCW, as well as in other NWA territories like St. Louis, and Florida's Championship Wrestling. His work rate and charisma made him a viable candidate for a title shot his father lobbied heavily for.

Following David's death, Fritz Von Erich was able to sway the rest of the NWA to give his son Kerry the championship. (Fritz sat on the NWA's board of directors and always held considerable influence when it came time to name a new champion.) While Kerry was not as experienced as David, he was nonetheless a legitimate babyface contender.

To capitalize on the pending win, Fritz Von Erich arranged for a show designed to honor the memory of his fallen son. Naturally, Kerry dedicated his effort to his late brother, with the story being this was Kerry's big chance to vindicate the family and win the prize his older brother seemed destined for. Fritz had appeared on WCCW television in the past, and talked of how one of his sons would one day lift the belt that had eluded him. It was like manifest destiny, Von Erich style. The Memorial was held in Irvin, Texas, at Texas Stadium. With business running strong and the strength of the Von Erich/Flair match, the card drew between 32,000 and 40,000 fans (depending on which number was accurate, it may have surpassed the attendance record of 1980's *Showdown at Shea*). Texans went home happy that day, with Von Erich using a backslide to pin the champion cleanly. After the match, Flair shook Von Erich's hand, acknowledging that Kerry was the better man that day. Von Erich's title reign would be short, however, with Kerry dropping the belt back to Flair less than three weeks later — ironically in Japan. It's been reported that Von Erich's unreliability led to the NWA only granting him a transitional reign.

The Texas supercard featured other matches that capitalized on popular feuds, including "Gentleman" Chris Adams teaming with Sunshine to defeat Jimmy Garvin and Precious; Kevin and Mike Von Erich teaming with their father Fritz (who came out of retirement for the bout) to defeat the Fabulous Freebirds for the WCCW six-man tag team championship; and Kamala fighting to a draw against the Great Kabuki. Further matches included the Junkyard Dog beating the Missing Link by disqualification; Butch Reed defeating Chick Donovan; and the team of Buck Zumhofe and "Iceman" King Parsons defeating the Super Destroyers (Bill and Scott Irwin) for the WCCW American tag team championship.

The supercard was not the first event to be known as the *Parade of Champions*: a 1972 event of the same name had been main-evented by none other than Fritz Von Erich challenging NWA champion Dory Funk Jr. That show was actually run by "Big Time Wrestling," the Texas promotion that was later bought out by Fritz and renamed WCCW. The success of the *David Von Erich Memorial Parade of Champions* would spawn future incarnations over the next four years, with the last being held on May 8, 1988.

WRESTLEMANIA III: BIGGER, BETTER, BADDER

As big and as important as the first *WrestleMania* was, *WrestleMania III* actually topped it. The third incarnation proved the event was no fluke, and it also made it clear that Vince McMahon was no one-hit wonder. If the first *WrestleMania* started the ball rolling, *WrestleMania III* shut the door on the WWF's competitors. When it was all said and done, no one questioned who the big dog was. (And even when WCW was pushing McMahon to the brink of bankruptcy during the Monday Night War, people still associated wrestling with the WWF.)

After the success of *WrestleMania I*, Vince McMahon took things to the next level. *WrestleMania 2* was to be bigger and better. Not only would the show feature three main events — it would actually be held in three cities simultaneously: beginning in Uniondale, New York's Nassau Coliseum, then traveling to Chicago's Rosemont Horizon, before concluding in Los Angeles at the Memorial Sports Arena.

> Wrestling magazines like *Pro Wrestling Illustrated* told everyone that the main-eventers, contrary to the hype, had met previously. Still, it was clear that Hogan vs. Andre was a true dream match. While the actual paid attendance of *WrestleMania III* has been disputed, it was clearly a record-breaking wrestling crowd.

And while *WrestleMania 2* was far from a disaster, it failed to meet McMahon's goals. Clearly, something had gone wrong. The bigger-is-better approach had failed, primarily by focusing too much on celebrity and the multiple site gimmick, rather than on the actual wrestling. While there were several good matches on the card, there was no blockbuster main event to capture the hearts of the fans the way the booking of *WrestleMania* had.

Billed as "Bigger, Better, Badder," *WrestleMania III* would deliver. It featured one of the most anticipated matches in wrestling history — an epic encounter between Andre the Giant and WWF champion Hulk Hogan. Andre, one of the most beloved wrestlers in WWF (and wrestling) history, was in the twilight of his career, perhaps even looking back at what might have been. The Giant had won countless matches and was considered "the King of the Battle Royal," but he had never held a world championship. Now, in the storyline leading up to the big day, Andre was seen as a bitter monster, looking for one last shot at glory and willing to do whatever was necessary to achieve it — including turning heel and aligning himself with one of Hogan's most bitter foes, manager Bobby "The Brain" Heenan. To the fans, Hogan talked of how Andre was the man who'd inspired him to become a wrestler, and of how he was shocked and disappointed by Andre's new attitude.

Wrestling is all about hype — and never was this made more apparent than in the run-up to *WrestleMania III*. Vince McMahon knew he had a great angle, and he wasn't about to let the facts get in the way of a good story. He touted the match as the first encounter between Hogan and Andre and claimed that Andre the Giant had never been pinned. Of course, none of this was true . . . but it made for a great story. The two *had* met before, but this time, clearly, the situation was very different and the storyline so much more powerful. WWF announcer Gorilla Monsoon would put it best, describing the match as "the irresistible force meets the immovable object . . ."

It was a case of the stars being in perfect alignment for the WWF. Andre vs. Hogan was promoted perfectly, painstakingly built toward in the months leading to *WrestleMania*. The fans' enthusiasm was shown at the box office. In the end, the show boasted a live attendance of 93,173, filling WWF coffers with a reported $17 million.

The match would be largely remembered for Hulk's bodyslam of the Giant, but in reality it was arguably, in terms of match quality, one of the worst main events in *WrestleMania* history. Fortunately there were several very good bouts on the undercard, including a legendary encounter between Ricky "The Dragon" Steamboat and "Macho Man" Randy Savage. The Steamboat/Savage battle is still considered by many fans as the greatest *WrestleMania* match ever.

Unlike *WrestleMania 2*, the third incarnation did not rely on a slew of unwanted celebrity appearances. While there were special guests, they didn't overshadow the pay-per-view. Some were even memorable: with Alice Cooper appearing in Jake Roberts' corner for his match against the Honky Tonk Man, Aretha Franklin singing "America the Beautiful," and goofy baseball Hall of Famer Bob Uecker being throttled by Andre.

Despite the wild success of *WrestleMania III*, the WWF did not contemplate another large stadium show for four years. The WWF originally scheduled *WrestleMania VII* for the Los Angeles Coliseum, but the show was moved to the Los Angeles Memorial Sports Arena at the last minute. (The WWF claimed security concerns caused the move; skeptics claimed it was poor ticket sales — due to the nature of the show's main event, which was said to exploit the Gulf War crisis between the United States and Iraq.) It wasn't until *WrestleMania XXIV* that the company's biggest PPV would be held in another outdoor stadium. The

2008 event saw more than 74,000 fans fill Orlando, Florida's Citrus Bowl, giving WWE its biggest *WrestleMania* ever in terms of gross ticket sales.

THE CROCKETT CUP

The 1980s saw an explosion in the popularity of tag teams, leading many to call the decade "the second golden age of tag team wrestling." The *Jim Crockett Cup* was an ambitious tag team tournament held to honor the legendary founder of Jim Crockett Promotions. For decades, Jim Crockett Sr.'s Mid-Atlantic promotion had revolved around tag matches, and even after the territory changed gears in the mid-1970s to focus on singles, it remained a hotbed of duo competition. It was only right, therefore, that the tournament named in his honor revolve around tag teams.

The Jim Crockett Sr. Memorial Cup was a showcase of the finest teams from not only JCP, but also from other promotions like the Universal Wrestling Federation (UWF). The show was took place at the Superdome in New Orleans, the site of many big Mid-South Wrestling (the promotion that evolved into the UWF) cards. The tournament featured so many tag teams that it was presented in two sessions, one in the afternoon and the finale in the evening. To add to the excitement, promoters created a storyline that would award the winning duo the prize of a cool million.

Twenty-five teams competed, with nine selected as the top seeds and given first round byes. At the time Jim Crockett Promotions worked closely with the editors of *Pro Wrestling Illustrated* (*PWI*) magazine to select the top seeds. These teams were the cream of the crop — either past champions or the top ranked competitors from North America and Japan.

The main event eventually saw the Road Warriors square off against Magnum T.A. and Ronnie Garvin. Although Magnum and Garvin weren't as experienced as the Roadies or other tag team specialists in the tournament, they were two of the most popular stars in the company. More importantly, Garvin had defeated the Road Warriors before (in Georgia Championship Wrestling, teaming with Jerry Oates to win for the national tag titles), a rare feat in those days — and something that made him a formidable opponent for Hawk and Animal. Despite a strong showing, in the end, the Road Warriors prevailed, adding the *Crockett Cup* to the impressive list of accomplishments they'd already achieved.

While tag teams were the focus, two singles matches were featured as well, with North American champion Jim Duggan defending his title against Dick

Slater, and Dusty Rhodes challenging Ric Flair for the NWA world championship. In both matches, the champions retained their belts.

Despite the hype and the lure of seeing tag teams from eight different promotions compete, the *Crockett Cup* was not the smash success the promoters had hoped for. The afternoon show drew a reported audience of only 3,000; the evening show fared better, bringing in 13,000 fans and $180,000. While it is estimated that 10,000 of the fans who saw the action were from outside the New Orleans area, the promoters had clearly planned on far more local support — or it's unlikely they would have booked the show at a stadium with a capacity of 70,000.

After the first *Crockett Cup*, the tournament focused mostly on JCP teams. By 1987, Bill Watts was running UWF on his own as promoters from around the country seemed to adopt an "every man for himself" approach to dealing with the WWF. As a result, subsequent *Crockett Cups* provided exciting tag team action, but nothing matching the scope and grandeur of the original. The *Crockett Cup* ran for three years until JCP was sold to Ted Turner and the company was rechristened World Championship Wrestling. Following the sale, the *Crockett Cup* was abandoned.

THE BIG EVENT

The combination of a white-hot feud involving Hulk Hogan, a city full of rabid fans, and an outdoor event culminated in a North American attendance record. But if you're thinking it was *WrestleMania III,* you're off by about a year. The year, in fact, was 1986, and the city was Toronto. The show dubbed *The Big Event* became an outdoor phenomenon and one of Toronto, Ontario's many great contributions to the world of professional wrestling.

Toronto has always been a wrestling hotbed (a tradition that continues to this day). For decades, the Tunney family promoted the city through Maple Leaf Wrestling, bringing stars from all over Canada and the United States to its home base in the fabled Maple Leaf Gardens as well as to its affiliates throughout the province of Ontario. Over time, Maple Leaf Gardens was home to many historic matches, including four NWA world heavyweight title bouts (the controversial win for Lou Thesz over Buddy Rogers that led to the formation of the WWWF actually took place in Canada). With Toronto so close to the U.S. border, Maple Leaf Wrestling maintained an international flavor while also featuring Canadian legends like NWA world champions Gene Kiniski and "Whipper" Billy Watson.

By the mid-1980s, the face of wrestling was changing drastically and promoter Jack Tunney finally aligned himself with the WWF after years of working closely with the NWA and JCP. The move proved wise, as the WWF ultimately put many of Tunney's old colleagues out of business. Tunney himself became an important part of WWF television, playing the figurehead role of WWF president for several years, and participating in important storylines such as the signing of the Hogan/Andre match for *WrestleMania III,* and in an angle where he was beaten up by "Bad News" Brown.

Given Toronto's large base of wrestling fans, the WWF anticipated a robust audience for *The Big Event.* It wasn't Toronto's first outdoor spectacle. In 1983, Jack Tunney held not one, but two events at Exhibition Stadium (the home of the Toronto Blue Jays at the time). Dubbed *The Night of Champions,* the July 10 and July 24 shows featured eleven titles being defended as well as several other matches. The two events proved successful, but they paled in comparison to *The Big Event.*

The key to that show's success was the feud between Hulk Hogan and Paul "Mr. Wonderful" Orndorff. Orndorff's betrayal of his former ally struck a nerve with Hulkamaniacs, making their subsequent feud a natural. In the United States, the rivalry fueled ticket sales and the program proved just as hot in Toronto. Before long, it was clear to everyone that ticket sales were going to be phenomenal. The combination of the main event, affordable ticket prices, and heavy promotion by the Molson Canadian Brewery were credited for the wrestling attendance record set by the 64,000 fans who packed the CNE.

Fans who attended that evening got their money's worth, both in terms of quality and number of matches (at least by 1980s WWF standards). At that time, many fans despaired that the WWF was built around short matches that lacked the technical wrestling seen in other promotions. While there were exceptions, the WWF's bouts were rarely considered technical masterpieces. A total of eleven matches were set for *The Big Event.* The main event ended in disqualification after Orndorff's manager Bobby "The Brain" Heenan ran in and hit Hogan with a wooden stool. For the unfortunate fans who could not attend, the WWF aired many of the night's matches on their *Prime Time Wrestling* show and released the supercard on VHS through Coliseum Video.

CHAPTER 3

THE TERRITORIES
(1977–1983)

Wrestling lore is full of tales about the ways outlaw promotions were controlled — extortion, blacklisting, or whatever else was necessary to keep a territory protected from outsiders. With few exceptions, promoters were largely successful in keeping rogue competition at bay — until Vince McMahon took the WWF national.

Before the WWF became dominant, dozens of wrestling territories dotted the United States. These unique fiefdoms operated in various regions, some successful, some less so. Each promotion was responsible for its own well-being, and over time the local promoter formulated a promotional style that worked his particular area. Memphis, for example, had an angle-driven style, with outrageous antics both in and out of the ring. Wild match stipulations, like hair vs. hair, the loser gets tarred and feathered, and scaffold contests were commonplace. At the other end of the spectrum was Sam Muchnick's St. Louis promotion, where elegantly dressed fans sat in a hotel ballroom for *Wrestling at the Chase*. Over time, a local promoter gauged the fans' taste and tried to provide the product that was best suited to his patrons.

The cardinal rule of the territorial system was that promoters operated only within their sphere of influence and agreed not to stray into others'. In many ways the NWA operated as a syndicate, with promoters protecting one another from anyone who violated their basic tenets. If an outlaw tried to run shows in an NWA territory, fellow affiliates would send in their top stars to help the local promotion squash them.

Whatever a territory's individual style, the bottom line was always the same: putting asses in seats. Thanks to the isolation that went with the day's limited technology, what worked in one territory could be rehashed in another, and few fans would be the wiser. While there were those who followed major storylines in newsletters and wrestling magazines, the majority had no idea what happened in other territories.

This system provided a training ground for young wrestlers. From the tiniest to the largest markets, newcomers developed their trade. And unlike today's game, back then, when a wrestler washed out in one territory he could always try his hand in another.

That rule applied to veterans as well. A wrestler might be getting stale in one town but there were always dozens of others that might eagerly embrace him. Wrestlers could reinvent themselves elsewhere — or even come back to a market with a new gimmick, attitude, or look. (This practice was not lost on Vince McMahon, who made a habit of repackaging established grapplers in a way he believed would sell; the best example being, perhaps, when he turned legendary NWA champ Harley Race into "the King of Wrestling.")

Fans will forever debate the pros and cons of the territories compared to today's business model. One thing is certain — they provided a host of venues for promoters to experiment with new ideas or spin variations on old ones. Angles so memorable they're still used today were produced there, as well as others that will be remembered forever.

Into the 1970s, things still seemed to be going well in the territorial system, so well that promoters routinely lent their talent to others. But change was on the horizon and most regional promoters seemed complacent or oblivious. When Vince McMahon made his move, few were prepared.

STEAMBOAT/YOUNGBLOOD VS. SLAUGHTER/KERNODLE

While there was only one world heavyweight championship belt in the NWA, several versions of the "NWA world tag team championship" (none of them officially recognized by the NWA) were housed in various territories, including San Francisco, JCP, and Central States. In 1992, the NWA finally recognized an official version of the NWA world tag team championship.

The team of Ricky Steamboat and Jay Youngblood was ahead of its time. Both men employed the kinds of fast-paced maneuvers that would define later teams like the Rock and Roll Express, the Fantastics, and the Midnight Express. Steamboat and Youngblood were also partially responsible for the creation of JCP's *Starrcade*.

By 1983, Steamboat and Youngblood had already achieved legendary status in Jim Crockett Promotions. Since arriving in JCP during the 1970s, Steamboat had established himself as an incredibly popular babyface as well as a top tag team competitor. His partnership with Jay Youngblood proved just as successful, and the duo won the JCP equivalent of the NWA world tag team championship on two occasions, as well as enjoying a run with the promotion's Mid-Atlantic tag team championship. When they challenged the team of Sgt. Slaughter and Don Kernodle for the belts, however, they faced their greatest challenge.

Slaughter had already established himself as a top heel after feuding with Wahoo McDaniel over the United States title. From there, he used his notoriety to help elevate the career of wrestlers Don Kernodle and Jim Nelson by taking them under his militaristic wing. Kernodle and Nelson had wrestled as supporting talent, but after their storyline stay in Slaughter's boot camp, they emerged as credible opponents, achieving championship success in the Carolinas. Pleased by the success of his students, Slaughter began teaming with Kernodle and claimed the NWA world tag team championship in what was essentially a fictional tournament.

After first crossing paths with Private Nelson and Kernodle, Steamboat and Youngblood eventually found themselves feuding with Kernodle and Slaughter. The team's toughness, as well as Slaughter's cobra clutch made them a difficult team to upset. During one match it seemed as if Steamboat and Youngblood had finally prevailed but the referee restarted the match after it became apparent that Slaughter's foot had been on the rope during the pin. After the match restarted, Slaughter leveled Youngblood with a clothesline off the top rope. But the injury only inspired the babyfaces. No doubt sensing that it was only a matter of time before the team scored a victory, Slaughter agreed to a title match — with the stipulation that if his rivals lost they could never wrestle as a team again. The teams eventually faced off in a bloody cage match that saw Steamboat and Youngblood finally emerge victorious.

The blowoff to this feud became a phenomenon. The Greensboro Coliseum was sold out, and fans who weren't lucky enough to get tickets rushed to closed-circuit television to watch the warfare. Traffic crawled to a standstill as over 6,000 fans were reportedly turned away. Slaughter and Kernodle were caught in the mayhem and almost missed the match themselves.

Fortunately for JCP, the heels made it to the arena and the match turned into a classic. After witnessing the success of the confrontation and the demand for closed-circuit access, JCP would soon embark upon their *Starrcade* supershow.

After the program ended, Slaughter would leave JCP for the WWF, where his career would soar after a babyface turn and feud with the Iron Sheik. Back in JCP, Kernodle would form successful tag teams with both "Cowboy" Bob Orton and Ivan Koloff. When Ricky Steamboat announced his retirement from wrestling (a short-lived hiatus; he soon returned to the ring in singles competition), Youngblood found continued success in the tag ranks, teaming with real-life brother Mark, and the legendary Wahoo McDaniel until Jay's untimely death in 1985.

HELL HATH NO FURY (PRECIOUS/SUNSHINE FEUD)

> *In revenge and in love woman is more barbarous than man.*
> —**Friedrich Nietzsche**

The 1980s saw women make their mark in wrestling as both valets and managers. Women had been a part of the business for decades, in the ring and outside the ropes. In some cases women were both wrestlers and valets. Long before she became known as the Fabulous Moolah, Mary Lillian Ellison, for example, served as a valet for Buddy Rogers under the name Slave Girl Moolah. It wasn't until the 1980s that women truly became a fixture of professional wrestling. These trailblazers would lay the groundwork for the divas of the 1990s, women who became as popular in the ring as men, and who even competed against men in one-on-one matches. One of the angles that precipitated the rise of women in the sport was the feud between the valets known as Precious and Sunshine.

"Gorgeous" Jimmy Garvin began working with a valet in GCW. Dubbed Sunshine, Garvin's real-life cousin Valerie French accompanied him to ringside, and like any heel valet worth her salt, was never afraid to help Garvin sneak to victory. But the couple really seemed to click when Garvin went to work in Texas for WCCW and began feuding with David Von Erich. It led to a classic angle where Von Erich won a match with the stipulation that the loser serve as the winner's servant for a day. (Von Erich would enjoy the services of both Garvin and Sunshine.) In a series of video vignettes on WCCW television, the two heels were seen reluctantly performing various mundane tasks at Von Erich's ranch.

Oblivious to the idea that "three's a crowd," Garvin hired a second valet to serve as an assistant to Sunshine. Dubbed Sunshine II, she was worked like a dog by the real Sunshine, who treated her with contempt. It soon became obvious that Sunshine wasn't the only person being served by the newcomer. When WCCW announcer Bill Mercer went to Garvin's home to for an interview, Sunshine II answered the door in a nightie, alerting fans to just how close she and Garvin had become. Not surprisingly, the ensuing battle for the affections of "Gorgeous" Jimmy led to the two women arguing. Things came to a head when Sunshine II blamed the original for costing Garvin a match. A fight broke out and Sunshine left Garvin, while Sunshine II adopted a new moniker: Precious.

In a perfect world, Sunshine would have left WCCW, but Garvin wasn't so lucky. She promptly aligned herself with "Gentleman" Chris Adams, one of the area's top babyfaces. Just as she had done for Garvin, Sunshine lent her support to Adams. Garvin was furious and taken aback. Not only was Sunshine privy to Garvin's secrets, her presence counteracted that of her replacement, Precious. When Garvin wrestled Adams, he no longer had an unfair advantage.

The feud led to a series of matches, with Precious and Sunshine helping their respective men. Sunshine would become a mainstay in WCCW, managing some of the promotion's top babyface stars. She even introduced a new player to WCCW: her tough, truck-driving "aunt," Stella Mae.

Precious would continue working alongside her real-life husband Jimmy Garvin and was the focus of many unforgettable angles, such as one in WCW where Ric Flair tried to woo Precious away from Garvin and even won a date with her after Garvin lost to him in a steel cage match. Sunshine would retire shortly after her run in World Class Championship Wrestling.

THE $25,000 BOUNTY ON RIC FLAIR

A man cannot be too careful in the choice of his enemies.
—**Oscar Wilde**

After wrestling for just two years, Flair was reportedly a candidate for the NWA championship in 1975 as Jack Brisco's title reign was winding down. He would be considered again in 1977 and eventually got the nod in 1981.

Despite having already held the National Wrestling Alliance world championship, Ric Flair's second title win was unquestionably more important. And it didn't just cement the Nature Boy's status as a bona fide star (as opposed to a one-hit wonder) — the journey toward the chapsionship was just as remarkable.

By the end of the 1970s, Flair had established himself as one of the biggest names in the business, after beginning in Verne Gagne's AWA, and establishing himself as a legitimate regional superstar in Jim Crockett Promotions. Flair's incredible charisma, coupled with his ability to get good matches out of the worst performers (wrestling insiders often joked that Flair could wrestle a broom to a five-star match) put him on the fast track to fame and fortune. It was only natural that he caught the eye of National Wrestling Alliance promoters.

On September 17, 1981, Flair defeated Dusty Rhodes in Kansas City for his first NWA title, thus claiming wrestling's ultimate prize. Flair's first title win occurred with wrestling legend Lou Thesz serving as special referee. Torturing the champion's leg with the figure-four leglock, Flair won the match after Rhodes' leg gave out as he attempted a suplex.

Flair's title win soon saw him leaving the Mid-Atlantic area to defend the NWA championship throughout the many territories of the NWA. For the most part,

Flair wrestled as a cocky heel, using the same style and mannerisms that had made him so hated in JCP during his early years. Flair would cut promos mocking his babyface opponents and boasting about the luxurious lifestyle he enjoyed as champion. The interviews helped make fans hate him — and made him a top box office star.

While Flair typically worked as a heel, he continued working as a babyface in JCP. Flair had been turned face in JCP after his incredible charisma and popularity with the fans made it all but inevitable during the late '70s. Flair was not the first NWA champ to work as both a babyface and heel. Harley Race, for example, worked as a babyface in his home Central States territory while working as a heel elsewhere.

An October 4, 1975, airplane accident ended the career of wrestler Johnny Valentine and seriously injured several others aboard the flight. Despite suffering a broken back and being told he'd never wrestle again, Flair would return to the ring and wrestle for another thirty-three years.

After nearly two years as champ, Flair dropped the belt to Race on June 10, 1983, in St. Louis. The match ended in victory for Race after he raised his shoulder during a pin attempt by Flair. JCP fans were crushed when they heard the news, but Ric promised to get the belt back (and in a move to appease Flair's fans in the Mid-Atlantic region, footage was shown of Flair raising his shoulder during his pin on Race to create controversy over the loss). Over the next few months, Flair campaigned hard for the belt. In order to put a stop to this, Race put a $25,000 bounty on Flair's head. Whoever eliminated Flair from wrestling would be a rich man. Race appeared on television and pleaded with JCP's top heels to take his money.

Undeterred by the bounty, Flair continued his quest for a second championship. During a title rematch on JCP television in late August 1983, Flair seemed to have the champion where he wanted him when the match was interrupted by Dick Slater. Flair knocked Slater off the apron and returned his attention to Harley Race. After locking the champion in the figure-four, it looked as if Flair's bid for the gold would be successful. However Slater reappeared, casting a dark cloud over Flair's imminent victory. Fortunately for Flair, his friend "Cowboy" Bob Orton Jr. jumped into the ring, ready to counter Slater's interference — or so it seemed. In a shocking move, Orton climbed the top rope and delivered an attack on Ric Flair. Slater joined him in the ring, and when the smoke had cleared, Flair had been laid out by a spike piledriver courtesy of Orton and Slater. Backstage, Harley Race gleefully rewarded Orton and Slater with the cash they'd been promised as JCP president Jim Crockett Jr. admonished him. Race couldn't care less, as he handed over wads of cash, confident Flair was finished. Flair's true friends, "Rowdy" Roddy Piper and Wahoo McDaniel, checked on him as medics rushed to the ring.

Not long after the attack, a somber Nature Boy appeared on JCP television from his home and thanked the fans for their support. Sporting a neck brace, the Mid-Atlantic hero told them that although he'd escaped without broken bones, the neck injury was the same injury he'd suffered in the 1975 plane crash that nearly ended his career. Flair also told fans he'd thought he wanted the world championship more than anything, but now he wasn't so sure. Flair then stunned the wrestling world by announcing his retirement.

If fans were shocked by Flair's retirement, they were even more stunned when he showed up during a JCP TV taping and ran in on a tag match featuring Orton and Slater. Wearing a neck brace and brandishing a baseball bat, he charged at both wrestlers, swinging like a madman. With Flair in hot pursuit, Orton and Slater ran for their lives. After they eventually made their escape, Flair cut one of the greatest promos in his career. As longtime JCP announcer Bob Caudle held the microphone, Flair promised revenge, warning Orton and Slater that he had a new tag team partner (the baseball bat) — and that they would pay for trying to take him away from the greatest sport on earth. Flair also promised payback for Harley Race, telling the champ that his revenge would come when he took his gold belt.

THE PRIDE OF TEXAS

> *Treat your friend as if he might become an enemy.*
> **—Publilius Syrus**

They were one of wrestling's oddest couples, the flamboyant Ric Flair and the tough-as-nails Texan Blackjack Mulligan. Flair, flash and technical, patterned himself after legendary NWA champ "Nature Boy" Buddy Rogers, while the burly vet Mulligan evoked Wild West outlaws. Regardless, the two heels had become the best of friends as they terrorized Jim Crockett Promotions, winning championship gold and earning the hatred of fans everywhere.

Mulligan had taken the up-and-coming Flair under his wing, guiding him as he won title after title. While the cocky Flair often teamed up with Greg "The Hammer" Valentine, he could count on Mulligan to stand beside him when the going got tough. But as the saying goes, when Flair's mouth began writing checks his body couldn't cash, Mulligan was there to collect. It began as Mulligan had just dropped the U.S. championship to Mr. Wrestling II, when his interview was interrupted by Valentine and Flair. The NWA tag champs berated the veteran heel for losing the belt. Mulligan left the studio grumbling about his so-called friends' comments.

Later, after winning the U.S. championship himself, Flair was riding higher than ever. When Blackjack came out to congratulate him on the win, he was rudely dismissed. The Nature Boy dressed down his former cohort, telling him he wasn't man enough to hold the belt. To show how little respect he had for Mulligan, Flair suggested he consider retirement then tugged on Blackjack's trademark mustache. That final act of disrespect sent Mulligan over the edge. The big Texan punched Flair, shocking both the Nature Boy and the fans watching the action.

But things were just getting started. Flair decided to strike back right away. During a match between preliminary wrestler Tony Russo and Mulligan, Flair walked into the studio wearing Mulligan's hat. It was no mere cowboy hat — it was a gift from country singers Waylon Jennings and Willie Nelson. Flair then began shredding the priceless gift while Mulligan wrestled. By the time Mulligan had finished off Russo, Flair's dirty work was done. A furious Blackjack vowed revenge.

Comeuppance came quick as Mulligan gave Flair a taste of his own medicine. While Flair was wrestling Ted Oates, Mulligan strutted into the studio wearing one of the U.S. champ's trademark feathered robes. Flair could only watch as his opponent did his best to keep him in the ring. As the Nature Boy struggled to get to him, Mulligan ripped the robe apart before tossing the tattered remnants to fans in the studio audience.

When Flair finally escaped the ring, Mulligan was on his way out of the studio, proud of his handiwork. An enraged Flair swore Mulligan was "a dead man." Not long afterwards, he appeared on *Mid-Atlantic Championship Wrestling* and offered a $10,000 bounty to any man who put Blackjack out of wrestling.

Despite the efforts of some of the territory's toughest heels, Mulligan remained standing. Flair's bounty was uncollected, but he took solace in the fact that he'd managed to avoid granting his former friend a title shot. Mulligan was gunning for Flair's belt, but Flair was ducking and dodging the big Texan at every turn. To many fans, it looked like Mulligan might never get the opportunity to wrestle Flair again.

That changed when Mulligan decided to expose the skeletons in Flair's closet. The two had logged thousands of miles together back in the day, traveling throughout the territory in a van they both owned. Mulligan showed up with a brown grocery bag full of items he wanted to return. Mulligan emptied the contents, revealing an assortment of foreign objects Flair had used in the ring over the years as well as a beat-up toothbrush and a blonde wig. The pièce de résistance was a pair of pantyhose Mulligan claimed to belong to the champ. Of course, it was about more than getting a laugh from the fans: Mulligan's endgame was revealed when an angry Flair agreed to a match.

The two then worked a memorable series, selling out several arenas in the process. Around this time, Mulligan bought a stake in the Amarillo promotion with Dick Murdoch, and he soon left the Carolinas to attend to his new business. This put the brakes on the feud and Flair managed to fend off Mulligan's bid for the belt. Mulligan would eventually return to JCP and mend their friendship (after a Flair babyface turn), leading to their reign as NWA world tag team champions.

SUPERSTAR VS. SUPERSTAR

"Superstar" Billy Graham and "The American Dream" Dusty Rhodes: two incredible talkers, perhaps the greatest of their time, and the kings of their respective mountains. Graham had skyrocketed to the top in the Northeast by winning the WWWF championship from Bruno Sammartino, while Rhodes had captured the hearts of the fans in Eddie Graham's Championship Wrestling from Florida promotion after turning babyface. While their physiques were a study in contrast, they both had a personal charisma and gift of gab that would become the stuff of legend.

While it wasn't uncommon for the top out-of-town talent to show up for a special event (such as Verne Gagne's battle royals in the AWA), before cable television and the Internet, a fan's exposure to wrestlers from other promotions was usually limited to what they read in wrestling magazines. Discovering a new wrestler was like discovering a new restaurant or musical artist. WWWF fans were some of the luckiest as promoter Vince McMahon Sr. brought in the biggest stars from around the world. For many wrestlers, working in "the Mecca of professional wrestling" was a sign that you'd truly arrived.

Given his incredible Florida success, it seemed inevitable that the American Dream would be asked to work in New York. Dusty's road to MSG was paved by the friendship between Florida promoter Eddie Graham (no relation to "Superstar") and Vince McMahon Sr. And when Rhodes finally got his opportunity to work in the Northeast, he didn't disappoint. From his first appearance at the historic Garden, fans knew they were seeing someone special. Rhodes was like the Pied Piper — he drew fans in with just the sound of his voice.

The program between Rhodes and Graham illustrated that, at its heart, professional wrestling is about showmanship. As the storyline progressed, it was obvious that the stars' promos were just as important as their matches.

Dusty's appealed to the common man. No one would ever mistake Rhodes for Arnold Schwarzenegger, but his determination to succeed took him far in the squared circle. Rhodes came to represent "the American dream" — that anyone could succeed given the right amount of drive and determination. The working-class fans who worked hard to buy a ticket saw him as one of their own, and every promo he gave made fans feel as if they knew him.

"Superstar" Billy Graham, in contrast, possessed not only the body of a Greek god but the charisma as well. While Graham worked as a heel, he was unlike anyone who had ever worked in the WWWF. A former preacher, Graham had been a bodybuilder since he was a teen. Patterning his interviews after legendary boxer Muhammad Ali (who, ironically, developed his style waching wrestling), Graham put the finishing touch on his image by wearing outrageous tie-dyed shirts and gaudy jewelry. While the WWWF was known for its larger-than-life heels, Graham stood alone (his work would inspire a generation of bodybuilders-turned-wrestlers, including Hulk Hogan and Jesse "The Body" Ventura). Both his look and the promos he cut set him apart from the pack, leading some fans to cheer him at a time when very few people supported heels. Listening to a Graham promo, you couldn't help but be fascinated by his character. Today, Graham would eventually turn babyface, but in the WWWF of the 1970s, that was simply not going to happen. His charisma led him to become the first heel to hold the WWWF championship for longer than a few weeks.

On paper, a series between Superstar and the Dream seemed a match made in heaven, and in reality it was. During their first encounter in Madison Square Garden, the Dream triumphed over Graham by count out. The September 26, 1977, event saw more than 25,000 pack the Garden (3,000 others watched the event on closed-circuit television at the Felt Forum) and a rematch was quickly organized. On October 24, 1977, a sellout crowd of 26,092 witnessed Graham hold on to his belt in a hard-fought Texas death match. The contest ended after both men collided in the center of the ring and Graham had the fortune of landing on top of Rhodes for the pin.

Before the Texas death match, Rhodes cut one of his many memorable promos, telling announcer Vince McMahon: "The man of the hour, the man with the power. I am the hit-maker, the record-breaker. I've got smiling grace and a lovely space. I make your back crack and your liver quiver. If you don't dig this mess, you have got the wrong address. And Superstar, while all the rest are in the back laughing and joking, the Dream's out front cooking and smoking."

After the match, Rhodes suggested promoter Vince McMahon stage a Texas bullrope match, promising a sellout. But the rubber match would have to wait nearly a year, as Graham was already booked to lose the title to Bob Backlund. When Rhodes and Graham continued their feud the following summer the match finally occured. The men were tied together with a bullrope, which they could (and did) use as a weapon. Rhodes won the bout after special referee "Chief" Jay Strongbow counted Graham out of the ring.

These matches and the hype behind them remain treasured memories for all involved. In the WWE DVD *Twenty Years Too Soon: Superstar Billy Graham*, Dusty Rhodes talks about how special they were, explaining that he and Graham made it a kind of contest to see who could put on the best show. Rhodes said he never wanted those matches to end, because of how much effort he and Graham had put in. Graham, simply, had this to say about Rhodes: "This man, by far, was my most favorite opponent." Vince McMahon called the matches: "Absolute magic. You never forget things like that."

While much has been said of the momentous encounters between Rhodes and Graham in the WWWF, few discuss their matches elsewhere. The truth is, Graham and Rhodes worked many matches in Florida, both prior to Graham defeating Bruno Sammartino for the WWWF championship in 1977, and following their legendary New York series.

The feud would be the apex of Graham's career. He would disappear from the WWWF soon after facing Rhodes, working in Japan and several other territories before returning with a new look. The tie-dyed shirts and blond hair were gone, replaced by a black karate gi and a shaved head. Although Graham was soon involved in a memorable program with WWF champion Bob Backlund, his new style never quite gelled with fans. Fortunately for those who loved the original Superstar, in 1986 the WWF brought him back in 1986, tie-dye and all. The return was short-lived, however, as Graham was forced to undergo hip replacement surgery. In time he would learn that the steroids he'd relied upon to build his phenomenal physique ultimately destroyed it, rendering him sterile as well as destroying his liver. Only a last-minute liver transplant would save Graham's life. Like many of his peers, Graham would find solace in religion, becoming an ordained minister. He also mended fences with Vince McMahon after years of feuding and was inducted into the WWE Hall of Fame in 2004.

Rhodes' career would continue well into the 1990s, with three reigns as NWA world champion and a run behind the scenes as booker for Jim Crockett Promotions. Rhodes would see his sons follow in his footsteps, with Dustin Rhodes achieving success as Goldust, and Cody Rhodes making his debut in the WWE in 2007 — the same year Dusty was inducted in the WWE Hall of Fame.

IT'S MILLER TIME (PIPER BREAKS A BEER BOTTLE OVER HIS HEAD)

> *If you've got the time, we've got the beer.*
> **—Miller beer ad**

Today, the wrestling promo might seem a dying art, but once upon a time they were the lifeblood of the sport. Wrestlers would do interviews about coming house shows that would air on weekly wrestling programs. Each interview would be specific to the town the wrestler was appearing in. For Memphis's Championship Wrestling Association the wrestler would cut individual promos for the promotion's regular shows in Memphis, Louisville, Birmingham, Huntsville, and Tupelo, referencing the program he was working in each town.

Long-time fans often found the promos the best part of the shows. Most promoters ran squash matches on their weekly TV programs (the conventional wisdom being that no one would buy a ticket to see a match if they could watch it on free TV), which meant that aside from run-ins the television offerings weren't particularly exciting. (This idea would finally be challenged when Eric Bischoff began routinely airing "main event" quality matches on *Nitro*. Interestingly, house show business actually grew as a result. While Bischoff wasn't the first promoter to feature main event matches on TV, he was the first to abandon squash matches entirely.)

Promos gave wrestlers their moment in the sun, and some made more of this opportunity than others. More important for the promoters, a good promo could convince fans to buy a ticket to a live event. And while most wrestlers learned to cut a decent promo, there were a select few who had the ability to "talk people into a building."

Wrestlers learned this skill the hard way. Typically, a promotion would earmark a specific day for mic time. If Dusty Rhodes, for example, was facing Roddy Piper in seven different towns, they'd each cut at least seven different promos. It could be challenging work, but it was also a valuable learning experience — younger wrestlers could listen to the really good talkers and learn the tricks of the trade. At times, it also became as competitive as anything that went on in the ring, as wrestlers tried to upstage each other.

Wrestlers have done some crazy things to make their mic time memorable, but perhaps nothing wilder than when Roddy Piper smashed a beer bottle over his own head — just to make a point. At the time, Piper and Rick Martel were feuding with the Sheepherders (Butch Miller and Luke Williams) in Vancouver's All-Star Wrestling. The Sheepherders had quickly developed a reputation as one of the toughest teams around and their matches became known for bloody violence. The fans in Vancouver had to wonder if Piper and Martel could hold their own.

Piper put the fans' concern to rest by demonstrating just how violently crazy he could be. With Martel looking on, Piper grabbed a beer while cutting a promo on the Sheepherders. Then he took the bottle and smashed it against his head. Glass and beer exploded and blood began to ooze. Piper simply continued talking, promising the Sheepherders a match they would never forget.

In true wrestling tradition, the Sheepherders followed with a promo of their own. They brought out a beer bottle, and for a moment, the fans wondered if they might try to outdo Piper's show of bravado. Rather than smashing it, however, one of the Sheepherders drank the beer. "That's what you do with a beer bottle," he said.

SANTA CLAUS IS COMING TO TOWN

Wrestling has seen its share of villains, but very few could be as twisted as Kevin Sullivan. Once upon a time, Sullivan was a beloved babyface in Championship Wrestling from Florida (CWF) and Georgia Championship Wrestling, but a strange transformation turned him from hero to heel.

Sullivan wasn't a run of the mill bad guy; he was pure evil. Eventually, he assembled a wild army of characters to terrorize the babyfaces of CWF. Things began when a mystery man offered a $1,100 bounty for every bone that was broken in the body of Barry Windham. Jake "The Snake" Roberts earned the money, breaking Windham's nose. When it came time to collect, the mystery man was revealed as Windham's tag team partner, Kevin Sullivan.

Plenty of wrestlers have turned heel by betraying their partners, but how many have claimed to worship mystical beings of darkness named Abudadein? Sullivan's ultimate goal was to destroy Dusty Rhodes, the embodiment of the American dream. There was nothing he wouldn't do to secure Rhodes' elimination.

The angle drew a fair amount of controversy — it was intense, even for wrestling. Sullivan's character pushed the limits of what fans expected from heels. Vignettes were aired on CWF TV showing Sullivan performing a mystical cere-mony in which he summoned a wrestler out of the ocean ("The Purple Haze" Mark Lewin) recalling the point in the Book of Revelations where the Beast emerges. Sullivan was said to control the minds of the wrestlers in his army, bending them to his will.

The controversial gimmick was only intensified by articles that suggested Sullivan worshipped the devil. Sullivan's super-hot companion, originally known as Fallen Angel, also drew attention. In real life, she was Nancy Daus, a young model who had originally came to watch the matches with her husband and who caught the attention of wrestling photographer Bill Otten. Before long, she would accompany Sullivan to his interviews in skimpy outfits. Their on-air rela-tionship incorporated elements of S&M that made the characters all the more provocative.

The program with Dusty Rhodes was a natural: the embodiment of the American dream versus its antithesis. Things between the two became explosive, with Sullivan perpetrating vile act after vile act on Rhodes and his friends.

The feud between soon reached the point where one of them just had to go. A "lights out" cage match was signed with a "loser-leaves-town" stipulation for a Christmas Day show in the Tampa Sportatorium. The encounter saw Rhodes battle not only for his chance to stay in Florida, but for his very life. During the match, "Santa Claus" was seen walking amongst the fans, handing out treats. Santa had a special treat for Sullivan — he handed him a foreign object, which the heel then used on Rhodes. Almost instantly, Rhodes collapsed. Then, Sullivan covered him for the pinfall.

The crowd was astonished, as much by Santa's actions as Rhodes's loss. A camera crew was sent to the back to try to ascertain the identity of Sullivan's accomplice. They discovered he was none other than Jake "The Snake" Roberts.

A dejected Rhodes apologized to his family and fans for losing. He vowed revenge on Sullivan, despite the fact that he was barred from wrestling in Florida for the next sixty days. Rhodes talked of how Sullivan had forced him to find a new way to support his family.

Not long after Rhodes had packed his bags, a new masked wrestler made his debut. The wrestler wore a bodysuit and mask, but his body shape looked, and his voice sounded, strangely familiar. Kevin Sullivan and the CWF's top heel manager J.J. Dillon cried foul. In their eyes, there was no doubt the Midnight Rider was Dusty Rhodes. They complained to NWA president Bob Geigel and demanded the Rider unmask. Geigel wouldn't bite. Dillon and Sullivan could produce no direct proof. Until they did, he would be allowed to wrestle. Geigel did agree, however, that if the Midnight Rider were ultimately revealed to be Rhodes, Rhodes would be banned from competing anywhere in the NWA for one year.

With Geigel's position firm, J.J. Dillon posted a bounty of $10,000 to anyone who unmasked the Rider. But despite numerous attempts, Sullivan and his Army of Darkness were unable to get the job done. In fact, the closest someone came was ironically the Midnight Rider himself. The unlikely scenario played out on February 9, 1983, in what came to be known as "The Night of the Mask."

The Midnight Rider's in-ring success led to a NWA world championship match against "Nature Boy" Ric Flair. J.J. Dillon upped the bounty to $50,000. The truth was that Flair probably would have unmasked the Rider for free, since he and Rhodes already had a stormy relationship. In any event, not even Flair could pull it off. Worse yet, the champ was pinned by the Rider, losing his NWA title — that is, until Geigel ordered him to unmask (NWA rules stated that a masked wrestler had to reveal his identity before receiving the title). To the fans' disappointment, the Rider refused the belt, leading to even more speculation.

The saga would take CWF fans on a wild ride. It became even more chaotic when Kevin Sullivan was himself banned from CWF for a year. In a move that was devilishly ironic, a masked man named Lucifer began working in Sullivan's absence. This masked man wouldn't be around long however, as he and the Rider wrestled in a mask vs. mask match. When the smoke cleared, Lucifer was defeated and revealed to be Sullivan — who was promptly banned from CWF forever.

Soon, the Rider disappeared, and Rhodes returned to CWF, having served his sixty-day suspension. Several years later, the mysterious masked man would ride again in JCP.

RODDY PIPER SAVES GORDON SOLIE FROM MAGNIFICENT MURACO

These days, TV announcers are routinely roughed up during interviews with wrestlers, but in the not-so-distant past announcers were considered off-limits. And while wrestlers occasionally menaced the men with the microphone, an announcer being touched, let alone accosted, was practically unheard of. So, when "Magnificent" Don Muraco began threatening Gordon Solie back in the day, fans were shocked. But their real surprise came when they met Solie's unlikely savior: "Rowdy" Roddy Piper.

Since his move from the West Coast, Piper had achieved incredible success in both GCW and JCP. He also achieved his fair share of notoriety for the heelish tactics he routinely employed. Piper's gift of gab was such that he was featured as a color commentator for GCW, working alongside Gordon Solie. While Piper wasn't the first heel announcer, he really knew how to fly with the position. Piper would make subtle digs at babyfaces while calling the matches, infuriating fans and wrestlers alike. The father-son team of Bob and Brad Armstrong felt Piper's sting when, week after week, he insinuated that the younger Armstrong was being held back by his father. The comments would lead to a physical confrontation between Piper and Bob Armstrong.

Gordon Solie had established himself as the finest announcer in all of professional wrestling, a versatile commentator who knew how to advance the storyline behind the matches while describing the action in the ring. Equally important, he knew how to do so without resorting to endless hyperbole. Solie's commentary and demeanor created a realistic environment for a business based on illusion. His work earned him the respect of the performers as well as the nickname "the Walter Cronkite of Professional Wrestling." Solie was so admired that he worked in CWF and GCW at the same time.

The incident in question began as Don Muraco (a top heel) had just finished a verbal joust with another wrestler. He then turned his attention to Solie. Muraco was irate at Solie for not acknowledging his many accomplishments (one of them being his self-professed claim of being the first man to ever reverse the figure-four leglock). Solie had no intention of getting into a physical confrontation. His job was to call the matches, not become involved in them.

The showdown between the wrestler and the announcer overshadowed colorman Roddy Piper, but when the Rowdy One saw his colleague in trouble, he soon made his presence felt. Piper and Solie had disagreed on occasion, but it was clear Solie had earned Piper's respect. At first, Hot Rod tried to gently coax his fellow heel away, but Muraco made it clear no one could stop him as he backhanded Piper and knocked him to the floor. Piper was dazed for a moment but the Scotsman soon was ready to pounce, and as the Magnificent One grabbed the announcer, Piper jumped on his back.

A wild brawl erupted in the studio as the fans cheered on the formerly hated Piper. Other wrestlers ran out to break things up, but it would be several minutes before any semblance of order was restored. If anyone doubted Piper's intentions, they learned he had turned over a new leaf when he also saved Tommy Rich from Muraco at a house show in the Omni. Unfortunately, Piper quickly left GCW for JCP so his face turn would not amount to much until he returned to the territory months later to feud with "Mad Dog" Buzz Sawyer.

YOU'LL BELIEVE A MAN CAN FLY (SUPERFLY SNUKA VS. BOB BACKLUND IN A CAGE)

Long before fans routinely cheered heels, "Superfly" Jimmy Snuka won a place in the hearts of WWWF fans despite the fact he routinely beat up the wrestlers they were supposed to love. Snuka was simply too good for fans to ignore. Case in point: Snuka's war with WWF champion Bob Backlund.

After a successful campaign in Jim Crockett Promotions that netted him the United States championship and the NWA world tag belt, Snuka headed north for one of wrestling's biggest prizes, the WWF championship. The title belonged to Bob Backlund, an all-American babyface who had held the belt since beating "Superstar" Billy Graham in 1978. Backlund had faced a variety of challengers, but no one like Snuka. Unlike the monster heels of his era, Snuka's eyes revealed both an evil craftiness and an unquenchable fire. While no one would confuse Snuka with a collegiate wrestler, his style was much more complex than Polynesian peers like the Wild Samoans.

It didn't take Superfly long to work his way up the ranks of challengers. Along the way, a transformation began. With "Captain" Lou Albano managing him, the fans had plenty of reason to hate Snuka, but the more they saw him perform, the more they respected his athletic abilities. Snuka boasted an impressive physique. Equally impressive was his speed — wrestling has always had its share of hype but when announcers talked about Snuka's catlike quickness, it was no exaggeration. Snuka was remarkably agile, the ultimate proof being his finishing move, the Superfly splash (or Superfly death dive). In an era when wrestlers did not routinely attempt maneuvers from the top rope, Snuka's flying bodysplash was a true spectacle.

Backlund, the WWF's all-American hero, had successfully defended his belt against the likes of Greg "The Hammer" Valentine, Ivan Koloff, and Pat Patterson, but he had never fought anyone quite like Snuka. Their first encounter in MSG saw Backlund both lose his cool and suffer a disqualification loss when he refused to break a chokehold. Their second encounter was unsuccessful for Backlund too, as Snuka won the match by count out.

Unlike other promotions, the object of a WWF cage match was to escape the cage rather than pinning your opponent in a locked cage. This difference in rules continues to this day.

As was often the case in the WWF, the climax of their feud was a stipulation match — Snuka and Backlund would meet in a steel cage. Fans couldn't miss the metaphorical situation set up for them: the civilized man trapped in a cage with a wild animal. As WWF champion, Backlund was no stranger to these kinds of matches, but once again, he found himself struggling. The champion fought gamely, but to those watching it was clear that he wasn't so much trying to win as simply survive. Despite amazing resiliency, Backlund seemed destined for yet another defeat. After delivering a tremendous amount of punishment, Snuka prepared to deliver the Superfly splash, a move that would surely make him WWF champion.

Normally, Snuka launched his dive from the top rope, but that was not enough for him here. He had scaled the steel cage to deliver his finisher, a sight never before seen in the WWF. As Snuka soared through the air, his glory became his downfall. Despite the savage beating he'd taken, the hardy Backlund had enough strength to roll out of the way. With Snuka dazed, he made his way out of the cage, winning the match and retaining his title.

The bout quickly became the talk of wrestling fans everywhere, whether they'd seen it on TV or read about it in wrestling magazines. Although he'd lost, Snuka's star had risen higher than ever. In an instant, Snuka's dive became legendary.

I NEVER WAS YOUR FRIEND, GORDON SOLIE

> *I was angry with my friend:*
> *I told my wrath, my wrath did end.*
> *I was angry with my foe;*
> *I told it not, my wrath did grow.*
> **—"A Poison Tree," William Blake**

The Omni Auditorium was the site of one of the most controversial turns in wrestling history. The reversal itself demonstrated the lengths to which Ole Anderson would go to exact revenge. At that moment, Ole finally completed a plan that had been more than a year in the making when he lured Dusty Rhodes into a cage from which there was no escape.

Dusty Rhodes found himself in the worst possible situation: facing five of the toughest men in professional wrestling and locked in a steel cage. The match was supposed to be a tag team bout between Dusty and Ole Anderson against the Assassins for the Georgia tag team championship. After a bloody feud, Ole and Dusty had mended their ways when Anderson turned babyface. After Anderson proved his sincerity, Rhodes asked him to team with him against the Assassins. Dusty and Ole had seen the belts slip out of their grasp night after night due to the Assassins' cheating, and only a cage match would allow Dusty and Ole a fair chance to secure victory. Such a match called for not one but two special referees — Ivan Koloff and Gene Anderson. Both Koloff and Anderson were hated, but they were tough as nails, and the fans knew they could keep order. Their presence would prove a necessary evil if Dusty and Ole were to become the champs.

While the cage match turned out to be a clever trap, it began with Dusty Rhodes locking up against the Assassins. As it progressed, Dusty also found himself battling one of the special referees, Ivan Koloff. After enduring a beating, Rhodes reached Anderson and tagged him in. Anderson looked at the Assassins for a moment then turned his attention to Rhodes. In talking about the match afterward on GCW's weekly TV show, Ole told announcer Gordon Solie that he had to make sure the Assassins didn't attack him, and that the only person who knew about his scheme was his trusted brother, Gene. Seeing that he was safe from attack, Ole began stomping on his former partner. The other men in the ring quickly realized what was going on and joined in the fun.

Ole Anderson boasted to announcer Gordon Solie that everyone had fallen for his scheme. To remind the fans of where Rhodes and Anderson had once been, Anderson showed an old interview where the American Dream swore "that it would never be over," referring to the epic blood feud between himself and Ole. Anderson described how he had waited nearly a year to spring his trap and told Solie of the lengths he had gone to win Rhodes over — how it had disgusted him to be in the corner of men like Tommy "Wildfire" Rich (a popular babyface), but that it was all worth it when Dusty finally asked him to be his partner. He then told Solie how it made him sick to call matches next to him, pretending to be his friend. "I never was your friend," he said, "and I never will be."

The double-cross was given the attention of a presidential assassination. Throughout the subsequent television broadcast, wrestlers gave their thoughts on the event and on Anderson's scheme. Ivan Koloff applauded Anderson's actions, commending him for putting Rhodes where he belonged — down and bloody.

Others like Kevin Sullivan and Stan Hansen talked of how Rhodes or someone else would make Anderson pay. It was an effective way to get the attack over and make the angle even bigger than it already was.

Of course, such an angle demanded a response from the victim, and Dusty rose to the occasion. He talked of how he had no one to blame but himself; how his fans had begged him to seek medical attention as he staggered, bloody and beaten, but that he wouldn't give Anderson the satisfaction. Rhodes vowed revenge, saying he would team up with Andre the Giant to face Ole and Gene.

Like many great angles, this one would be revisited in another promotion. Several years later, Rhodes found himself betrayed again, this time after saving Ric Flair from the Koloffs. Once again, Ole Anderson would play a key part in the attack.

THE FREEBIRDS BLIND THE JUNKYARD DOG!

If ever a wrestler captured the hearts of a territory's fans, it was the Junkyard Dog in Mid-South Wrestling. After several years honing his craft in places like Stu Hart's Stampede Wrestling, Sylvester Ritter saw his star rise to new heights when promoter Bill Watts decided to take a chance and book an African-American as his number one star. Given wrestling's treatment of minorities, this was an unprecedented move. Watts, however, recognized Ritter's tremendous charisma, and understood that a large part of his audience was African-American. Watts' gamble quickly paid off as the JYD became the promotion's biggest draw, helping to create unprecedented successes in the New Orleans Superdome. In the end, the Dog became more than just a hero to African-Americans — he became a hero to wrestling fans everywhere, embodying many of the same Superman qualities Vince McMahon would use in building Hulk Hogan.

While the JYD was involved in many feuds throughout his Mid-South run, the biggest angle (perhaps of the Dog's entire career) began the night he fell victim to the Fabulous Freebirds and found himself blinded. After winning a hair vs. hair tag team match with partner Buck Robley against the Freebirds, the JYD was ready to watch the vanquished opponents get shorn. Sadly, he would not see that happen. Before the stipulation could be carried out, Freebird Michael Hayes rubbed hair removal cream (forever known afterwards as Freebird Hair Removal Cream) in his eyes.

After the attack, the fans in the Mid-South area were informed that the Junkyard Dog was blind. Bill Watts made sure the angle was played to the hilt, filming vignettes of the JYD struggling to cope with his vision loss. The story was made all the more tragic when it was revealed the Dog had recently become a father and was now unable to see his newborn daughter.

As if the Freebirds' treachery wasn't bad enough, the three wrestlers boasted about how they had ended the Dog's career. But Michael Hayes would soon regret his arrogance: the caustic substance may have robbed the Dog of his sight, but not his courage. After weeks of being mocked on Mid-South television, the JYD challenged Hayes to a match where his sight would not matter — a dog collar match. An overconfident Hayes arrogantly accepted.

The headline bout would draw a record wrestling crowd to the Superdome. The heat was so intense that the Freebirds had to contend with death threats. One fan became so enraged he actually jumped into the ring and pulled a gun on Hayes. Fortunately, the Freebirds managed to escape serious harm.

Like many other supposed career-ending wrestling injuries, the JYD would experience a miraculous recovery. Following the success of the angle, Ritter's fame soared to new heights. Eventually, word of his popularity would reach New York, and when Vince McMahon moved to take the WWF to the next level, the Junkyard Dog would be one of the all-star talents chosen to lead the charge.

TIME TO PAY THE PIPER

When Jack Brisco laid down ten grand to exact revenge on Roddy Piper, fans thought "the Rowdy Scot" would finally get what was coming to him — a beating in the middle of the ring and the loss of the Mid-Atlantic heavyweight championship to the former titleholder. Sadly, Brisco's desire for revenge backfired, much to the delight of Roddy Piper.

After establishing himself as one of the hottest heel acts on the West Coast, Piper left for the East Coast where he worked simultaneously for JCP and GCW, two of the hottest territories in the early 1980s. While he could play an effective babyface, Piper was always at his best when he played the cowardly heel, inciting crowds with incredible promos. Fans gladly laid down their money to see him get his comeuppance at the hands of the local hero, whether it was JCP icon "Nature Boy" Ric Flair or GCW's Tommy "Wildfire" Rich. Thanks to smart booking in both promotions, Piper usually found a way to cheat his way to victory, setting the stage for a number of lucrative rematches.

Jack Brisco was Roddy Piper's polar opposite: a soft-spoken, scientific wrestler who spent much of his career achieving success through a combination of all-

American amateur wrestling skills and a middle-class work ethic. A two-time NWA world champ, Brisco was cheered by JCP fans instantly.

It was only natural that Piper and Brisco would cross paths. After cheating his way to a victory over Brisco for the Mid-Atlantic heavyweight title, Hot Rod made the feud even hotter by injuring Brisco's brother. Jerry Brisco was wrestling a preliminary wrestler, and seemed to have the match won when he placed his opponent in a submission leglock. Piper ran out and jumped off the top rope onto Brisco's leg, putting the younger Brisco on the shelf.

After the attack, Jack Brisco was hopping mad. Ever the crafty ring general, Piper refused to wrestle Brisco until he put up $10,000 in prize money. At first, Brisco couldn't raise the funds, but fellow babyfaces Ricky Steamboat and Wahoo McDaniel threw in their own money (they had had their own run-ins with Piper and were anxious to see him get pummeled). This intricate piece of booking was typical for the Mid-Atlantic promotion, which not only featured some of the biggest names in wrestling but also knew how to use them to maximum effect.

The angle played out on TV, with Brisco signed to face Piper in a title match during *Mid-Atlantic Championship Wrestling*. Before the match began, Piper made it clear to announcer Bob Caudle that both Ricky Steamboat and Wahoo McDaniel were barred from the studio. If either wrestler as much as stepped in the ring, Brisco would forfeit the match as well as the prize money. Anxious to get Piper in the ring and confident in his ability to handle him one-on-one, Brisco agreed. Like many a babyface before him, Brisco had underestimated Piper's guile.

The match featured a smooth mix of wrestling and brawling with Brisco and Piper trying to wear each other down. Brisco took the early lead with a headlock. While many fans today may dismiss it as a boring rest hold, veterans like Brisco and Piper knew how to make the move look dangerously effective (as anyone familiar with martial arts knows, it can be deadly when applied correctly). The psychology behind the hold was brilliant, with the first five minutes of the match consisting of Piper trying to break free. As he struggled, announcers Bob Caudle and David Crockett pointed out how Brisco's strength made the headlock a potential match-ender. He pulled hair, tossed Brisco into the ropes, and even attempted an acid drop, but Piper could not break the hold. Finally, Piper wrestled himself into a position to suplex Brisco, staggering the former world champion and freeing himself.

After just experiencing the effects of the hold, Piper put Brisco in a headlock of his own, turning it into a rear-front facelock. Brisco fought his way out only to find himself in Piper's dreaded sleeper. As the sleeperhold took its toll, referee

Sonny Fargo checked on Brisco to make sure he hadn't passed out. Taking a page from Piper's book now, Brisco finally used a suplex to escape. The match was building up steam.

Things went back and forth. Finally, their hatred for each other, no doubt coupled with their frustration over their inability to put each other away, led to a wild brawl outside the ring. When the match returned to the ring Brisco closed in for the kill with his own sleeperhold. But then, just before he lost consciousness, Piper raked Brisco's eyes. The two brawled some more and then Piper rolled outside to catch a breather. But Brisco didn't let up, ramming Piper's head into the mat apron. As the referee tried to keep Brisco in the ring, Piper reached into his trunks for a foreign object. Then it happened: Brisco caught a right hand and fell back into the center of the ring. Piper went for the pin while Brisco lay motionless, surrounded by coins.

The Brisco Brothers

To the announcers and anyone else watching the match it was obvious Piper had used a roll of coins to knock Brisco out. The referee, however, missed the chicanery and the win was awarded to the heel. A jubilant Piper grabbed his title belt and Brisco's cash and gloated to Bob Caudle that he had beaten Brisco and taken Steamboat and Wahoo's money. Thanks to this well-crafted angle and match, Piper's heat with Brisco had intensified, while new feuds were created by Piper's theft of McDaniel and Steamboat's money. For anyone looking to book a successful, productive angle, this would be a good place to start.

CHAPTER 4

TELEVISION

Television is chewing gum for the eyes.
—**Frank Lloyd Wright**

Wrestling was on the small screen from the beginning, and just as the medium has evolved, so has wrestling's television presence. The larger-than-life characters, as well as wrestling's other showbiz elements, made it a perfect fit for TV; it quickly became a network fixture, and the national exposure helped establish new stars. While Gorgeous George's name is often mentioned, he was but one of many wrestlers who became national figures because of the small screen.

As often happens in the world of TV, wrestling was eventually overexposed and ratings fell. Naturally, the major networks cut programming. Wrestling promoters soon struggled to find stations to air their product. They'd come to rely on the medium to promote arena matches, and now it was almost impossible to find a broadcaster willing to offer airtime. The end result was that promoters struck whatever deal they could, even if it meant paying to have their programs aired. UHF stations in local markets became the last bastion of the sport.

For thirty years, local stations were the only place a fan could watch wrestling. Cable television changed all that. Suddenly there were more channels, all with timeslots to fill. The owners and operators of the new channels quickly discovered professional wrestling was an inexpensive way to draw ratings.

Cable TV provided professional wrestling with national exposure for the first time since the 1950s. Fans with channels like WTBS and the USA Network could now watch wrestling from promotions outside of their market. In the past, promoters agreed to stay out of each other's territory, and the only time a fan had access to more than one promotion was when an outlaw tried to set up shop. This all changed when TBS began airing Georgia Championship Wrestling. Anyone with access to the Superstation could now watch GCW in addition to their local programming.

Cable would revolutionize the wrestling business, but the industry was slow in recognizing the breakthrough. While GCW stars now enjoyed national exposure, the promotion took no steps to expand outside of their traditional territorial boundaries (although the idea was reportedly considered). It would not be until the mid 1980s, when the WWF began airing on the USA Network, that a promoter used the exposure to make a bid for national expansion.

Eventually, the shows that aired on local stations became less and less important. As wrestling's popularity grew, the cable networks offered advertising revenue for promoters and started paying them for their programming. Over time, local shows became nothing more than highlight programs, and then they were dropped for good.

While television continues to be the major outlet for promoting professional wrestling, changes in technology threaten its position as the best medium for reaching fans. As the Internet expands in use and availability, more and more promoters are hyping and in some cases, airing, their shows online.

WRESTLING ON THE SUPERSTATION

When Ted Turner first put professional wrestling on his fledgling WTBS, it was a cheap way to fill a couple hours. The decision quickly paid off and wrestling would forever hold a special place in his heart. It was a big reason for his network's success, and this triumph is one of the most important developments in wrestling history.

Turner's airtime also worked wonders for the promoters of Georgia Championship Wrestling. Although GCW made no effort to promote outside of their territory, they enjoyed the boost in exposure the national timeslot gave them. The wrestlers also benefited, reaching new audiences and more importantly, promoters in other regions who might be interested in their work.

World Championship Wrestling would become a fixture on Turner's Superstation. Hosted by Gordon Solie and Freddie Miller, the program is still fondly remembered by fans fortunate enough to watch. The two-hour show featured an all-star roster and many memorable feuds. The show became a must-see event.

The world of GCW would see many interesting angles play out in the 1970s and '80s but nothing as shocking as the real-life story that developed when promoter Vince McMahon bought out the company. On Saturday July 14, 1984, fans tuning in to watch *World Championship Wrestling* were stunned to see Freddie Miller introduce the WWF's Vince McMahon. The day became known as Black Saturday among wrestling fans — their disenchantment with the WWF product was so strong. Hardcore acolytes of GCW didn't care for the WWF's style, and it showed in the show's disappointing ratings. Despite the excellent timeslot, their show flopped, while a Mid-South Wrestling telecast, aired in a graveyard slot, scored much higher.

The WWF had purchased GCW because of its timeslot, hoping to add the national exposure of the Superstation to the national coverage they already enjoyed on the USA Network. In order to get the timeslot, McMahon had to convince several of the company's owners to sell their shares. Ole Anderson, for one, didn't know of the move until after it had happened. Needless to say, he wasn't happy.

Anderson wasn't the only one. Turner reportedly expressed his concern with the product since *World Championship Wrestling* was supposed to air original content. Turner threatened McMahon with legal action, and McMahon sold the timeslot to Jim Crockett Promotions. Legend has it that Crockett told him, "You'll choke on that million dollars." The timeslot hosted JCP's (and later on, WCW's) flagship program. Not long after, the stars of both Georgia Championship Wrestling (brought back by Ole Anderson for a short time) and JCP competed on WTBS.

Professional wrestling would be a Superstation fixture for years. But when Ted Turner lost the hands-on control he'd once enjoyed (after the company merged with America Online), the new executives dismissed the sport. When Eric

Bischoff attempted to buy WCW, the deal fell through because he was told the Superstation would no longer air wrestling.

TUESDAY NIGHT TITANS

When Vince McMahon decided to take the WWF national, rival promoters had no idea what to expect. Anyone who'd ever tuned in to McMahon's Tuesday night talent showcase, *Tuesday Night Titans*, should have realized that his new brand of professional wrestling was unlike anything that had ever been seen.

In order to go national, McMahon realized he needed to get his product out to as many homes as possible. The USA Network had been airing a program for the Southeast Championship Wrestling promotion, but questionable content (or payment issues, depending on who you believe) caused them to drop the show. McMahon didn't wait long to seize their spot.

When the WWF kingpin launched *Tuesday Night Titans* fans expecting to see a traditional wrestling program were in for a surprise. While *TNT* featured matches, the focus was an interview segment in the mode of *The Tonight Show* with former wrestler–turned–color commentator Lord Alfred Hayes playing Ed McMahon to Vince's Johnny Carson. Wrestlers would arrive on the set to be interviewed, showcasing the characters McMahon wanted them to play.

TNT allowed McMahon share his vision of professional wrestling with a national audience, something he would eventually call "sports entertainment." The WWF, his programming said, was more than just wrestling. There were musical performances from WWF personalities such as "Mean" Gene Okerlund and Hulk Hogan (who performed "Tutti Frutti"); George "The Animal" Steele underwent shock treatment; "Mr. USA" Tony Atlas gave a bodybuilding exhibition; advice for the lovelorn came from "Classy" Freddie Blassie; and Jesse "The Body" Ventura (who sang vocals on the heavy metal–tinged "Body Rules") starred in a music video.

An animated series (which included some live action segments with WWF wrestlers) called *Hulk Hogan's Rock 'n' Wrestling* ran from 1985 through 1987 and featured Hogan and his fellow babyfaces battling Roddy Piper and his assemblage of heels. Brad Garrett of *Everybody Loves Raymond* fame was the voice of Hulk Hogan.

Like anything that challenges convention, the show received more than its share of criticism from wrestling traditionalists. Some fans derided the variety show format, as they felt McMahon was turning his wrestlers into cartoon characters and the WWF into a circus. But other fans enjoyed a change of pace that presented wrestling with tongue placed firmly in cheek.

Of all of the interviews and vignettes shown on *TNT*, none proved as popular as the series of segments involving wrestler "Magnificent" Muraco and his manager Mr. Fuji. Muraco and Fuji were truly an odd couple, showcasing their acting skills in parodies of television shows and movies. Whether it was *Fuji Vice* (a spoof of the then-popular cop show *Miami Vice*) or *Fuji General* (the good-natured poke at medical soap operas such as *General Hospital*), their skits are still fondly remembered by WWF fans.

While *TNT* helped showcase the WWF's stars and style to a national audience, the show was relatively short-lived, airing from 1984 to 1986. Although the studio/talk format would be revisited briefly on the WWF's *Prime Time Wrestling* program in 1991, subsequent WWF offerings were more traditional wrestling programs.

SATURDAY NIGHT'S MAIN EVENT

When Vince McMahon gambled his company's future on *WrestleMania*, his bravado caught the attention of more than just wrestling fans. Intrigued by the public's growing fascination with wrestling, as well as by McMahon's unique spin on promotion, NBC executive Dick Ebersol decided to bring professional wrestling back to network television, something that hadn't happened in roughly thirty years. The result would be *Saturday Night's Main Event*, a series of regular specials that would air on NBC from 1985–1991 (*SNME* would subsequently air twice on the Fox Network before returning to NBC in 2006.)

There were growing pains. NBC made it known that if the WWF wanted to enter the realm of the not-ready-for-prime-time players, it would have to do something about its production values. With Ebersol's help, they stepped up the production side, learning much from the experience and eventually gaining the reputation of having the slickest-looking programs in wrestling.

Before the days when *Monday Night Nitro* began airing main-event matches on a regular basis, every episode of *SNME* was a major event. While there were occasional squash matches, the shows featured an abundance of all-star bouts, something fans rarely saw from the WWF. Like any good promoter, McMahon used the show as a means to inspire viewers to order his pay-per-views or attend house shows. While some scores were settled on *SNME*, more often than not the fans appetite was whetted rather than sated.

For the next few years, *SNME* became the place where big matches were set up and feuds simmered to perfection. Whether it was King Kong Bundy sneak-attacking Hulk Hogan (setting up their match at *WrestleMania 2*) or Jake "The Snake" Roberts delivering a DDT to Ricky Steamboat on a concrete floor, WWF fans knew they could expect something exciting.

SNME was typically hosted by McMahon himself, with either Jesse "The Body" Ventura or Bobby "The Brain" Heenan providing color commentary. McMahon would have his hands full covering the action while Ventura or Heenan bewildered him with their outrageous take on what was happening in the ring. Both color commentators favored heels, always quick to point out the villain's side of things.

The ratings for *SNME* proved strong and the show soon became a semi-regular part of NBC's Saturday night programming. The success would also lead to two prime time wrestling specials, bringing the sport of kings back to prime time audiences for the first time in decades.

THE CLASH OF CHAMPIONS

As Vince McMahon began to squeeze regional territories out of business, his rivals slowly realized he was playing for keeps. At the end of the day, McMahon's strongest opponent turned out to be Jim Crockett Promotions. While there were still other territories operating, Crockett's organization was considered to have the best chance of competing with the WWF. As the war between JCP and the WWF intensified, Jim Crockett Jr. would discover how far McMahon was willing to go.

Flush with success from *WrestleMania III* (an event that had all-but-cemented the WWF's dominance), McMahon now held considerable influence with pay-per-view providers. In the fall of 1987, McMahon decided to use that influence by striking a blow against one of JCP's biggest sources of revenue, *Starrcade*. The JCP pay-per-view aired every Thanksgiving and it had become the company's biggest show of the year. The company always relied on the revenue from the event, but never before was as much at stake: they'd just bought out Bill Watts' Universal Wrestling Federation (UWF).

Vince McMahon decided to run his own Thanksgiving show, labeling the event *Survivor Series*. The *Survivor Series* would consist of all-star teams of faces battling against heels in elimination-style matches — a team would wrestle the other until all of their members had been eliminated by pinfall, submission, count-out, or disqualification. This would be the first time the WWF would go head-to-head with JCP during a pay-per-view.

Or so everyone thought.

While most people expected a pitched battle, Vince McMahon had other plans. He contacted the pay-per-view providers and let them know that he was offering them *Survivor Series,* with one catch. Any company that wanted *WrestleMania IV* also had to order *Survivor Series.* . . . The result was that JCP would be locked out.

JCP protested, but the end result was that the WWF ran *Survivor Series* widely, while very few companies chose to carry *Starrcade*.

Seeing what he'd successfully achieved with *Survivor Series,* Vince McMahon set out to sabotage another JCP event. This time, McMahon aired a free show called *The Royal Rumble* against the JCP's *Bunkhouse Stampede* PPV. McMahon's free battle royal aired on the USA Network, cutting into JCP's viewership.

In 1988, Crockett Promotions responded with *The Clash of Champions*. The WWF had robbed JCP of its number one show; Jim Crockett planned to do the same to McMahon by running a free show against *WrestleMania IV*. This would be no regular wrestling show; it would feature marquee matches, much like *Saturday Night's Main Event,* and capitalize on the success of a new star, Sting.

Sting (Steve Borden) was a wrestler who had worked in Bill Watts' Universal Wrestling Federation. After buying the UWF, JCP had acquired the company's impressive talent roster, but inexplicably, they had treated most of the company's stars as canon fodder for JCP talent. The main exception was Sting, who was given a huge opportunity against NWA world champion Ric Flair. An angle had been set up in which a celebration for Flair had been spoiled by Sting, prompting a faceoff between the rookie and the veteran. This would be no run of the mill title match either. Flair's manager James J. Dillon would be placed in a cage to prevent interference. In the event of a tie, a five judge panel would choose a winner.

Crockett was convinced that there were still plenty of fans who wanted to see old school wrestling, rather than the more cartoonish fare of the WWF. Now, fans would get to see such action for free and JCP would get their chance to stick it to the WWF.

The Clash of Champions was held at the Greensboro Coliseum in Greensboro, North Carolina. The show drew a very impressive rating of 5.6 for Superstation TBS and it was well received by everyone in attendance and watching at home.

The main event saw Sting and Flair wrestle to a forty-five-minute draw. The match became an instant classic and it is considered by many as the beginning of Sting's run as a bona fide superstar. After time ran out, the decision went to a panel of judges, but in the end they too were deadlocked. As a result, Flair retained his NWA championship.

The March 27, 1987, show featured several other big matches, including the Fantastics vs. the Midnight Express, Dusty Rhodes and the Road Warriors vs. the Powers of Pain and Ivan Koloff in a barbed wire match, the team of Barry Windham and Lex Luger defeating Arn Anderson and Tully Blanchard for the NWA world tag team championship, and Mike Rotunda defending his world television title against "Gorgeous" Jimmy Garvin in a match based on amateur wrestling (three five-minute rounds with a one count being enough for a pin).

JCP's show seriously cut into *WrestleMania IV's* audience. Crockett had scored one of his rare victories against McMahon — but the glory would be fleeting. The pay-per-view companies were furious when the buyrates for *WrestleMania IV* came in and it was clear how much JCP's free show had negatively affected revenue. As a result, they sent a strong warning to both McMahon and Crockett that they would tolerate no further sabotage.

Despite the moral victory, the damage to JCP had already been done. Its *Starrcade* losses and mounting debt eventually forced Crockett to sell his assets to Ted Turner in late 1988. Turner's new venture would be rebranded as World Championship Wrestling.

The Clash of Champions would continue in Turner's WCW, as a semi-regular program on Superstation TBS. Before the Monday Night Wars made star-studded wrestling TV a regular occurrence, *The Clash* served as WCW's version of *Saturday Night's Main Event*. Once *Monday Night Nitro* started providing weekly marquee matches, *The Clash* lost its luster and became just another show. With WCW airing more and more programming on free TV, it wasn't long before the show that had upset *WrestleMania* was sent packing.

MONDAY NIGHT NITRO

For years, WWF Monday night programming was competition free. *Raw* (like its predecessor *Prime Time Wrestling*) was the WWF's national flagship, just like WCW's Saturday night show, *World Championship Wrestling*. In 1995, the debut of WCW's *Monday Night Nitro* changed everything.

The amazing thing about *Nitro* was that the show was created by accident rather than by design. The idea came during a meeting between Eric Bischoff and Ted Turner. Bischoff began working for WCW in 1991 as an announcer; by 1993 he was running the company. He had an uphill battle, trying to bring the company out of the red as well as shake its image as a poor man's WWF. After years of hard work, Bischoff believed he had the final component necessary to get WCW into the black: a deal to air WCW overseas. The problem was that the programming would be carried on Star TV, an overseas network owned by Ted Turner's archrival Rupert Murdoch. To push the deal through, Bischoff arranged for a meeting with Turner. As Bischoff made his pitch, he was interrupted by the owner of Turner Broadcasting, who asked Eric point blank, "What do we need to do to become competitive with Vince?" Bischoff quickly came up with the one thing WWF had that WCW didn't: prime time television. Shockingly, Turner immediately told TNT executive Scott Saasa to give WCW two hours of prime time.

A stunned but excited Bischoff went to work on creating a show that would not only air on prime time, but head-to-head with *Monday Night Raw*. Many industry insiders thought Bischoff was insane. The conventional wisdom was that the show would either fracture the wrestling audience on Monday night, or become an outright ratings disaster. What Bischoff's critics didn't count on was new fans actually tuning in.

Targeting a new audience rather than fighting with the WWF for the traditional wrestling demographic was a key element of Bischoff's vision. In his autobiography, *Controversy Creates Cash*, Bischoff explained: "WWF at the time had a core audience that was pretty young. We went after an older group, eighteen to thirty-nine-year olds, and we got them. The buzz we generated got a lot of new people sampling us. That's why I believe the majority of our growth came from an audience that hadn't been watching."

But how would WCW reel them in? Bischoff and his team worked hard, analyzing what had succeeded in the past for what might work in the present. One thing was clear, his show had to be different. Things began to click when Bischoff scrutinized the findings of a study conducted by Ted Turner's research department. Wrestling fans and non-fans alike suggested their favorite part of professional wrestling was unpredictability.

If the audience wanted unpredictable, then that's what they would get. WCW *Nitro* would be about keeping people on the edge of their seats, wondering. *Nitro's* goal was far-reaching: what next; what about next week; next month?

The Internet made it impossible to keep secrets as long as a wrestling show was taped. In the early 1990s an online community of wrestling fans grew. They began sharing the results of wrestling events they'd attended (much as fans had done in the '70s and '80s by regular mail), and the information spread at a breakneck speed. Bischoff had learned this the hard way after taping WCW shows weeks and even months in advance only to see the results already posted on websites, spoiling his storylines. *Nitro* would be live, a show that could not be spoiled.

Monday Night Nitro debuted on September 4, 1995, a night when there was no competition. It was a carefully planned move. The cagey young Bischoff booked the show's debut on a night when *Raw* was pre-empted. Fans looking for wrestling wouldn't find the WWF — but if they channel-surfed they would discover *Nitro*. And those who did were treated to a roller-coaster ride.

If you tuned in that night you saw one of the biggest talent jumps in history when Lex Luger appeared. The former WCW star had been employed by the WWF for some time after leaving WCW to pursue a career as a bodybuilder in Vince McMahon's World Bodybuilding Federation (WBF). But Luger's contract with the WWF had just expired. Still, as far as Vince McMahon was concerned, Luger was still working for him. In fact, the night before *Nitro's* debut, Luger had worked a show for the WWF in Canada. He had already sent a letter to the WWF stating he considered himself a free agent once his contract expired, but for whatever reason, the WWF paid no heed. One day later, he was parading around on WCW's new show. Bischoff's goal had been accomplished: fans were shocked. The WWF now had some real competition.

Nitro's debut rating was a successful 2.9, but how would the show do once *Raw* returned to the air? The head-to-head matchup took on a life of its own, becoming a main-event contest in its own right. The buzz on the Internet and in the wrestling dirtsheets was intense, with fans wondering who would come out on top in this unprecedented Monday night battle.

Following the opening salvo of Lex Luger's debut, people speculated about what kind of stunt Bischoff might pull for the first head-to-head with *Raw*. First, *Nitro* began a few minutes before *Raw*, rather than at the same time. The biggest surprise, however, came when announcer Eric Bischoff shattered the notion of kayfabe and told viewers what was going to happen later that evening — on *Raw*. Thanks to the WWF pre-taping its shows, Bischoff knew exactly what matches and angles would take place. He deliberately spoiled the results of *Raw's* matches, then invited fans to be surprised by a live, unpredictable *Nitro*.

Bischoff's gamble paid off: the first battle between the two shows saw *Nitro* earn a 2.5 rating against *Raw's* 2.2. Not a crushing victory, but Bischoff had won the first battle when most people believed his show had little chance of surviving, let alone competing. In the following weeks, the shows traded rating victories as they jockeyed for viewers. Bischoff would continue his tactics, spoiling the WWF's

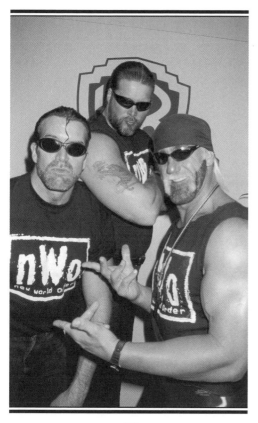

nWo

taped shows and forcing them to air more live editions of *Raw.* He would also carefully counter-program *Nitro* by trying to ensure that *Nitro* aired matches while *Raw* was running commercials.

As one might expect, the folks over at the WWF were concerned. Former WWF executive Michael Ortman talked openly about it in *Sex, Lies, and Headlocks:* "We also had a sense that there was enough room for everybody under the tent. After Eric gave away the results of our matches, Monday night became a war." Vince McMahon, particularly, was not happy. But the head-to-head competition proved to be a blessing for fans. As the rivalry heated up, both promoters explored new ways of stealing away their foe's audience. Gone were the perpetual squash matches as they wooed viewers with top caliber cards. Over time, each show expanded (in *Nitro's* case to three hours) and eventually spun off other prime time wrestling shows (*Smackdown* and *Thunder*).

For the next six years, Bischoff and McMahon would wage an all-out war.

CHAPTER 5

THE ROCK AND WRESTLING ERA (1984–1989)

He who rejects change is the architect of decay.
The only human institution which rejects progress is the cemetery.
—Harold Wilson

The 1980s was a time of great change for wrestling. New technologies would revolutionize the way promoters did business. Change in the sport itself came both in the form of a rebirth in tag team wrestling and in the influx of bodybuilders. For the fortunate few, regional territories blossomed into national promotions. But many other promoters saw the end of businesses they'd spent a lifetime building.

During a meeting with promoter Jerry Jarrett, Bill Watts was asked, "Where are the blow jobs?" Soon after he brought in the Fantastics — to appeal to female fans.

Thanks to cable television, promoters were free to promote shows in more than one arena, and profits increased dramatically. It didn't take the innovative minds long to reach for the stars.

Like all times of change, there were positives and negatives. Tag team specialists blossomed — lightweight competitors, typically, who executed lightning fast moves and developed team finishing maneuvers. (Ironically, however, the most successful tag team of this era — perhaps any era — was a heavyweight duo who practiced a power-based style, the Road Warriors.) With the success of pretty boy teams like the Fabulous Ones and the Rock and Roll Express, promoters wisely recruited their own teams to draw in a new type of fan: teenage girls. Even promotions like Mid-South Wrestling, which prided themselves on tough, rugged action, realized that young women were an untapped source of revenue — and likely to come to the show accompanied by teenage boys.

The physiques of wrestlers also changed, primarily after the incredible success of Hulk Hogan and the Road Warriors. Again, promoters rushed to duplicate the success of the hard bodies. Some fans felt this wasn't necessarily a good thing: as appearance rather than wrestling ability seemed to be the new criteria for stars, it often lead to poor in-ring performances.

More than anything else, one man changed the business.

When Vince McMahon bought the WWF from his father, few people had any idea what to expect. There were warnings that Vince Jr. was going to do things differently — but most promoters wrote off his big ideas as a pipe dream. McMahon knew differently. He launched a careful campaign to transform the WWF from a northeastern territory into a promotion that spanned the United States and Canada.

McMahon was not the first person to try running on a national scale. During the 1970s, the IWA took a shot, but the ambitious undertaking failed. He wasn't the first person to recognize the potential of cable television either. During a meeting of the NWA in 1979, promoters Mike LeBell and Jim Barnett warned their colleagues that cable television would change the way business was done.

The unfortunate truth was that many promoters had become complacent. When McMahon began airing matches from promotions across the United States, fans were in heaven. Rival promoters didn't seem to mind supplying

McMahon with footage of their top stars, probably viewing the practice as free advertising. Had they known McMahon's true motives, they might have reconsidered. It wasn't long before McMahon's rationale became clear. All of the stars McMahon was featuring would soon work for him. Wrestlers hyped on WWF shows oftentimes disappeared from their promotions overnight.

> Wrestlers have reported that as they were brought into the WWF, they were told to leave the promotions they had been working for without notice. This broke another taboo: promoters traditionally got wrestlers on their way out to do jobs to put over wrestlers who were staying. This left rivals with egg on their face, as wrestlers announced for house shows suddenly were unavailable and storylines already in place had to be dropped prematurely.

The reaction to McMahon varied. In some cases, promoters were bought out; others simply folded. A few refused to sell and went to war. The NWA and AWA had a longstanding policy of banding together when an outsider tried to compete in their territories. They created Pro Wrestling USA, a promotion made up of top stars from both companies. Pro Wrestling USA got off to a good start (and even ran a show in the WWF's backyard, at the New Jersey Meadowlands) but infighting between the various promoters eventually led to its demise.

The WWF's success in the mid-1980s was astonishing. And while Vince McMahon made his share of mistakes, his triumphs outstripped them and the WWF steamrolled its competition.

Despite the WWF's incredible rise in the Rock and Wrestling Era, not everyone was happy. After the demise of JCP, the traditional style of wrestling which emphasized realism and athletics took a backseat to the "show over substance" approach of the WWF. The days of bloody matches and sixty-minute broadways faded as short matches centered on muscular wrestlers with flashy gimmicks became the norm.

TITO SANTANA REGAINS THE INTERCONTINENTAL BELT FROM GREG VALENTINE

By 1984, Tito Santana had become a WWF fixture. The popular Latin-American wrestler had achieved considerable success, winning the tag team championship with "Polish Power" Ivan Putski and grabbing the Intercontinental title from the

Magnificent Muraco. With a babyface having a stranglehold on the WWF championship, Santana had gone as far as he could. Still, the adoration of the fans and the gold around his waist meant life was good.

Santana's climb to the top had been arduous, but nowhere near as hard as the climb back up would be. In September 1984, Santana's world came crashing down when Greg "The Hammer" Valentine defeated him for his Intercontinental belt, hospitalizing him in the process. The scene was London, Ontario, and Santana was set to square off against Valentine in a title defense. The son of legendary grappler Johnny Valentine, the Hammer's reputation as a wrestler who liked to hurt people preceded him. Santana knew he was in for a hellacious title defense but he hadn't counted on Valentine's ace in the hole — "Captain" Lou Albano. The ever-crafty manager distracted Santana before the match, allowing Valentine to blindside him and clip his knee. At 100 percent physical capacity, Santana would have been in for a tough battle; injured, he proved to be no match for the heel and Valentine won the belt despite the champ's spirited defense. After the pin, Valentine clamped his figure-four leglock on Santana's already injured leg, hoping to end his opponent's career.

As a result of that attack, Santana's knee had to be surgically repaired. (Of course, Santana was already scheduled for knee surgery — the injury was used to set up his absence during recovery.) At *WrestleMania*, Santana returned and defeated the Executioner. Later in the card, he made an appearance during Valentine's title defense against the Junkyard Dog, sending the message that he was ready to take back what Valentine had stolen.

While the Hammer may have underestimated Santana's resilience and willpower in their first encounter, he didn't aim to repeat his mistake. Once Tito had worked his way back into title contention, Valentine threw every trick in his arsenal at him. He used all the advantages of being champion in defending his belt, getting himself disqualified or simply bailing out of the ring to avoid defeat. But when a lumberjack match (a match where wrestlers surround the outside of the ring to prevent the combatants from bailing out) against Santana was finally signed, it seemed like Valentine had nowhere to run. Still, thanks to an assist from fellow heel "Big" John Studd, Valentine managed to steal a victory.

Valentine's questionable tactics were not unnoticed by WWF officials. So when Tito Santana demanded a cage match, there were no qualms about sanctioning the bout. Valentine would be locked inside four walls of steel, with no one to rely on but himself.

The match was held at the Baltimore Civic Center in July 1985. Cornered, Valentine proved more dangerous than ever. He understood the rules he had bent to his advantage were useless in a cage. In the WWF, pinfalls and submissions were meaningless; the match could only be won by beating an opponent senseless and escaping over the walls or through the door.

The match went down to the wire. Both men had beaten each other to the point where the fans wondered how either could still stand. Somehow, Santana found the strength to climb the cage while Valentine took the easier path to victory, crawling toward the door. As Santana lowered himself over the fence, it looked like Valentine would escape first. But in an ingenious move, Tito had positioned himself near the cage door. And on his way over he kicked the door into Valentine's head. The champion was stunned. Santana's feet touched the floor and he became the Intercontinental champion for the second time.

Santana held the championship for seven more months before falling prey to Randy "Macho Man" Savage. This would be Santana's last WWF singles reign, but tag team gold still loomed. In 1987, Tito would win the WWF tag team championship with Rick Martel as a member of Strike Force. In 2004 he was inducted into the WWE Hall of Fame.

Valentine's run as a singles champion ended here as well, but like Santana, he found championship success in the tag ranks when he teamed with Brutus Beefcake to form the Dream Team. In 1985, Valentine and Beefcake defeated Mike Rotunda and Barry Windham (a.k.a. the U.S. Express) to win the WWF tag team championship; they held the belts for nearly eight months before dropping them to the British Bulldogs at *WrestleMania 2*. In 2004 Valentine's career would mirror Santana's once more when he too was inducted into the WWE Hall of Fame.

THE LAST STAMPEDE

When Bill Watts brought manager Jim Cornette to Mid-South Wrestling, he wasted no time in casting the youngster as one of the area's top heels. Cornette, a lifelong fan of the squared circle, had become a manager in CWA after working as a photographer, adopting the gimmick of the spoiled rich kid. Unfortunately, it was hard to manage standing in the shadow of the area's number-one heel mouthpiece, Jimmy Hart.

Things changed when Cornette came to work in MSW in a talent trade. Cornette began managing the Midnight Express (Dennis Condrey and Bobby Eaton) and soon, championship gold was theirs.

To celebrate, a party was held on *Mid-South Wrestling*, complete with cake

Andre the Giant

Rock meets wrestling

Dick Murdoch in St. Louis

Andy Kaufman and
Jerry "The King" Lawler

The Iron Sheik

Bob Backlund

Terry Funk and Dusty Rhodes

HOWARD BAUM

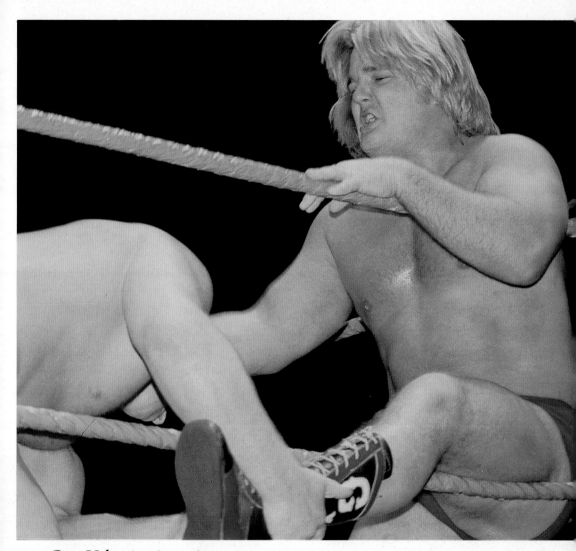

Greg Valentine in action

"Cowboy" Bill Watts and Krusher Kruschev

Big John Studd

Black Jack Mulligan

"Superfly" Jimmy Snuka

Ric Flair

Ricky "The Dragon" Steamboat

Paul Orndorff

"Rowdy" Roddy Piper

The Von Erichs

"The Million Dollar Man" Ted DiBiase and Virgil

Jake "The Snake"
Roberts DDTs
Sting

A Freebird, A Rebel,
Michael Hayes

HOWARD BAUM

"Hot Stuff" Eddie Gilbert

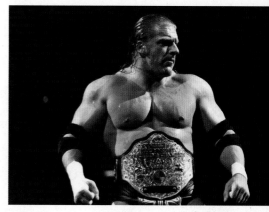

Triple H

*The American Dream
and Magnum T.A.*

KEVIN GUTHRIE

Kane

MIKE RICKARD AND MELISSA ROTHMAN

The Undertaker

Stone Cold

Shane Douglas and Tazz in ECW

and champagne. Cornette and his men reveled in their victory, taunting the fans at ringside. But the celebration turned sour when the Rock and Roll Express (Ricky Morton and Robert Gibson) snuck up from behind and shoved Cornette's face in the cake.

MSW promoter Bill Watts loved the incident so much he decided to replay it every week. Cornette was furious — no one did such a thing to him! The boisterous manager made it clear that he was going to sue, sue, sue. No one in Mid-South Wrestling would escape his wrath, not even the Irish McNeil Boys Club (the site where *MSW* was taped every week). Bill Watts had enough of Cornette's threats and confronted him. Then Cornette made the mistake of a lifetime when he made fun of Watts' son Joel. An angry "Cowboy" slapped Cornette, ending the confrontation.

But the quarrel wasn't over in Cornette's mind. The next week he appeared on *Mid-South TV*, replacing Watts as the show's host. The fans were curious; Watts was a regular part of the program. Soon they understood. During a taped interview with Butch Reed, Watts had been jumped by the Midnight Express and beaten like a dog. The attack was so heinous Reed (who was arguably the promotion's top heel) shook his head and walked away.

Like many before him, Cornette underestimated the Cowboy. Watts' best years were behind him but he wasn't going to let the assault go unanswered. During an interview with Jim Ross, Watts told the fans that he knew fining Cornette would be ineffective. (Cornette's spoiled mama's boy gimmick included a fabulously wealthy mother as part of its backstory.) Instead, he would challenge the Midnight Express and their manager to a match known as "the Last Stampede."

More promos followed, with Watts promising he'd find the toughest partner he could. Watts was seen visiting his long-time friend the Junkyard Dog. The Dog was serving out a ninety-day suspension after losing a loser-leaves-town match, but he led Watts to someone who could help him, a mysterious masked wrestler known as Stagger Lee. Stagger Lee was a controversial figure in the Mid-South region. His resemblance to the Junkyard Dog was uncanny, to the point that the area's top heels accused the Dog of donning a mask and working as Lee to circumvent his suspension.

Eager for revenge, Watts threw out match stipulations to sweeten the victors' pot. If Cornette's team won, the heel manager would gain control of Mid-South Wrestling for six months. Watts having to work for Cornette would only add to his satisfaction. However if Watts won, Cornette would be forced to wear a dress.

On April 7, 1984, a sellout crowd of over 23,000 saw the Cowboy exact his revenge. Watts and Lee started off strong, using the Midnight Express as their personal punching bags. Eventually though, the double-team tactics of the Express, and Cornette's interference, gave the heels the upper hand, putting Watts' anticipated victory in doubt. But when Bobby Eaton tried to throw powder into Watts' eyes, his scheme backfired — thanks to the timely intervention of Stagger Lee. Watts moved in for the kill, scoring the pinfall victory. Knowing what was coming, Cornette did his best to get out of Dodge, but Watts, Lee, Magnum T.A., and Pierce Boyd surrounded him. Cornette was stripped, doused with baby powder, and forced to wear a diaper. The crybaby manager now looked the part he habitually acted.

HOW'S ABOUT A COCONUT?

When "Rowdy" Roddy Piper came to the wwf in 1984, the promotion was in a state of flux. Vince McMahon had recently taken control, and he prized showmanship above all else. Stars who had been the bedrock of his father's company were being phased out in favor of newcomers. Given his incredible charisma and showmanship, Piper's success in the wwf was all but guaranteed. At first, McMahon used him as a manager for "Dr. D" David Schultz and Paul "Mr. Wonderful" Orndorff, and the Rowdy One quickly earned the hatred of wwf fans. While Piper was no stranger to the role of manager, it was a role beneath a worker of his caliber. Still, he quickly jumped into the spotlight, hosting a weekly talk segment called "Piper's Pit." The mini-show allowed him to show off his mic skills as he routinely insulted the wwf's top babyfaces. He angered their fans, too, and often set up matches with his patter. Fans quickly became accustomed to Piper's biting wit — but nothing could prepare them for the day when Piper interviewed "Superfly" Jimmy Snuka.

By the time Superfly appeared on "Piper's Pit," he was one of the most beloved wrestlers in the wwf. He'd recently completed a feud with the Magnificent Muraco and he was at the peak of his popularity, a fame rivaling that of Hulk Hogan at the time. What better way for Piper to make himself a main-eventer than to cross paths with Snuka?

When Snuka arrived on his show, an unusually gracious Piper told him he wanted to make him feel at home. Piper produced a grocery bag and began to empty its contents. He reached into the brown bag and a pineapple emerged. He then reached in and pulled out a bunch of bananas. Piper suggested the tropical fruit would remind Snuka of his Fiji Islands home, but all his antics seemed to do was bring Snuka's blood to a boil. With Snuka watching on in disbelief, Piper continued the charade, revealing some coconuts. Snuka stood in silence as Piper told him this was his chance to talk, his chance, in Piper's words, "to be a big shot." It was clear from the look on Snuka's face he wasn't amused. But Piper continued antagonizing his guest. He falsely apologized, feigning sadness because he didn't have a tree for the Superfly to climb.

Snuka had finally had enough, and he asked Piper if he was making fun of him. Clearly aware Snuka's patience had reached its end, Piper grabbed one of the coconuts and cracked it over his guest's head. Snuka fell back onto the backdrop, knocking it over as Piper asked, "Am I making fun of you?"

But the assault had only just begun. Piper proceeded to humiliate Snuka, rubbing a banana in his face and screaming, "You want a banana?" Then he circled around the fallen wrestler, repeating Snuka's "Are you making fun of me?" Next, he screamed, "You want to be a big shot?" and as Snuka crawled toward him, Piper whipped him with a weight belt, tearing the skin off Snuka's back.

"Everybody wants to be a big shot," Piper taunted.

Piper continued the verbal and physical beating; finally Snuka rose to his feet and let out a blood-chilling battle cry. Piper left through a door and locked it — but not before making a rude gesture at Snuka. Snuka rushed for the door and smashed against it, but Piper was gone. Wrestlers from the dressing room (including Tito Santana and B. Brian Blair) came onto the scene and stopped Snuka from doing something he might regret for the rest of his life.

Thanks to this event, "Rowdy" Roddy Piper and "Superfly" Snuka created an instant feud. The two would battle repeatedly, including a match that led to a storyline where Piper broke Snuka's neck, sidelining the popular star. While Snuka recovered, his cousin, the Tonga Kid, showed up seeking revenge. Snuka and the Tonga Kid would work tag team matches against Piper and "Cowboy" Bob Orton (Piper's storyline bodyguard), adding more fire to the already hot feud.

The Snuka feud established Piper as the WWF's number-one heel. He became the villain Vince McMahon would build the main event of *WrestleMania* around. Unfortunately for Jimmy Snuka, personal problems soon pushed him out of the spotlight.

THE KING GETS CROWNED!

Memphis-area fans remember the wild stipulation matches that were a big part of the promotion's perennial charm. In CWA, wrestlers fought over more than titles (though there were plenty of those to go around), often putting money, property, or their careers on the line. But most of the time, in Memphis a stipulation match meant you put up your dignity, with the loser having to undergo any manner of humiliation: being powdered and diapered, tarred and feathered, or shaving off their hair. One man who was no stranger to stipulation matches was Jerry "the King" Lawler. In particular, he excelled at the hair vs. hair match. Many an opponent walked away shorn after falling victim to the King. Lawler's record in hair vs. hair matches was highlighted by a victory over "Superstar" Bill Dundee, after which Dundee's *wife* had to have her head shaved. It seemed like Lawler was unbeatable in these matches, but everything changed on the night of April 27, 1987, when he battled Austin Idol.

With the nickname "The King of Memphis," it was clear Lawler was the top man in the territory. Whether he wrestled as a heel or a face, he played second banana to no one. More often than not, that led to conflict with the other top stars when it came time for title shots, especially world title shots. Back in the '70s and '80s, the National Wrestling Alliance (NWA) and American Wrestling Association (AWA) world champion toured the country. In the case of CWA, a world champion might show up only once or twice a year to defend the title. Naturally, this meant world title shots were a huge deal, and the competition was so fierce it could turn friends into enemies.

That was just what happened between Austin Idol and Jerry Lawler. Idol, a notorious hothead, took offense when the powers that be decided Lawler would receive a title shot against the AWA champion Nick Bochwinkel. His anger led to a chain match in which Lawler prevailed in under a minute, completely humiliating Idol in the process. Furious, Idol enlisted the help of Tommy Rich in an attempt to exact payback. The blonde bombers tried to take Lawler out on several occasions but found him an elusive target. After several frustrating encounters, Idol agreed to a steel cage match against Lawler. It was more than a cage match though — it was a hair vs. hair cage match. Worse, if Idol lost, the fans would have their tickets refunded — thanks to Idol putting up $50,000 of his own money as security.

Longtime CWA announcer Lance Russell introduced the two combatants. Idol's manager Paul E. Dangerously was forced outside the cage, despite his protests. Lawler wasted no time getting down to business, determined to settle things for good. At one point, the referee was knocked out, but neither man seemed in a hurry to score a pinfall. Things were looking pretty good for the King, until Idol's friend Tommy Rich appeared out of nowhere and blindsided Lawler. (Rich had hid under the ring earlier in the day, playing possum for hours until it was time to strike.) Rich piledrived Lawler and then Idol joined in the fun, double-teaming Memphis's other favorite son with a spike piledriver.

> Through the years, shrewd promoters incorporated real-life injuries into wrestling angles. Jerry Lawler remembers the famous match with Idol and how he worked an upcoming surgery into an angle: "They did the number where they each took one of my legs and pulled me into the post. I got posted. It looked like it wrecked me. Well, the truth of the matter was that I was scheduled to have a vasectomy reversal the following morning. We had cameras at the hospital, filming me going into surgery to have my testicles worked on. It was a real-shoot operation, but we did the angle to play off it, to utilize the operation. I had to be off a couple of weeks anyway. It turned out to be one of the hottest angles. It looked great when they ran me into the post. I kind of turned my ass up when they did it so it hit my butt, more or less, but I got a big bruise."

The fans were furious, but there was nothing they could do but watch in horror as their beloved hero was eventually pinned. After winning the match, Idol and Rich each grabbed one of Lawler's legs and rammed his groin into the ring post. By now, Lawler had no idea where he was. The King was summarily escorted into a chair and a barber executed the match's haircut stipulation. Lawler's personal barber was on hand to administer the haircut as Paul E. Dangerously collected Lawler's hair into a plastic bag. While Lawler had lost, he actually received more of a brush cut than a complete shave. Nevertheless, fans were shocked that he had lost hair, as well as a good portion of his dignity, to the hated heels.

As Dave Meltzer reported in the *Wrestling Observer*, the Memphis Coliseum fans were close to rioting. Rich and Idol were safe as long as they stayed in the cage — but the crowd didn't seem to be in any hurry to go home. Eventually, security managed to run the heels to safety.

GIRLS JUST WANT TO HAVE FUN

For a brief moment, the Rock and Wrestling Connection made Wendi Richter a bigger star than even WWF champion Hulk Hogan. On the night of July 23, 1984,

Richter wrestled the Fabulous Moolah for the WWF Woman's Championship in a match nicknamed *The Brawl To Settle It All*. The confrontation would help pave the road to *WrestleMania* and make the WWF a pop culture phenomenon.

The match's roots extended months back, to when rising pop star Cyndi Lauper had asked long-time heel manager "Captain" Lou Albano to appear in her video "Girls Just Want to Have Fun." Never one to pass up a chance in the spotlight, the charismatic Albano agreed and his appearance in the video earned him mainstream fame as MTV viewers delighted in Albano's over-the-top performance as Lauper's father. Soon, Albano was everywhere, riding the waves of success.

After a noted career as a wrestler, Albano had smoothly transitioned from wrestler to manager, becoming one of the unholy trinity of heel managers in the WWWF (with "Classy" Freddie Blassie and the Grand Wizard). Albano was known for managing team after team to the WWWF tag championship. His outrageous interviews and colorful appearance were eclipsed only by the equally off-the-wall duos he managed, including the Wild Samoans. Not surprisingly, Albano's charisma caught the eye of Hollywood.

Following his success with Lauper, Albano appeared on "Piper's Pit" to boast about his newfound career in music. Albano talked up his accomplishments, mentioning the periodicals he'd appeared in and claiming a key role in Lauper's success. After further self-congratulation, Albano was asked by Piper if he might be able to get Lauper to show up on "Piper's Pit."

For weeks, Albano promised to produce Lauper, but after repeated no-shows, fans were beginning to wonder if this was just more of the usual baloney they'd come to expect from the Captain. Then the moment that would forever change the face of women's wrestling finally occurred — Lauper appeared on "Piper's Pit." During the buildup to Lauper's appearance, When Lauper finally appeared, she thanked Albano for his help, but told Piper and his audience that Albano was not her manager. An enraged Albano began shouting and screaming at Lauper (of course, shouting and screaming was Albano's normal tone of voice), berating her and once more claiming responsibility for her success.

Richter would later have problems with WWF management, which led to the company taking the belt off of her and putting it back on Moolah by subterfuge. This controversial finish predated wrestling's infamous "Montreal Screwjob" by twelve years and has become known as the "Original Screwjob."

Albano was clearly of the mindset that a woman's place was in the home, and he began patronizing Ms. Lauper. "The Manager of Champions" was in for a shock when Lauper yelled back and shoved him out of her personal space. A stunned Albano looked on as Lauper left him to rethink his actions.

WWF fans had come to know that Albano wasn't satisfied unless he got the last word. And when Lauper popped his balloon, he swore revenge. Albano had boasted of his tremendous success as a manager and argued for the superiority of men over women. But the young singer was not going to back down and she issued a challenge. They would each select a wrestler to manage, and their match would determine who was the superior manager. The erstwhile battle of the sexes led to Lauper selecting a wrestler named Wendi Richter to face a wrestler of Albano's choosing. A cocky Albano selected the legendary WWF women's champion, the Fabulous Moolah. Moolah had held the title for the better part of twenty-seven years, and he was confident Lauper's charge had no chance.

Thanks to Lauper's connections in the music industry, it was natural for MTV to be involved. Lauper's videos were in heavy rotation, and with the help of her manager/boyfriend David Wolff, she was able to get the spectacle aired on MTV. Thanks to the publicity, a woman's match would headline Madison Square Garden as a WWF main event. *The Brawl To Settle It All* opened with Lauper accompanying Richter into the ring as "Girls Just Want to Have Fun" played on the loudspeakers.

The match itself was nothing memorable, but the hype surrounding it made it a phenomenal success both for MTV and the WWF. In the end, Richter triumphed, winning the women's championship and ushering in a new era of women's wrestling.

After the match, Albano saw the error of his ways and slowly began the turn from heel to hero. Albano's switch would be cemented after he worked with Lauper to raise money to fight multiple sclerosis.

THE GIANT AND THE HAIRCUT

Ken Patera broke into wrestling alongside "Nature Boy" Ric Flair in Verne Gagne's AWA. In his autobiography *To Be the Man*, Flair joked about the results of their bodybuilding regimes: "Before the Olympics, he was trying to become as big as possible. I began eating like him. We'd drink two gallons of milk and eat two dozen eggs — yolks and all — then go to Burger King for five Whoppers. He transformed everything into muscle. In my case, 40 percent of what I ate became fat."

While *WrestleMania I* is best known for the main event, featuring Hulk Hogan, Mr. T, Roddy Piper, and Paul Orndorff, it also featured a highly publicized match between Andre the Giant and "Big" John Studd. The $15,000 Body Slam Challenge had Andre putting his career on the line against Studd's money, with the winner being the man who was first able to body-slam his opponent. What led to this match was an angle known as the haircut match, and it was one of the biggest angles of the Giant's career.

After arriving in the World Wrestling Federation, manager Bobby "The Brain" Heenan set out to make a name for himself and his wrestlers (collectively known as "The Bobby Heenan Family") by taking out the biggest man in the WWF. Heenan knew he had his work cut out for him, but he also knew he had two of the toughest men in the game — "Big" John Studd and "The Olympic Strongman" Ken Patera.

Ken Patera was a former Olympic weightlifter who had been the first American to clean-and-jerk 500 pounds. He was also a skilled wrestler and, while not as big as John Studd, a powerhouse in his own right.

Heenan put out a challenge for Andre and a partner of his choosing to face off against Patera and Studd. Who would be Andre's partner? There were many greats who would jump at the chance to team with the legend, but no one could have predicted he would choose "Special Delivery" Jones. Jones, a journeyman with a less-than-stellar win-loss record, was an undercard wrestler and probably the last man fans would have expected. Perhaps Andre was sending a message, telling Studd and Patera that he didn't need anyone's help. But Andre would soon learn otherwise.

The match started off strong, with Jones holding his own against Patera. Jones then tagged in Andre who dominated Patera. When Jones returned to the ring he lost his momentum, being overwhelmed by the power of Studd and Patera. When the opportunity to escape presented itself, Jones wisely tagged out. Unfortunately, on his way back to his corner, Jones was tossed from the ring by Patera, and when he hit the floor hard he was knocked senseless. Now on his own, Andre went after the Olympian. Andre threw Patera into the corner, then smashed his 500-pound frame against him. However, when he tried the move a second time, Patera lifted his knee and stunned the giant. Patera then climbed the turnbuckle and delivered a devastating kneedrop across the back of Andre's head.

Patera was quickly joined by his tag partner. Studd entered the ring illegally and joined Patera in beating Andre senseless. Heenan's henchmen pummeled Andre mercilessly and, in an impressive feat of strength, lifted Andre up for a body slam. Andre crumpled to the mat as Studd and Patera continued their thrashing, dropping elbows and knees until the Giant was unconscious.

When Bobby "The Brain" Heenan mounted the mat apron, it suddenly became clear that the challenge had actually been a set-up. Heenan handed Studd a pair of scissors, and the big man began clipping the Giant's bushy head of hair while Patera held him down. In one of the greatest bits of hyperbole ever heard in professional wrestling, announcer Vince McMahon cried out: "This is humiliation. This is sheer humiliation. . . . Studd and Patera are raping the dignity of Andre the Giant."

After the assault, Patera grabbed some of Andre's hair and held it up for the fans to see.

For the next few weeks, Studd and Patera traveled across the country with a bag of Andre's hair. Fans couldn't wait to see the Giant get his revenge. Andre's started with Patera. After defeating the Olympic Strongman, he next targeted John Studd, issuing the body slam challenge for the first *WrestleMania*. Despite Patera's loss, Heenan was confident in Studd's ability, putting up a $15,000 guarantee that Andre wouldn't be able to slam him. When Vince McMahon asked Andre on *Tuesday Night Titans* why he hadn't put anything on the line for the match, the Giant became enraged and announced he'd retire if he didn't slam Studd.

The match at *WrestleMania* saw Andre make short work of Heenan's man, slamming Studd in less than six minutes. Andre began disbursing Studd's cash to the fans at ringside — until Bobby Heenan snuck up behind him and stole the duffel bag containing the money. (Heenan would later make the outrageous claim that Studd had been hip-tossed rather than slammed.) But Andre's victory proved that he was still professional wrestling's only true giant.

Looking back, the haircut match holds up as one of the greatest angles of all time. Few wrestlers possessed the size or strength to be legitimate opponents for Andre, but Patera and Studd fit the bill. Studd's size and Patera's power made Andre being beaten unconscious believable. Bobby Heenan helped sustain the heat by appearing on WWF television week after week, bragging about what his men had done. Studd and Patera got instant heat whenever they pulled out the bag of Andre's hair. With the exception of the buildup between Andre and Hogan that led up to *WrestleMania III*, this was unquestionably the greatest angle of the Giant's career.

THE DEBUT OF THE FABULOUS ONES

Top coat, Top hat,
And I don't worry coz my wallet's fat.
Black shades, white gloves,
lookin' sharp and lookin' for love.
They come runnin' just as fast as they can
coz every girl crazy 'bout a sharp dressed man.
—**"Sharp Dressed Man," ZZ Top**

One of the many innovative promotional techniques used by Jerry Lawler and Jerry Jarrett was the music video. According to Lawler, "We started doing music videos with our wrestlers, which few promotions had really done before. We used them to get people over. Taking the most popular songs of the day, we'd add some wrestling footage and shots of the guys getting into a Corvette with girls. A two-minute video got some guys over much better than a fifteen-minute match or an interview."

It's difficult to place the exact moment when tag team wrestling took off again. There were always good teams to be found, but by the early 1980s, tag specialists were in vogue in just about every promotion. Ricky Steamboat and Jay Youngblood have often been credited for the tag team resurgence. And certainly the Road Warriors were a tremendous draw, wherever they went, in the 1980s.

One pivotal duo is often overlooked in discussions of what made tag team wrestling so popular during the '80s. This team spawned a legion of imitators: the Rock and Roll Express, the Midnight Express, the Fantastics, and the Rockers.

Not surprisingly, the team was developed in Memphis's Continental Wrestling Association, a promotion always ahead of its time in terms of booking and angles. In the early 1980s, heel manager Jimmy Hart introduced the latest of the many tag teams he had formed to taunt the area's faces (and more importantly, their fans). Dressed in white tuxedos and top hats, the combination of the Love Machine and Rick McGraw were known as the New York Dolls.

In typical Jimmy Hart fashion, he promised his new team would win a championship in their first title match or he would leave the Memphis area. Eager to see the hated manager exiled, Memphis fans were disappointed when the Dolls defeated Spike Huber and Steve Regal for the World Wrestling Association (WWA) world tag team championship, one of the many titles used in the CWA promotion.

Even angrier though was local legend Jackie Fargo. Fargo had wrestled solo in the 1950s, and with his "brother" Don Fargo as "The Fabulous Fargos" he had gone on to big regional success in the Tennessee area during the '60s and '70s. Fargo took exception to Hart's team, feeling that they were nothing but cheap imitations. So, in true wrestling form, Fargo formed his own team to send against Hart's New York Dolls.

Behind the scenes, the Fabulous Ones had been born when CWA promoter Jerry Jarrett happened upon MTV and the station's cutting edge music videos. The CWA had combined music and video before, but Jarrett wanted to take things to the next level. After pairing veteran wrestler Steve Keirn with Stan Lane (a protégé of "Nature Boy" Ric Flair), he costumed them in top hats, tuxedos, and canes and shot a video set to Billy Squier's "Everybody Wants You." Soon after, the Fabulous Ones debuted — and they began working against the New York Dolls.

The Fabulous Ones became the hottest tag team in the CWA, combining wrestling, brawling, and a touch of Chippendales to win the attention of male and female fans alike. The Fabs' popularity saw them eventually compete in the AWA against world tag team champions the Road Warriors. The Fabs were even booked by promoter Verne Gagne to win the championship, but the Road Warriors refused to put them over. Over time, the Fabulous Ones wrestled in several regional promotions, including Florida Championship Wrestling, until the team disbanded in 1987 with Steve Keirn's short-lived retirement from wrestling.

While the Fabulous Ones made their mark, their biggest contribution to wrestling was perhaps in the legion of teams who emulated their style. After the Fabs proved box office draws, local promoters did what promoters always do — they copied the Fabs ad nauseam. First came the Rock and Roll Express — Ricky Morton and Robert Gibson. Morton and Gibson wrestled on the CWA "B" shows while the Fabs wrestled on the "A" shows. Other promoters formed their own versions as well. By the middle of the 1980s the Fabulous Ones' success had created a chain reaction, with tag teams becoming popular across the nation. The British Bulldogs, the Hart Foundation, the Fantastics, the Midnight Express, and the Midnight Rockers were just the tip of the iceberg.

STEAMBOAT VS. FLAIR

Professional wrestling has had its share of classic rivalries, and while Jack Brisco vs. Dory Funk Jr., Triple H vs. Michaels, Austin vs. Rock, and Hogan vs. Savage all come to mind, there was nothing quite like Flair vs. Steamboat. These two epitomized the NWA style of wrestling, creating money-making programs whenever they locked up. Better yet, their matches have long been considered some of the finest in wrestling's history.

As with many of the great feuds, it's hard to choose a favorite program. Steamboat and Flair first met in Jim Crockett Promotions, where Steamboat quickly won fans. His speed and technical prowess, coupled with his good looks, made him a natural babyface. (Steamboat would remain a babyface throughout his career, one of the very few individuals in the sport's history to manage the feat.) Putting Steamboat in a program against the area's top heel, Ric Flair, was a no-brainer.

Their matches were built up with angles that would be repeated throughout their careers. One of the most memorable was when Flair attacked Steamboat and drove his face into a concrete floor in an attempt to destroy Steamboat's good looks (the angle would be revisited during the 1980s during Flair's program with Ricky Morton). Steamboat would avenge himself by attacking Flair during an interview and stripping him of his custom-made suit.

The two men would meet in the squared circle countless times over the next two decades, sometimes against each other, sometimes wrestling together. During the late 1980s, WCW decided to revisit the feud after Steamboat's WWF run. Steamboat's WCW return came when "Hot Stuff" Eddie Gilbert enlisted the aid of a mystery partner against the tandem of Flair and Barry Windham. After unveiling Steamboat as his partner, Gilbert and the fans saw Steamboat pin Flair in the center of the ring. The message was received: not only was Steamboat back, he was gunning for the belt that had previously eluded him — the NWA world championship.

What followed next was one of the most celebrated series in professional wrestling. Steamboat captured the belt in an epic match at the *Chi-Town Rumble* pay-per-view on February 23, 1989. He held the title until May 7, when Flair regained it at the *Wrestlewar* pay-per-view. Along the way to *Wrestlewar,* Flair and Steamboat set the wrestling world on fire with show-stopping matches across the country and on television. Their two out of three falls match at *Clash of Champions VI* is still considered by many fans to be one of the finest matches ever broadcast on television.

I QUIT!

The harder you work, the harder it is to surrender.
—**Vince Lombardi**

Despite the widespread popularity of the wwf, not all wrestling fans enjoyed the product. Fortunately, there were still promotions offering the gritty, traditional style of wrestling people had grown up with. No match epitomized this better than the classic "I quit" confrontation between Magnum T.A. and Tully Blanchard.

Both Blanchard and Magnum had seen their stars rise in jcp and their eventual feud propelled them to true stardom as they battled over the U.S. title. Magnum had earned the prestigious belt after defeating Wahoo McDaniel in a steel cage match. He was later cheated out of the title thanks to Tully's bodyguard, Baby Doll. Disguised as a security guard, Baby Doll was able to pass a foreign object to Blanchard during a title match, giving him the edge he needed to win. Baby Doll's interference continued throughout Blanchard's title defenses against the popular T.A., making it seem as if Magnum would never regain the belt.

Magnum was no stranger to adversity. His work in Bill Watts' msw had made him tough, whether it was enduring a tar and feathering at the hands of the Midnight Express or being whipped after his partner Mr. Wrestling II walked out on him in a fit of jealousy. He continued campaigning for the U.S. title, even going as far as disguising *himself* as a security guard to attack Blanchard.

An exasperated Blanchard decided to end the chase by agreeing to a title defense inside a steel cage. But this would be no ordinary cage match. Both Blanchard and T.A. stipulated that the only way to win the match was to make your opponent quit. A referee would be in the cage with a microphone, and unlike in traditional matches, his only role would be to check and see if one of the competitors was ready to give up.

With Baby Doll locked outside, Magnum finally had his chance to face Blanchard without interference. Blanchard knew Magnum would be looking for payback as well as the United States championship. The men beat each other senseless, with neither man giving ground. And as often happens in cage matches, the structure itself became a weapon.

As the match progressed, it became clear that Blanchard still needed something extra. He naturally looked to Baby Doll. Although she was unable to enter the locked cage, the crafty Blanchard knew she could still be of use. He instructed her to throw a chair into the structure, and then he smashed it and used a piece of the broken chair leg against T.A. Before the referee could even protest, Tully kicked him, knocking him to the mat.

A bloodthirsty Blanchard then jumped on top of his opponent, shoving the jagged wood toward his eye. Magnum T.A. grabbed Blanchard's hands and fought back with every ounce of strength he had. With the referee out of action, Magnum must have known Blanchard was trying to end his career. He held Blanchard's hands back and finally positioned himself so he could take his opponent out. Using his free leg, Magnum kneed Blanchard in the side, finally knocking the champion off of him. Magnum scrambled for the chair leg and grabbed it. Wasting no time, he jumped behind Blanchard and drove the sharp piece of wood down onto his head. After Blanchard's attempt to take out his eye, Magnum wasn't holding back. Within seconds, Blanchard gave up, no doubt aware that his career was in jeopardy if he didn't surrender.

The "I quit" match would be remembered as one of the highlights of JCP during the 1980s. The "I quit" concept was strong enough that it would be brought back time and time again. One of the most memorable of these matches would involve "Nature Boy" Ric Flair and Terry Funk.

THE COSMIC COWBOYS VS. THE DYNAMIC DUO

In Fritz Von Erich's World Class Championship Wrestling, the Von Erichs reigned supreme. The brothers' individual stars outshined all others in the promotion, but there was one outsider who came close to achieving the Von Erichs' popularity. "Gentleman" Chris Adams had earned the respect and love of Texans, becoming so closely aligned with the Von Erichs that he was considered part of the family. A native of England, Adams' good looks, dazzling ring skills, and English charm made him very likeable.

Imagine the fans' horror then when Adams turned on the Von Erichs and joined forces with hated manager Gary Hart. Hart was one of the most despised men in WCCW, managing some of the territory's nastiest heels and constantly making life miserable for the Von Erichs. He was also successful, something that did not go unnoticed by Adams. Despite Hart's background, Adams told the fans to give him a chance as he was sure the manager would guide him to greater success. Against the wishes of both the fans and the Von Erichs, Adams hired Hart.

Eventually, everyone's worst fears came true as Adams turned his back on long-time friend Kevin Von Erich. In a tag bout against Gino Hernandez and

Jake Roberts, interference from Stella Mae French backfired, and Adams became enraged. French had taken over for her storyline niece Sunshine while Sunshine was injured, but her well-intentioned interference had cost her team dearly. And when Gary Hart began berating French, Kevin Von Erich intervened — only to catch a superkick in the face from Adams.

Von Erich was willing to let bygones be bygones if Adams fired Hart. Adams' response was to break a chair over Kevin's head. This led to a lengthy war, with both men doing their best to put the other out of action. Not long after that, Adams fired Hart and began teaming with Hernandez, forming a tag team nicknamed the Dynamic Duo.

The Dynamic Duo quickly became a thorn in the side of the Von Erichs. At the 1985 David Von Erich Memorial Parade of Champions, they spoiled Kevin Von Erich's victory when they destroyed a brand new car he had won in a tag team contest. This led to a series of matches with the Von Erichs, but neither team could score a conclusive victory.

Around this time, the Dynamic Duo began cutting the hair of defeated opponents. Adams and Hernandez would bring golden scissors to the ring and use them to add insult to injury. Emboldened by their success, they challenged Kevin and Kerry Von Erich to a hair vs. hair match. Their cockiness cost them their locks, however, as they lost the match and were shorn in front of thousands of fans in the Cotton Bowl.

Adams and Hernandez vowed to use the misstep to their advantage — and that they did, by wearing identical masks into the ring and using them to get the upper hand. Whether it was loading the masks with foreign objects or tricking the referees by their similar appearances, Hernandez and Adams continued to plague the Von Erichs.

After taking the Dynamic Duo's hair, the Von Erichs next focused on their belts. After thwarting the brothers' numerous attempts to capture the tag titles, Adams and Hernandez finally refused to fight them anymore. With the Dynamic Duo unwilling to wrestle, the Von Erichs tried a different tack. A match was signed between the Dynamic Duo and a new team of masked men named the Cosmic Cowboys. Just as the match was set to begin, the Cowboys took off their masks, revealing themselves as the Von Erichs. As the match progressed, it was clear that the tag team titles were in jeopardy. At the same time, the Dynamic Duo's partnership began to crumble before the fans' eyes when Gino Hernandez refused to take a tag from Chris Adams, acting as if his knee was injured.

Sensing that everything was going awry, Adams got his team intentionally disqualified. While the titles were saved, the partnership ended that night. When

Hernandez's knee injury miraculously healed, Adams exploded, superkicking his partner and effectively dissolving the team.

Adams and Hernandez would go on to have a brief feud, but it was cut short when Hernandez died from a cocaine overdose. Those who worked with Hernandez, however, have doubts about whether Hernandez's death was an accident. Although Adams would continue wrestling for another two decades, he too would see his life cut short. On October 17, 2001, Adams was shot to death after a drunken brawl.

NO MORE MR. NICE GUYS

As confusing as it may sound, a six-man championship is actually held by only three wrestlers. "Six-man" refers to the fact that two teams of three compete in these matches.

From the start of their JCP debut, the Road Warriors were cheered. Hawk and Animal's brutal style wowed the Carolinas, just as it had wowed audiences wherever they'd wrestled. Of course, it didn't hurt that the Roadies battled some of the promotion's most hated heels, including the Russians and the Four Horsemen. But to the Road Warriors being on the side of the angels mattered little, especially when one triumph proved elusive — the NWA world tag team championship.

Their style hadn't really changed, but the Roadies felt that they had grown soft playing to the fans. Their failure to win the NWA title seemed to call for a new approach — or rather a return to the take-no-prisoners style that had served them so well early on. Unfortunately for the man called Sting, he was in their way.

While the Road Warriors didn't possess the belt they wanted, they did share the NWA world six-man tag team championship with "The American Dream" Dusty Rhodes. When three were scheduled to defend their belts against the Varsity Club (Mike Rotunda, Kevin Sullivan, and Rick Steiner), Rhodes was unable to participate (he was reportedly at the Special Olympics). His friend, Sting, agreed to fill in for him. Things were looking rough for the Roadies and Sting until Animal tagged in Hawk. As often happens in these matches, all six men soon found themselves in the ring and the referee quickly lost control. After Sullivan and Steiner were tossed out, Sting slapped the scorpion death lock on

Rotunda. Inexplicably, Hawk pulled him off the TV champion. Sting confronted him, only to be waylaid by Animal. Rotunda was thrown over the top rope, prompting a disqualification by referee Tommy Young. Paul Ellering directed traffic while the Roadies beat down Sting, culminating in a "doomsday device" (a double-team move by the Road Warriors where one would hold their opponent in a bearhug and the other would hit a clothesline off of the top rope), that saw Sting do a 360. A stunned Lex Luger ran in to make the save, only to get clothes-lined and beaten down himself until the babyface dressing room emptied.

Backstage, announcer Tony Schiavone asked the Road Warriors to explain the attack on their own partner. An angry Animal said Sting had no business coming in and that the Legion of Doom (LOD) was tired of carrying guys like Sting and Dusty, tired of being the team newcomers jumped to make a name for them-selves. From now on, he explained, the only people he needed were Hawk and Ellering. Hawk echoed Animal's comments, while manager Precious Paul blamed Dusty for shirking his commitments and helping out "special kids."

Sting, it seems, was just in the wrong place at the wrong time.

It didn't take the LOD long to go after Rhodes. On an episode of WCW, Dusty squared off against Animal in an impromptu bout. Rhodes held his own, but he was soon attacked by Hawk. As Dusty and Hawk battled, Animal unscrewed a spike from the LOD shoulderpads and struck Dusty in the head. Things became even nastier when Animal jabbed the spike into Rhodes' eye. Once again, an army of babyfaces charged the ring.

Speaking from the announcers table at *Clash of the Champions IV*, Lex Luger said it best when he talked about how the fans loved to cheer for the bad boys of professional wrestling. But the Road Warriors' new attitude was different. They were now out to end people's livelihoods, whether it was their attempt to break Sting's neck, or take out Dusty's eye. The Road Warriors had to be stopped.

After everything that happened, there was no way the NWA six-man champs would remain partners. This resulted in a match at *Clash of Champions IV* where Rhodes battled Animal to determine who would hold the six-man belts. If Rhodes won, he would get to choose two new partners; if Animal were victorious the Roadies would control the title. The match began with Rhodes eliminating Ellering with a bionic elbow, then going after Animal. With his face painted to mimic the Road Warriors' look and his injured eye heavily bandaged, the Dream fought fiercely. It was clear to anyone watching that Dusty was more interested in revenge than any championship. Rhodes grabbed Animal's leg and smashed it against the ring post several times before clamping on the figure-four leglock in an attempt to break his former ally's leg. Rhodes continued the assault, drawing concern from the referee. When Tommy Young tried to stop Rhodes' brutality, he was elbowed and hurled out of the ring. With Young dispatched, Animal's teammate Hawk rushed in and the two began double-teaming Rhodes.

The arrival of Sting saw the odds evened. Sting battled Hawk outside the ring, leaving Rhodes to attend to Animal. Rhodes continued his quest for payback as he grabbed a chair and beat Animal with it. Referee Young had seen enough, and Rhodes was disqualified. The Warriors ultimately chose Genichiro Tenryu as their new partner, but the six-man belts were soon retired.

As a booker, Dusty Rhodes was put to pasture after the spike incident, with wcw officials facing stiff criticism over the violence from executives at Ted Turner's Superstation TBS executives. The Road Warriors' heel turn would soon end as the fans just couldn't bring themselves to boo the team, no matter what tactics they used or who they fought.

DANNY DAVIS IS SUSPENDED FOR LIFE

> *There was a crooked man, and he went a crooked mile,*
> *He found a crooked sixpence against a crooked stile:*
> *He bought a crooked cat, which caught a crooked mouse,*
> *And they all lived together in a crooked little house.*
> **—Nursery rhyme**

"Danny Davis is suspended for life!"

With those words, WWF President Jack Tunney barred long-time WWF referee Danny Davis from ever officiating another match. In the words of Gorilla Monsoon, a "miscarriage of justice" had taken place because of Davis' biased officiating during a WWF tag team championship match between the British Bulldogs and the Hart Foundation.

The storyline — a crooked referee costing the tag team champions their belts — underscored a classic series between two of the greatest teams in WWF history. In one corner the British Bulldogs: Davey Boy Smith and the Dynamite Kid. In the other, the Hart Foundation: Bret "The Hitman" Hart and Jim "The Anvil" Neidhart.

Even before the British Bulldogs had captured the WWF tag team titles from the Dream Team (Greg "The Hammer" Valentine and Brutus Beefcake) at *WrestleMania 2*, the Bulldogs had scrapped with the Hart Foundation in fast-paced exciting matches across the United States and Canada. The four men were no strangers to each other, each having worked in Stu Hart's Stampede Wrestling before coming to the WWF.

By the time the title was to switch hands, the Dynamite Kid was wrestling in agony — the result of injuries he had suffered over the years. Dynamite was respected for his high-risk maneuvers, but years of performing stunts with no regard for his body had finally taken their toll. In essence, he was unable to wrestle — but the title still had to change hands. Despite his injuries, a scheme was hatched that would allow the Bulldogs to drop the belts without Dynamite having to step into the ring.

Around this time, the WWF had been running a storyline about a crooked referee, Danny Davis. Although this type of angle had been tried before, it was something the WWF had never explored. Smartly, the WWF took its time establishing Davis as corrupt. At first, his questionable calls were ignored. Then a pattern began to develop. Davis would disqualify babyface wrestlers, or make fast counts on them for no apparent reason. Curiously, all of his bad calls seemed to favor the heels. Eventually, Gorilla Monsoon pointed out that Davis seemed to live a nicer lifestyle than other referees — the announcer was implying the ref was on the take.

Eventually, Davis' calls became so bad that it was obvious that he was in cahoots with the heels. In a match between Randy "Macho Man" Savage and Billy Jack Haynes, the ref disqualified Haynes when *Savage* kicked him (when a wrestler strikes a referee, it is usually grounds for immediate disqualification, resulting in a loss). The call was impossible to justify, but Davis made it nonetheless. Soon after, Davis would involve himself in a title match between Savage and Ricky Steamboat, breaking up a count made by another referee when it looked like Savage was going to be pinned.

So by the time the Bulldogs/Hart Foundation match came along, the fans knew Danny Davis was on the take. What happened next, therefore, wasn't unexpected. The Bulldogs came to the ring with Davey Boy Smith carrying Dynamite (who couldn't walk) on his shoulders. Before the match could begin, Dynamite was struck with Jimmy Hart's megaphone, and knocked out cold. As Dynamite lay outside, Davey Boy wrestled alone against Hart and Neidhart. Despite the two-to-one disadvantage, he held his own. As the match progressed, it became apparent that Davey Boy was actually at a greater disadvantage: Danny Davis did nothing to stop the Hart Foundation from working over Smith *together*. Instead, Davis spent most of the match checking on the Dynamite Kid. It was clear the referee was simply turning a blind eye to the Hart Foundation's tactics.

At one point it looked like Smith might even win the match. After knocking

Bret Hart out of the ring, he power-slammed Neidhart and covered him for the pin. Alas, there was no one to make the count; Davis was still outside, "checking on Dynamite." A frustrated Smith reached his hands through the ring ropes and dragged Davis in by the hair. As he did, Bret Hart smashed into Smith from behind, knocking him down. From there, the Hart Foundation regained their bearings and worked Smith over mercilessly, double-teaming him while Danny Davis again disappeared from the ring.

Davis ultimately ignored the carnage until the Hart Foundation hit their finishing move (Neidhart held Smith in a bearhug while Hart clotheslined him). Then, finally, he returned — to count to three and crown the Hart Foundation the new wwf tag team champions.

Following the match, wwf President Jack Tunney reviewed Davis's actions and suspended the ref for life. It was too little, too late; the Hart Foundation's title win remained on the books.

Danny Davis would return to the ring soon thereafter. This time as a wrestler: "Dangerous" Danny Davis. He teamed with the Hart Foundation to defeat the Bulldogs and Koko B. Ware at *WrestleMania III.*

In true wrestling fashion, Davis returned to refereeing after his career as a wrestler cooled, once again proving that nothing lasts forever in the world of the squared circle.

THE ULTIMATE CHALLENGE

At WrestleMania, *I bring you The Ultimate Warrior. I Bring you The Ultimate Challenge. I bring you, Hulk Hogan . . . Ultimate Reality.*
—**The Ultimate Warrior**

With each *WrestleMania,* the wwf found it more difficult to top itself. Hulk Hogan had defeated Andre the Giant at *WrestleMania III* and guided Randy Savage to win the wwf championship at *WrestleMania IV;* circumstances dictated Hogan challenge Savage at *WrestleMania V* after the MegaPowers exploded. What more could they do?

For *WrestleMania VI,* the wwf made the unprecedented move of pitting the Hulkster against another babyface. As befitting the main event of the wwf's flagship pay-per-view, he would meet no ordinary babyface — it was the Ultimate Warrior, a man who seemed destined to cross paths with Hulkamania.

The wwf knew they had to build the matchup carefully. Face vs. face battles were rare, and the company couldn't risk damaging either superstar. Hogan's popularity was a given, but the Ultimate Warrior's rise had been nearly as impressive. Soon after debuting, the Warrior shot to the top of the federation. He boasted a body that was even more impressive than Hogan's — in his autobiography, the Hulkster talked about how he was blown away by the Warrior's physique — and undeniable charisma. At the same time, however, his promos, while unique, were often incomprehensible — and his matches had to be kept short. Incredibly, he possessed even less wrestling ability than Hogan. Nonetheless, the wwf made him a top star.

After winning the Intercontinental Championship, the Ultimate Warrior seemed to have plateaued: fans were long used to the wwf keeping its top babyfaces from meeting. But in this case Vince McMahon decided to smash the glass ceiling. Events were put into motion that would lead to Hogan vs. Warrior.

The 1990 *Royal Rumble* saw the first rumblings. During a pre-match interview, the Warrior talked of a very special opponent competing in the *Rumble*: "If they refuse to understand that the power of the Ultimate Warrior has spread like a virus through the wwf then let them continue to walk as normal as they seem. But if those twenty-eight normal men want to have special attractions such as the *Royal Rumble* then you and I, as the Warriors, the most powerful force in the wwf, will continue to see it only as another challenge, only as another day of combat. Twenty-eight of those normal men stacked one on top of another can't come close to the billions and the destinations from parts unknown. You realize, as I do, that the twenty-ninth man, you Hulk Hogan, walk with a different force field around you, walk on horizons that are close to where I've been. But no one in the *Royal Rumble* shall form a team. Every man will fight for what he feels is within himself. And I, the Ultimate Warrior, will fulfill another destiny."

The Ultimate Warrior relished the chance to meet a competitor of Hogan's stature and soon got his wish. It was a classic battle of strength with neither man keeping the upper hand for long. In the end, however, Hogan won the match, eliminating the Warrior, albeit from behind.

Things were teased on wwf television, until finally wwf President Jack Tunney made the announcement: a confrontation that would become known as "The Ultimate Challenge." Over the next few weeks, Hogan and the Warrior began watching each other's backs. Neither man wanted the other to be at anything less than 100 percent.

Like Andre vs. Hogan, the hype was huge. The two biggest stars in the wwf were facing each other, not to settle a grudge, but to determine who was the very best. And unlike Andre vs. Hogan, this match would feature two competitors in their prime.

Toronto, Ontario's SkyDome hosted *WrestleMania VI*. A crowd of about 68,000 was on hand, including a young fan by the name of Adam Copeland, a.k.a. current WWE superstar Edge. The event featured a strong undercard as well. Although some questioned just how good the main event would be given both wrestlers' limitations, the match was surprisingly good. In the end, the unthinkable happened. Hogan went to deliver his famous finisher legdrop — and the Warrior rolled out of the way. Seconds later, Hogan was on his back, with the Warrior covering him for a three-count.

The throng at the SkyDome and those watching at home were in shock. Hogan had never surrendered a clean pinfall during his entire WWF reign. The Ultimate Warrior was the new WWF champion. How would Hogan react? Outside the ring, Hogan grabbed the WWF title belt and paused. Was he going to turn heel? As Hogan entered the ring, fans wondered. It wouldn't be the first time someone had gone to the dark side after losing to another babyface. Fortunately for the Warrior, Hogan simply handed the belt to him, passing him the torch.

Behind the scenes, Hogan wasn't convinced that the Warrior could shoulder the burden. In his autobiography, he writes: "68,000 people in SkyDome watched me go. Ultimate Warrior held the belt over his head in victory and no one cared. It turned out I was right about Ultimate Warrior. He couldn't carry the load as heavyweight champion, not the way Hulk Hogan had. Vince's attempt to move in a different direction hadn't been the success he had hoped it would be."

The Warrior would hold the belt for nearly a year before ultimately losing it to Sgt. Slaughter at the 1991 *Royal Rumble*. At *WrestleMania VII*, the Hulkster would regain the championship. After the 1991 *Summer Slam* PPV the Warrior would leave the WWF over a pay dispute.

CHAPTER 6

THE MATCHES

Wrestling has always pushed the idea that "bigger is better." Whether running weekly house shows or monthly events, promoters were always on the lookout for something to make a wrestling event seem more special. No matter how hot a feud or program is, the fear lurks: what if the fans grow bored?

Over the years, promoters developed various techniques for keeping things fresh. Sometimes this meant wrestlers would work in a territory for just a few months before moving on to a new employer; sometimes it meant turning a babyface heel (or vice versa). Other approaches included putting a singles wrestler into a tag team competition, or splitting a team to form a new combo.

Another tactic was to develop variations on traditional matches. The need for novelty has led to all sorts of interesting matchups — mixed tag team matches, no disqualification matches, steel cage matches, and even wrestlers vs. animals. You name it, and promoters have probably thought of it. Of course, not all the concepts have had staying power. When was the last time you saw a shark cage match or a bear vs. wrestler match?

Many "new matches" are simply variations on old ones. A Punjabi prison match is, for all intents and purposes, a cage match — except the cage is made of bamboo. Texas death matches are now better known as last-man standing matches. That's not to say that variations haven't been successes. The Royal Rumble, a modification of the traditional battle royal, has become an annual tradition in the WWE (and it's spawned its own variation in TNA's Gauntlet for the Gold).

But promoters have also learned that bigger isn't always better. It's proven difficult for the wrestling business to leave well enough alone: hence the evolution of coal miner's glove matches to turkey-on-a-pole matches and, the ultimate in awfulness — the Judy Bagwell-on-a-pole match. Nevertheless, wrestling has seen some interesting variations added to the rich legacy of the sport. What follows are some of the best innovations of the last thirty years.

MICHAELS VS. RAMON (LADDER MATCH)

The hardware store has always played a special role in the world of professional wrestling. Whether it's ladders, scaffolds, or salt miner's gloves, the denizens of the squared circle have always found new ways to use tools meant to build things to destroy their opponents. Perhaps the greatest of these weapons is the ladder: over the years, it's provided wrestlers with a myriad of ways to play daredevil and reach new in-ring heights of both heroism and depravity.

The ladder match's origins date back to 1972, when, ahead of its time, Calgary's Stampede Wrestling featured a ladder in a match between Tor Kamata and Dan Kroffat. For a decade, the match was all but forgotten, and seemingly did not surface again until 1983, when Bret Hart battled Bad News Allen, once more in Stampede Wrestling. Hart himself bought the concept to Vince McMahon when he began working for the WWF, and during the early 1990s McMahon decided to try it. Hart would battle Shawn Michaels on July 21, 1992, at a house show, in the WWF's first ever ladder match.

Word of the strange battle began to spread amongst diehard wrestling fans, but it wasn't until *WrestleMania X* that the ladder match really made a name for itself, mostly because of the tremendous performances of Razor Ramon (Scott

Hall) and Shawn Michaels. The two had been feuding over the Intercontinental championship ever since Michaels returned from a storyline suspension. HBK had held the strap prior to his forced absence, but in the interim, Ramon won the belt in a tournament. Everything seemed fine until Michaels appeared with the original belt, claiming to be the legitimate champion. The ladder match would crown the true champ, with the Intercontinental belt suspended over the ring during the match.

Michaels gained early control, thanks to the assistance of his bodyguard Diesel (Kevin Nash). However the referee soon took notice of Diesel's interference and sent him back to the dressing room, leaving Michaels to battle Ramon one-on-one. The match became a classic, with fans seeing action like never before.

Through the years, the ladder match has become a wrestling staple. Promoters have wisely limited its use both to keep it fresh and because of the toll the match can take on its participants. The match has also evolved, leading to tables, ladders, and chairs (TLC) matches and TNA's King of the Mountain ladder match. Recently, the WWE added the ladder match as a special feature at *WrestleMania*, creating the Money in the Bank ladder match. The winner of this particular match earns a WWE title shot that they can cash in whenever they want. The Money in the Bank prize has proven extremely lucrative. So far, every winner has won the title after cashing in their prize.

THE EMPTY ARENA MATCH

Given the importance of audience participation, it's not surprising that wrestling promoters have always booked matches they feel will draw strong crowd response. However one legendary confrontation would be booked with the express purpose of excluding fans: the empty arena contest between Memphis legend Jerry "The King" Lawler and Terry Funk.

The wild and crazy Funk had come up short during previous matches with Lawler, and there was only one reason — the fans. After complaining that he couldn't get a fair shake in the Memphis Coliseum, Funk sent a sealed envelope to Lawler offering a time, place, and date to meet once more — without the presence of anyone but an announcer, cameraman, and referee. Funk knew Lawler's pride would make the battle irresistible, despite his unorthodox conditions.

Funk had selected the Mid-South Coliseum as the place. With no fans to throw their support behind Lawler, as expected, the match quickly degenerated into a wild brawl that ranged throughout the arena. Lawler and Funk fought their way through the empty seats, with neither man showing any mercy. Funk's desire to win at any cost was apparent when he produced a stick and tried to use it against the King. Unfortunately for the Texan, Lawler kicked his elbow, knocking the stick into Funk's own eye. Showing his true colors, Funk began to cry out for medical help as Lawler looked on, not sure if he should continue battering his helpless foe. Given the problems Funk had caused, Lawler had every reason to finish the villain off, but he relented. Announcer Lance Russell entered the ring and checked on Funk's condition before making arrangements to get medical attention for the fallen star.

This highly unorthodox match was the talk of the wrestling community for years, and it got extensive coverage in magazines such as *Pro Wrestling Illustrated*. The novelty of the contest, coupled with its wild brawling and exciting finish, made it a must-have item for fans who traded wrestling tapes. Once again, Memphis Wrestling had developed an innovative match: but this time it was largely ignored by other promoters — the nature of the match made it counter-productive to selling tickets.

A generation later, the concept would be brought back for a special Super Bowl halftime show produced by the WWF. This time, WWF champion the Rock would defend his belt against Mankind. Their wild brawl also spilled into an empty arena, and highlights included the Rock beating Mankind down in an office. Announcer Shane McMahon called the match, which culminated with Mankind using a forklift to pin the Rock to win his first WWF Championship.

THE ROYAL RUMBLE

While there's little question the *Royal Rumble* was conceived to stick it to Jim Crockett Promotions, the match itself would go on to become a WWE favorite. The *Royal Rumble* now stands as one of the most anticipated pay-per-views — the show has become directly tied to *WrestleMania* ever since the winner of the *Royal Rumble* earned a main-event sport at *WrestleMania*.

But long before the *Royal Rumble* was even conceived, the battle royal was a special event, pitting a promotion's top stars in a free-for-all where the winner was the last man standing. As with many specialty matches, the rules varied from promotion to promotion, but generally the battle royal winner had to either throw his opponents over the top rope or pin them to score an elimination. Verne Gagne's AWA and Roy Shire's Big Time Wrestling are just two promotions that used the battle royal to great success. Shire ran eighteen-man battle royals annually at the Cow Palace from the late '60s until 1981, touting them as the Super Bowl of wrestling. These matches often awarded fantastic storyline prizes to the winner, everything from cash and cars to world title shots.

Battle royals were typically all-star events, with promoters flying in top wrestlers from across the country to compete. One wrestler who made the match a specialty was Andre the Giant, who earned the reputation as the king of the battle royal (while Andre had his fair share of victories and was always considered a top contender, he was not as dominant in battle royals as legend would have it). His presence always added an extra level of excitement, causing fans to speculate about who, if anyone, could eliminate the monstrous man.

As I've said, the first *Royal Rumble* was a free show that aired on the USA Network, directly against JCP's *Bunkhouse Stampede* pay-per-view. Both shows used the concept of the battle royal, with each company imposing its unique spin. *The Bunkhouse Stampede* was more traditional, though in JCP's version it was an "anything goes" event. Wrestlers could use whatever weapons they wanted. WWF's *Royal Rumble* differed in that it started with two wrestlers and then saw a new combatant enter the fray at regular intervals, as opposed to the traditional battle royal, which began with ten, fifteen, or twenty wrestlers in the ring from the opening bell.

The *Rumble* would earn impressive ratings, and clearly cut into the buyrate of *Bunkhouse Stampede*. It would become a pay-per-view event one year later, while the *Bunkhouse Stampede* would disappear forever when JCP was sold to Ted Turner.

Over the years the *Rumble* has made history, with fans witnessing truly epic encounters. In 1992, Ric Flair captured the WWF championship, the only time the title was decided at the *Rumble*. In 1993, the *Royal Rumble* added the stipulation that the winner would go to *WrestleMania*, cementing the event's position as one of the most important matches in the WWE. One of the novelties of the *Rumble* was that it was "every man for himself." As many a wrestler has learned, there are no friends in the *Rumble*, just because a wrestler helps you one minute doesn't mean that same person won't be trying to eliminate you the next.

HELL IN A CELL

Once upon a time, the cage represented professional wrestling's most brutal match. Whether it was the WWF, where a wrestler won by escaping, or the NWA's version, where opponents wrestled inside the structure until someone won by pinfall or submission, fans understood the cage match was the grand finale of any feud — a place where wrestlers settled the score once and for all. In the cage match, two men walked in, but only one man walked out. Bob Backlund vs. Jimmy Snuka, Sgt. Slaughter and Don Kernodle vs. Jay Youngblood and Ricky Steamboat, and Tito Santana vs. Greg "The Hammer" Valentine — these were the matches that lived up to the hype, and still stand out today as all-time classics.

By 1997 the cage match had lost its luster; it was just another wrestling gimmick. It was largely a result of promoters no longer treating it with respect. There had been too many occasions where wrestlers broke into the cage or hid under the cage to interfere and tip the balance in one wrestler's favor. World Championship Wrestling put several spins on the cage match in an effort to restore some of its mystique — the War Games event, the Thunderdome match, and the infamous "doomsday" cage match from 1996's *Uncensored* pay-per-view — with mixed results.

The cage match had become even more pathetic in the WWF. Run-ins had become so commonplace that the cage was little more than an inconvenience. Granted, the WWF sometimes tried to make things interesting — the time the Undertaker reached through the mat apron and pulled Diesel underneath it during his match with Bret Hart is one example — but overall, what was once a special event had become just another match.

But everything changed on October 5, 1997. At the *In Your House: Badd Blood* pay-per-view Shawn Michaels squared off against the Undertaker in a match known as "Hell in a Cell." Patterned loosely on the WCW cage matches of old, where wrestlers were locked inside the cage to battle for a pinfall or submission, Hell in a Cell added one important feature: a cage roof.

The Michaels/Undertaker feud began after HBK work as special referee for a match between 'Taker and Bret "The Hitman" Hart and cost the Dead Man his WWF Championship. During the match, Michaels accidentally struck the Undertaker with a chair. A none-too-happy 'Taker challenged Michaels, only to face repeated interference from the Heartbreak Kid's cohorts in Degeneration X. To put an end to this, Hell in a Cell was created.

The inaugural Hell in a Cell was a great success, and it spawned many sequels. Cut off from his Degeneration X teammates, Michaels eluded the Undertaker for as long as he could — but in the cage, there was nowhere to run. The Undertaker eventually caught him, and beat Michaels senseless. Just when it looked like HBK was going to go down early, the Undertaker missed a move and hit the steel. Michaels capitalized on the misstep and went to work, using every weapon he could find. Steel chairs and the ring steps were just two implements of destruction. During his counterattack, Michaels also laid out a cameraman for no apparent reason. He pressed on, bringing the Undertaker into the ring and preparing him for his coup de grace — the superkick. Michaels unloaded on the Undertaker with his patented finishing move only to watch in horror as the Undertaker sat up and escaped.

At that point, Michaels' genius began to shine. During his offensive flurry, WWF officials (including then-commissioner Sgt. Slaughter) unlocked the structure's door to tend to the injured cameraman. When Michaels saw his opening, he bolted for what he thought was safer ground. Little did he know he was merely leaving one hell for another. The Undertaker followed and delivered a second round of offense, using the cage to punish Michaels further. Not once, but twice, the Undertaker picked up the Kid and launched him into the steel structure like a human javelin.

A bloodied Michaels somehow found the strength to climb the cage in a desperate bid to escape. Once he reached the top, he found himself under the gun once more. The Undertaker threw his opponent across the roof, sending him close to the edge. As the frenzied Michaels tried to climb back down, the Undertaker kicked him off. Michaels hurtled onto the unforgiving announcer's table far below. After bouncing off the edge, Michaels lay shockingly still. Announcer Jim Ross cried out, "My God, he may be broken in half!" (Less than a year later, the Undertaker would also throw Mankind off the top of the cage and *through* the announcer's table. Mankind's fall has taken on mythical proportions, but watching Michaels', you have to wonder if it wasn't equally bad, considering he all but missed the announcer's table on the way down and there was ultimately little to cushion his impact.)

Without a moment's hesitation, the Undertaker continued the punishment, battering the leader of Degeneration X as he carried him back into the cage. The Undertaker took his time finishing Michaels off, superplexing him and blasting him with a chair before giving the signal for his tombstone piledriver. A great moment in wrestling became even greater when the lights went out and a pyrotechnical flash signaled the arrival of Kane, Undertaker's long-lost brother.

Led by Paul Bearer, the Undertaker's traitorous former manager, Kane walked to the cage and ripped the door off its hinges as if it were a toy. A stunned 'Taker looked on as the brother he believed had died years earlier was now standing in front of him. Kane made the now-familiar motion that set off more ringside pyrotechnics, then proceeded to tombstone the Undertaker into the mat before leaving. A barely conscious Heartbreak Kid found the strength to drape his arm over his fallen foe and take the match.

Despite the fact that the first Hell in a Cell involved someone escaping the cage and outside interference, it instantly earned its place in the fans' hearts and minds. While the Hell in a Cell has had a couple of speed bumps in its path to immortality, it has for the most part guaranteed both blood and excitement. When fans hear Hell in a Cell, they know they are in for something special.

WAR GAMES: THE MATCH BEYOND

> *Remember where you are — this is Thunderdome,*
> *and death is listening, and will take the first man that screams.*
> *—Beyond the Thunderdome, Mad Max*

By the summer of 1987 it was clear that no ordinary match could contain the explosive violence between the Four Horsemen and the Super Powers/Road Warriors. When wcw booker Dusty Rhodes needed a match to sell the *Great American Bash* at Atlanta's Omni, he began thinking outside the box, or in this case, the cage. *War Games: The Match Beyond* was the result.

Two rings would be used to stage the battle. Surrounding them, a monstrous cage. The rules were announced before the event, creating even more anticipation among the fans in attendance. The match began with one competitor from each team facing off. Every five minutes, a coin toss would determine which team received a temporary two-on-one advantage. And if this wasn't brutal enough, the real match did not begin until all ten wrestlers were in the ring (whether or not they'd be in any condition to wrestle was another story) with submission being the only way to win.

Let the games begin!

And so they did, with the American Dream squaring off against "The Enforcer" Arn Anderson. While Rhodes' main opponents from the Horsemen were Ric Flair and Tully Blanchard, Anderson had interfered in Rhodes' matches enough to earn his scorn. Arn fought gamely but Rhodes shrugged off his offense and hit him with a low blow, proving that this was war indeed. Anderson earned a respite when the Horsemen won the coin toss and Tully Blanchard entered. The tag team partners went after Rhodes but the Dream fought back with his favorite maneuver, the bionic elbow. As is usually the case in these situations, the numbers game eventually caught up with Rhodes and the Horsemen double-teamed their opponent effectively. Finally, Animal rushed in, smashing through Anderson and Blanchard like a one-man wrecking crew. His attack gave Rhodes a chance to recover and get back in the game.

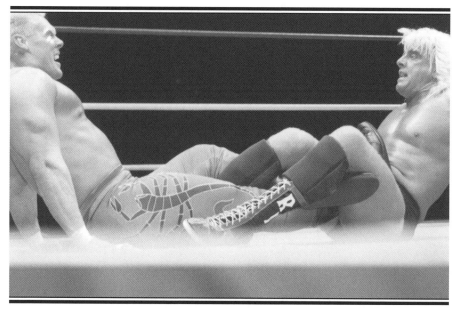

Ric Flair and Sting

The war continued like this until ten wrestlers were in the ring. With that, the match morphed into the Match Beyond — a brutal affair in theory and in reality. The Road Warriors and the Super Powers were finally declared the winners after James J. Dillon was unable to continue. Dillon, the manager of the Four Horsemen, would pay the price when he was legitimately taken out of action by the Roadies, suffering a dislocated shoulder after being hit with the Warrior's doomsday device.

The War Games match was a smash hit, and it would be brought back year after year for big WCW pay-per-views. It's still highly regarded by fans and it is considered one of the greatest gimmicks ever. The format would go on to be copied or modified by many other promotions, including ECW, Ring of Honor, and TNA.

CHAPTER 7

THE BEATDOWNS

In the immortal words of WWE Hall of Famer Jim Ross: "He's getting beat like a government mule." And while J.R. certainly didn't coin the phrase, he made it popular among wrestling fans describing the many beatdowns he's witnessed in the squared circle. While the ring ropes generally confine the action, wrestlers have often found themselves battling it out wherever they can.

Pro wrestling is about emotion and anger is a big part of the business. Wrestlers have never been known for their "live and let live" attitudes so it's no surprise things can (and often do) get out of hand. When the competition begins to get heated, you can expect to see men and women doing some terrible things to each other: all manner of attacks before or after a match, ambushes, and gang warfare have become commonplace.

Behind the scenes, it's simple enough. One of the biggest motivators in wrestling is revenge — someone stole a title belt, someone betrayed a partner, that kind of thing. It's a sure-fire catalyst for a feud. And the bloodier the beatdown, the better the chance fans will want to see a wrestler get what's coming to him.

I BROKE WAHOO'S LEG

Fans who grew up watching Jim Crockett Promotions will forever remember the T-shirt worn proudly by Greg "The Hammer" Valentine. It read *I BROKE WAHOO'S LEG* and it symbolized both the arrogance of Valentine and the contempt he held for both fans and opponent alike.

The angle began during a cage match between NWA world tag team champs Greg "The Hammer" Valentine and "Nature Boy" Ric Flair and the Anderson Brothers, Gene and Ole. The heel vs. heel matchup was just the latest exchange in a war that had raged for months. Special referee Wahoo McDaniel was pressed into service to try to keep a modicum of order. Controversy erupted, however, when Valentine was tripped by McDaniel and the Andersons secured victory.

This wasn't Wahoo's first run-in with the Hammer — it wasn't even his first run-in with a wrestler by the *name* of Valentine. In the not-so-distant past, McDaniel had feuded with Greg's father, Johnny Valentine. Both men liked to work stiff, and their bad blood had them battling across the country, exciting fans with a brutal, no-holds-barred style of combat.

Greg Valentine was a chip of the old block, and his matches with Wahoo inevitably turned bloody. Ric Flair also got into the action, working singles matches with Wahoo as well as tag team programs where he and Valentine fought with McDaniel and Paul Jones.

Valentine was not a man to let a perceived wrong go unanswered. So it was no surprise to JCP fans when he vowed revenge on his family's hated opponent during a televised match in the summer of 1977. The bout saw Wahoo put his Mid-Atlantic heavyweight championship up against $2,000 put up by Valentine. In the past, Valentine had put up 1,000 silver dollars against anyone who could defeat him, but McDaniel forced him to up the ante by another thousand to get a title shot.

McDaniel should have smelled a rat when Valentine came up with the extra money. Fifteen minutes in, the Hammer made it clear this wasn't about money or titles — it was about injuring Wahoo. The crafty Valentine introduced a new move to his arsenal (David Crockett would refer to the hold as a "leg-ankle suplex," while McDaniel described it as the European version of the figure-four

WRESTLING'S GREATEST MOMENTS

leglock): he grabbed McDaniels' leg and then fell backwards upon it. As Wahoo howled in agony, the referee awarded the match to Valentine. McDaniel's leg, it was announced, had been broken. Ric Flair joined Valentine in the ring to celebrate the double victory — Valentine's title win and Wahoo's serious injury.

The next week, Wahoo returned to television to update fans on his condition. The break was so bad he needed a wheelchair to get around. The proud Native American could not hide the shame he felt. To no one's surprise, Valentine and Flair arrived to add insult to injury. The partners mocked McDaniel's condition, wondering whether the wheelchair had to be special-ordered to carry Wahoo's fat frame. McDaniel vowed revenge, but Valentine and Flair laughed off his threats. Over the next few weeks, Valentine would continue joking at McDaniel's expense as he began sporting a custom made "I Broke Wahoo's Leg" T-shirt.

McDaniel would have the last laugh two months later. The series of revenge matches that ensued would become classics.

EDDIE GILBERT DRAPES RUSSIAN FLAG OVER BILL WATTS

All warfare is based on deception.
—**Sun Tzu**

"Cowboy" Bill Watts was a Mid-South Wrestling fixture. He'd been a popular star in the area, battling the promotion's top heels and imposing his own form of justice. After retiring from the ring, Watts remained active as the television announcer for Mid-South's weekly show (behind the scenes, he actually owned Mid-South Wrestling). Calling the action, he often saw things that aggravated him and he was occasionally tempted him to re-enter the ring and settle matters. Most of the time, he was able to resist the urge.

While doing his best to stay out of the fray, Watts was never afraid to voice his opinions — especially about Russian wrestlers who used interview time to propagandize and, even worse, drape the Russian flag over fallen foes. With the Cold War raging, the Russians' ring antics were enough to make the red-blooded American livid.

Even more disgusting to the Cowboy was the sight of U.S. citizen Eddie Gilbert carrying on with the Ruskies. The Koloffs and Korchenko were one thing, but Watts was appalled by Gilbert selling out his own country for the sake of a buck. It didn't take long for his comments to infuriate Gilbert, and the manager/wrestler to call out Watts during a television broadcast.

At first, Gilbert pleaded for forgiveness. He invited Watts into the ring and the retired grappler obliged. But as he did, two of Gilbert's wrestlers, the Blade Runners, arrived as well. Watts was immediately suspicious, but Gilbert said there was a logical explanation for their presence — he would continue to manage the Blade Runners, but from this day forward, he was through with the Russians. Gilbert said he had been wrong to side with the Koloffs and Korchenko and as a sign of good faith he gave Watts the Russian flag he'd obtained from his past dealings with them. Watts took the flag — and then the Russians rushed out. As the Russians hit the mat, Gilbert attacked Watts; his olive branch was an elaborate set-up. Watts was beaten down, and Gilbert's Blade Runners ran interference, keeping Steve Williams, Ted DiBiase, and Jim Duggan from rescuing the MSW legend. Gilbert and the Russians used a chain and shovel to punish Watts — to complete the humiliation, they draped the Russian flag over his battered body.

These events led the former wrestler to announce, via videotape, that he was coming out of retirement to exact revenge. Watts' quest led to a match against Blade Runner Sting, with the stipulation that Watts get Gilbert if he won. There would be no stopping the Cowboy, and he earned his shot at redemption.

But true revenge was not in the cards. Gilbert had planned ahead and secured the services of the Fabulous Freebirds; his match with Watts had barely begun when Michael Hayes, Buddy Roberts, and Terry Gordy stormed the ring. Watts was no stranger to the Freebirds and all three men eagerly beat up their former nemesis. Once more, Watts was undone by the craftiness of Eddie Gilbert.

The attacks on Watts would serve as a springboard for the promotion's top babyfaces to seek revenge on his behalf. It would be yet another memorable angle for a promotion that has been regarded as one of the all-time greats in the history of the industry.

CAR WARS: EDDIE GILBERT RUNS OVER JERRY LAWLER

By 1989, "Hot Stuff" Eddie Gilbert had earned the dubious honor of being one of the most hated heels in wrestling. Fans in Memphis' Championship Wrestling Association were well aware of his antics, dating back to his feud with former tag team partner Tommy Rich. Now, Gilbert had finally crossed the line, incurring the wrath of promoter Eddie Marlin. After referring to Memphis as a "bush league promotion," Gilbert was fired by Marlin during an episode of *Championship Wrestling*.

Fans were delighted, but Gilbert clearly was not. He began a shoving match with the promoter. Marlin, a former wrestler, held his own, but he was clearly outgunned by the much younger man. Finally, Gilbert began beating Marlin down in the parking lot outside the television studio. Fortunately, Jerry Lawler caught wind of what was happening and raced outside to Marlin's rescue. Gilbert headed for his ride as Lawler attended to his friend.

But the villain wasn't through. Rather than driving off, Gilbert aimed his vehicle at the promoter and the King. Lawler had little time to react as the vehicle sped toward him, but he was able to get Marlin out of harm's way. Unfortunately, he wasn't so lucky himself.

The angle made for exciting television and was featured in all the wrestling magazines. The car hitting Lawler looked almost *too* realistic. Normally, in wrestling, this isn't a problem — but when your TV tapings are done right across the street from a police station, things can get . . . complicated. Some of those watching the show actually called the authorities.

Memphis fans had seen their share of strange happenings, but over the next several weeks, the parking lot became as much a part of the action as the ring inside the studio. One week, as Gilbert and Lawler were brawling, Gilbert body-slammed Lawler through a windshield. The next, Lawler won a car from Gilbert and was ready to drive off with it when Gilbert smashed the windshield, injuring his rival.

The car wars saga continued until Gilbert believed he had put Lawler on the shelf. He then made a mistake familiar to many of Lawler's opponents: under-estimating the King. TV announcer Lance Russell was talking with Lawler on the phone when Gilbert interrupted. Hot Stuff mistakenly believed Lawler was at home, and he told Russell he had finished off most of the legends in Memphis — but there was one left. Gilbert began menacing the announcer until Russell finally revealed that Lawler wasn't at his home; he was at the studio. The King appeared and started pummeling Gilbert, proving that he was equal to Gilbert's guile.

The angle itself would be revisited in the WWF several years later when the WWF needed to write its top star "Stone Cold" Steve Austin out of the picture. Austin was facing a lengthy hiatus from the ring after some much-needed surgery. With the Texas Rattlesnake about to miss almost a year, the WWF needed a convincing explanation for his absence. They developed a storyline that had Austin run down by an unknown driver at the *Survivor Series* pay-per-view. The attack would not only explain Austin's absence, it would set the stage for a feud upon his return — in the end, it would be revealed that Hunter Hearst Helmsley had masterminded the vehicular assault.

"HE SAID I WASN'T GOOD ENOUGH" (TERRY FUNK BREAKS RIC FLAIR'S NECK)

After chasing Ricky Steamboat and the NWA world championship for three months, Ric Flair finally triumphed. Now, suddenly, the new champion was lying in a heap of broken wood — with an equally broken neck. Flair's moment of celebration turned to turmoil after a bitter Terry Funk decided the only way he could recapture his glory days was to commit one of the most heinous acts in wrestling history.

It began with Funk, a former world champion, serving as a ringside interviewer. As he congratulated Flair on his title win, it appeared, on the surface, as if two all-time greats were about to share a moment of mutual respect.

But Funk's motives were much darker.

No one can be sure when or why he decided to make his move. Perhaps the sight of Flair recapturing the title made him wonder if he was capable of one last run at the top himself; perhaps he'd just snapped (Funk's reputation — as "middle-aged and crazy" — certainly can't be ruled out). Whatever the rationale, Funk made his move. After congratulating Flair on his victory, the former champ asked for a title shot of his own. A gracious Flair dodged the question, but after repeated queries, he told Funk flat-out that he had to consider the wrestlers ranked in the top-ten first. An insulted Funk asked, "So you think I'm not good enough?"

Flair said no, he didn't think that at all, and moved to shake Funk's hand. Funk seemed appeased and offered his hand in a conciliatory gesture. Then he pulled Flair in, punched him, and threw him out of the ring. Funk's best years may have been behind him, but he was still a dangerous opponent and Flair was in no position to defend himself after having just wrestled a grueling match. Before he knew it, Naitch found himself piledrived through a wooden table. In a time when such moves were extremely rare, fans were stunned. It also shocked the man going through the table — while Funk took every step to protect Flair, the move was still dangerous. "He almost killed me," Flair recalls. "It's pretty hard to protect a guy when you're both crashing through a table. I couldn't turn my head for weeks."

It was later announced that Flair's neck had been broken and that he would be out of commission for at least thirty days. Jim Ross interviewed the champ from his mansion, where Flair acknowledged the severity of his neck injury. The NWA would allow Flair an additional thirty days before he had to defend his title — NWA rules dictated that a champion had to make at least one title defense every month

— but Flair said he didn't know if he'd even be able to wrestle again. Still, he was sure of one thing — whether it was a month or a year, he would exact revenge.

The fans rallied behind the Nature Boy. Ric found an unexpected ally in Sting, who helped him battle Funk and members of the J. Tex Corporation. During a tag team affair between Flair and Sting and "Mad Dog" Buzz Sawyer and Muta, Funk attacked again, taking a plastic bag and pulling it over Flair's head, attempting to smother him. Flair lost consciousness and medical personnel were required to revive him.

In his autobiography, *Terry Funk: More Than Hardcore*, the Texas legend remembers the controversy: "We had a deal where I attacked Flair by putting a plastic bag over his head and suffocating him. That deal could have been extremely hot if TBS had gone along with it. They ended up getting so many complaints about it, they never replayed it. People were calling in and complaining about it so strongly, you'd have thought I was really trying to murder Flair. Maybe the complaints were from Vince McMahon, because that angle did get over."

The attack was the lead-in to one of the most celebrated matches of all time — the Funk vs. Flair "I quit" match.

It was a brutal encounter that ended with the "Nature Boy" forcing his opponent to submit. After the match, Funk shook Flair's hand, as he had agreed to do if he lost. Funk told Flair he was the better man, putting an end to their feud. As a result of the storyline, Flair would wrestle as a babyface in WCW for the first time in years. Funk would continue to work as a commentator for WCW and go on to reinvent himself in Extreme Championship Wrestling as one of the innovators of hardcore wrestling. He'd also play a pivotal role in ECW getting over by lending his credibility to the fledgling promotion and taking risks that were unthinkable for a man half his age.

POWERS OF PAIN LAY OUT THE ROAD WARRIORS

In the eyes of many wrestling fans, the Road Warriors were unbeatable. With their size and power, who could stop them? Factor in that the team's pinfall losses were few and far between and their tag team championships many, and you had two true juggernauts of professional wrestling.

The Road Warriors had originally been booked for short squash matches to build up their mystique and hide their in-ring weaknesses. And although their ability improved over the years, their matches were still generally kept short, with the Roadies almost always going over strong.

While the tag team was immensely popular wherever they went, their successes created a problem for bookers. Given Hawk and Animal's aura, it became difficult to book teams against them because fans had trouble believing they could lose.

Two men who didn't present this problem were the Warlord and the Barbarian, collectively known as the Powers of Pain. At 6'3" and 323 pounds, the Warlord was an impressive physical specimen, as was the Barbarian who stood 6'2" and weighed 295 pounds. Both men had worked in regional promotions before coming JCP, and they clearly matched Hawk and Animal in terms of strength and size. With manager Paul Jones by their side and "The Russian Bear" Ivan Koloff in their corner, it made them formidable foes for the Legion of Doom.

Now that JCP had a team that posed a realistic challenge, it was time to lay the ground for a program. Since all four men were weight lifters, a test of strength seemed like a good way to get things started.

When two strongmen decide to test their strength, wrestling has many options to exploit before they ever face off in the ring. Arm wrestling, pose-downs, weight lifting — the possibilities are endless. And because it's pro wrestling, all manner of violence is possible as well.

Such was the case when the Powers of Pain challenged the Road Warriors to a weight-lifting contest. Never one to back down from a challenge, the Roadies agreed. With Ivan Koloff assisting the Powers, the Roadies and manager Paul Ellering were outnumbered four to three. The bench-pressing competition proceeded without any real conflict. Both teams showcased the power that had made them successful, with each team's representative (Animal and the Barbarian) bench pressing an impressive 475 pounds. Then, Powers of Pain manager Paul Jones taunted the Warriors, accusing Animal of barely being able to lift the weight. The trash talking had begun.

Normally, such a contest would see each team progressively work their way up in weight until one team could go no further. The next level should have been 500 pounds, but the Road Warriors' manager "Precious" Paul Ellering (no stranger to weight lifting himself) requested that they skip straight ahead to 600. Ellering confronted Jones and said, "Desperate money never wins." Ellering suggested they stop wasting the fans' time and go to a real challenge. Jones refused, saying that since it was his challenge and his money the contest would continue as planned. Ellering upped the ante by slapping Jones in the face, leading to a close call as Animal and Hawk backed him up against Barbarian and Warlord. With Animal mimicking a chicken and Jones' ego bruised, the Road Warriors request was granted.

Knowing how much money was at stake, and knowing the kind of man Paul Jones was (Jones had earned a reputation as a notoriously fickle wrestler after turning on many of his tag team partners throughout his career), they should have been more careful. Overconfident, Hawk turned his back on Jones and company as he spotted Animal's attempt to lift 600 pounds. Sensing an opportunity to make a kill, Ivan Koloff grabbed a wooden box of powdered chalk (used to help the competitors maintain a good grip on the weight bars), and threw the powder into Hawk and Animal's faces.

The chalk blinded both men, setting them up for a vicious beating. The Barbarian laid out Hawk with a nasty boot to the face as the Warlord grabbed Animal and rammed his head into some barbells, knocking the weight bench over. Koloff smashed the wooden box over the back and head of Hawk and Ellering respectively. The Warlord then grabbed Hawk and held him as the Barbarian smashed a steel chair over his head. An angry Paul Jones grabbed his money and declared his team the winners.

The feud escalated with the Powers of Pain making several improvised attacks. A six-man barbed-wire match at the first *Clash of Champions* settled nothing. Both teams seemed equally matched in terms of size and power. The Road Warriors were the more experienced team but the added presence of Ivan Koloff and Paul Jones at ringside made up for this. JCP seemed to have the makings of a money-making feud.

The program looked like it could turn into an epic confrontation, but it was cut short when the Powers of Pain bolted to the greener pastures of the WWF (legend has it that they balked when JCP booked them against the Road Warriors in a scaffold match). They would actually work as a babyface team against Road Warrior imitators Demolition before turning heel and joining forces with Mr. Fuji.

UNDERTAKER LOCKS ULTIMATE WARRIOR IN COFFIN

Men fear death as children fear to go in the dark; and as that natural fear in children is increased by tales, so is the other.
—Francis Bacon

"Never in the history of the World Wrestling Federation . . ." *Superstars of Wrestling* announcer Vince McMahon's anguished words captured the sense of horror fans experienced as they watched the strange ordeal of the Ultimate Warrior — locked in a coffin with WWE officials scrambling to rescue him.

The eerie events had begun on "The Funeral Parlor," a talk segment hosted by the Undertaker's manager Paul Bearer. While Bearer's ghoulish look — white makeup and a mortician's suit — was nothing compared to that the Undertaker, he still inspired a sense of dread whenever he spoke. With his creepy intonation, Bearer served as the perfect mouthpiece for the Undertaker, and his "Funeral Parlor" often brought the Dead Man and his opponents together.

With the set done up for a wake, Bearer welcomed his guest for the day — the Ultimate Warrior. The ghoulish manager told the Warrior he thought he'd never show up, and spoke of how the Undertaker had worked night and day to prepare a gift just for him. Bearer wasted no time in unveiling that gift — an ornate coffin, decorated with the Ultimate Warrior's symbol.

The pine box seemed to unnerve the Warrior as the host spoke. Bearer went on about how natural the Warrior would look at rest and boasted that the coffin was double-sized to accommodate his massive physique. He accused the Warrior of being scared of death as well as meeting the Undertaker in the ring. Taunting further, he told the "Little Warriors" (as Jim Hellwig's young fans were known) that their hero was afraid. With a look of resolve, the Ultimate Warrior grabbed Bearer and told him he mistook his look of fear for the fear Bearer felt himself. At *WrestleMania VII*, the gods had spoken to the Warrior and told him his time to return to Parts Unknown had not yet arrived. Paul Bearer ignored this and told him *he* would be scared, but the Warrior said he and his warriors did not fear death itself.

At that point, another wooden coffin on the set opened and the Undertaker emerged, attacking the Warrior from behind. He unleashed blow after blow, smashing the Warrior with forearms and big boots. To finish him off, he blasted a metal urn over the Warrior's neck. The Warrior was then stuffed inside "his" coffin, with Paul Bearer assisting the Undertaker in sealing it. Sensing his fate, the Warrior fought desperately to keep the lid from being closed. He stuck his leg out; the Undertaker unleashed more blows. Finally, the Warrior lost the fight, the Undertaker pressed the coffin lid down and Paul Bearer turned the key.

As the events played out, announcers Vince McMahon, "Rowdy" Roddy Piper, and "Macho Man" Randy Savage clearly couldn't believe their eyes. Piper pleaded for someone to get down there to help, and McMahon expressed disgust. Even Savage (who had seen his career ended by the Warrior at *WrestleMania VII*) showed sympathy when he realized just how desperate the situation was.

WWE official Tony Garea raced to the scene and attempted to open the coffin, but thanks to Paul Bearer, it was locked tight. Another official soon showed up (Blackjack Lanza) but he too was unsuccessful in lifting the coffin lid. Referee

Dave Hebner arrived with a crowbar, raising hopes that the Warrior might soon be freed. But the crowbar proved ineffectual. Piper noted that nearly a minute had elapsed and every second counted. Another official (Rene Goulet) used a hammer and chisel, but even his efforts proved fruitless. The broadcast team conveyed the frustration the Little Warriors must have felt, and the situation grew more critical as more time elapsed. Someone brought out a power drill — to no effect.

After several minutes, emergency personnel finally managed to break the coffin open. The still form of the Warrior left everyone wondering if it was too late. The coffin had been ripped apart from the inside, signs of the Warrior's futile bid to escape. He seemed lifeless. Fortunately, referee Dave Hebner performed CPR, reviving the fallen wrestler.

Nothing like this had ever been seen in the WWF, and the angle helped launch two superstars. The Ultimate Warrior and 'Taker would do battle, with the feud culminating in body-bag matches. Equally important, the angle helped establish the Undertaker as one of the darkest characters in WWF history.

THE MASKED SUPERSTAR BREAKS MULLIGAN'S HAND

For years, Blackjack Mulligan had terrorized Jim Crockett Promotions, but now that he was on the side the angels, he was making things awfully difficult for the area's top heels. Mulligan's size and strength was augmented by his wild, brawling style, and he won championships wherever he wrestled. The combo sent "Big" John Studd packing, with Mulligan soundly defeating him in a loser-leaves-town match.

Studd's ignominy was Mulligan's most recent triumph. The big Texan was riding high in JCP and his timing couldn't have been better. The promotion was holding a tournament to crown a new television champion. Mulligan became a favorite to win — a scenario that did not go over well with a wrestler by the name of the Masked Superstar (Bill Eadie, who would later go on to become "Ax" of the WWF's Demolition).

The Masked Superstar was a formidable competitor whose technical skills alone were enough to secure victory; but he also wasn't above cheating when necessary. The burly masked man had terrorized babyfaces in Georgia Championship Wrestling and he looked to expand his success to the Mid-Atlantic region. For the power and wealth a JCP TV title reign could bring, the Masked Superstar was determined to win the tournament at any cost.

Knowing that his biggest competitor would be Blackjack, the Masked Superstar looked for any edge. To get it, he would rob Mulligan of the most deadly weapon in his arsenal — the claw. Mulligan's version of the hold had won him many matches — the move made all the more effective by Mulligan's size and the extra leverage he was able to apply. Without the claw, Mulligan would be hamstrung.

The Masked Superstar also enlisted the aid of a familiar-looking henchman, a wrestler known as Superstar #2. Although Superstar #2 wore a mask, the fans had a pretty good idea who the large man was: "Big" John Studd. Until the second Superstar was unmasked, however, no one could stop him from competing.

During a match, Mulligan was brutally beaten down by both Superstars. The two men took turns stomping on Mulligan's hand until it was little more than a pile of broken bones. The claw was no more.

Or was it?

Despite his injury, Mulligan appeared in the TV title tournament finals against the Masked Superstar #1. While Mulligan was unable to use his favorite hold, he had a new weapon: his injured hand was now encased in a hard cast. Mulligan beat the Superstar using the new tool, leaving his opponent to wonder if he'd have been better off against the claw. As Mulligan continued his assault on Superstar #1, his rival found a way out of his predicament. The technically sound Superstar went back after Mulligan's injured hand, pounding away at the cast.

But the Superstar's attack seemed to anger the big Texan more than it hurt him. Finally, the Superstar struck a nerve and Mulligan went berserk, throwing him over the top rope. Unfortunately, according to the rules of the promotion, this meant an automatic loss via disqualification. The Superstar was the new JCP TV champion.

Although Superstar #1 won the TV title, Mulligan would gain a measure of revenge later by defeating Superstar #2, who was subsequently unmasked and, of course, revealed as "Big" John Studd. As for the original Masked Superstar, he would later turn babyface after an altercation with manager Gene Anderson and his wrestlers Jimmy Snuka and Ray Stevens.

RICKY MORTON GETS BENCHED!

In the largest territories, it was not uncommon for promoters to run more than one show a night. One card, made up of the promotion's top stars, would run in a large arena, while secondary stars would perform in a smaller one. These events were commonly known as "A" and "B" shows. In some promotions, a third show might even be added (a "C" show).

The team of Steve Keirn and Stan Lane (a.k.a. the Fabulous Ones) had quickly become a top box office draw in Memphis' Championship Wrestling Alliance. It only made sense to book them as often as possible. While promoters Jerry Lawler and Jerry Jarrett possessed amazing promotional talent, even they couldn't make a wrestler appear in two places at once. So they came up with the next best thing — a Fabulous Ones clone known as the Rock and Roll Express would work "B" shows while the Fabs worked the "A" shows.

Although the Rock and Roll Express (Ricky Morton and Robert Gibson) were originally conceived as a knockoff, their charisma and skills as a tag team quickly earned them their own fans (in fact, the Rock and Roll Express would go on to even greater fame). One of the programs that helped the Express win hearts was their long battle with the brother team of Randy "Macho Man" Savage and Lonny Poffo. Managed by their father, Angelo Poffo, the two heels had come to Memphis after their father's "outlaw" promotion, International Championship Wrestling (ICW), had folded.

Memphis' Mid-South Coliseum was the scene for one of the great moments in wrestling, a harbinger of the hardcore movement of the 1990s. As was often the case, the Rock and Roll Express found themselves facing a bigger and stronger team. Savage and Poffo had things going their way; with Ricky Morton cut off from his partner victory seemed imminent. Lanny Poffo went to finish Morton off with a swanton, only to see him roll out of the way. Seizing the moment, Morton made the hot tag to Robert Gibson, who proceeded to "clean house" (a routine the Rock and Roll Express would later hone to perfection). Gibson then threw Poffo into the ropes — only to fall prey to Savage's heelish tactics. With expert timing (no doubt developed in his years as a baseball player), Savage pulled the ring rope down just as Gibson bounced into it, sending him flying over the rope and onto an unforgiving concrete floor.

The referee immediately disqualified Savage and Poffo. Angered by the loss, the heel brothers vented their frustrations on a helpless Gibson. Only the timely intervention of his partner Morton saved him from a horrible two-on-one beating.

But the rescue came at a terrible cost for the rescuer. Turning their attention, Savage and Poffo worked Morton over. Savage then took the lead by ramming Morton's head into a wooden bench at ringside. Finally, he threw Morton on top of the bench, setting him up for what was, at that time, one of the wildest moves ever seen in wrestling. The Macho Man picked Morton up and piledrived him

— through the bench. Morton collapsed, leaving Savage and Poffo to revel at the havoc they'd unleashed.

Savage's piledriver shocked fans around the country. The CWA faithful had been conditioned to view the piledriver as a devastating move that could end a match instantly (so devastating that its use earned an automatic disqualification). A piledriver *through a bench* was something unimaginable. Morton sold the move like he'd been hit by a truck, adding fuel to the fire. Ten years later, such moves would be routine in promotions like ECW, but for the time, this was an extraordinary event. It became a highlight reel clip, ending up as one of the featured moments on *Pro Wrestling Illustrated's Ringmasters* videotape, and further cementing its place in wrestling legend.

This was just the beginning of all four men's careers. The Rock and Roll Express would soon leave Memphis for Bill Watts' Mid-South Wrestling and eventually work their way to national success in Jim Crockett Promotions. Savage and Poffo were recruited by the WWF, with Savage becoming a true superstar. Although Lanny's career paled in comparison, he still attained a level of national success as "Leaping" Lanny Poffo, and later, "The Genius."

STEAMBOAT'S TURNING PURPLE!

> *Tyger! Tyger! burning bright*
> *In the forests of the night,*
> *What immortal hand or eye*
> *Could frame thy fearful symmetry?*
> **—William Blake**

While the Steamboat/Savage match from *WrestleMania III* is unquestionably one of wrestling's greatest, the angle leading up to it was equal to the moment. Macho Man Randy Savage had been Intercontinental champion for several months when he faced his greatest challenge: Ricky "The Dragon" Steamboat. Steamboat, fresh off of a feud with the Magnificent Muraco, was at the top of his game and he quickly showed Savage just how good he was.

Matched move for move by the challenger, it became apparent to the frustrated Macho Man that he had to take drastic action if he was going to hold on to his championship. The problem was that Steamboat wasn't giving Savage the opportunity to counterattack. After referee Dave Hebner was accidentally knocked to the mat, Steamboat caught Savage with a flying body press off the top rope for what looked to be a pin. Still groggy, Hebner was slow to make the count, and even when he did, the arrival of controversial referee Danny Davis broke up the pin. To the casual viewer, it looked as if Davis was checking on Hebner's condition, but to anyone familiar with the storyline, it was clearly a case of Davis helping out the heel champ. As Steamboat began arguing with Davis, Savage regrouped and realized what he had to do. Without hesitation, the Macho Man launched his counterattack, moving the action outside of the ring where he could make maximum use of his superior brawling skills. After knocking a distracted Steamboat from the ring, the Macho Man then targeted Steamboat's neck, blasting him over the metal security railing and delivering a flying axe-handle for good measure. As the referee began counting him out, it was clear the challenger had suffered a serious injury. Steamboat clutched at his throat as Savage was awarded the countout victory.

If fans thought the champion was living up to his name, they were in for even more savagery as the Macho Man grabbed the metal timekeeper's bell and launched it (and himself) off the top rope — once more into Steamboat's throat. The crowd gasped in horror as Steamboat began thrashing about, struggling for air. The damage was done, but Savage still wasn't finished. He climbed the top rope again and prepared to deliver another blow, but referee Hebner was able to prevent Savage from leaping off, in one of the few moments where a ref has been able to do anything of consequence, other than counting to three. Thwarted, the Macho Man left the ring as medical personnel rushed in.

Commentator Vince McMahon's over-the-top announcing style seemed particularly well-suited to describing the attack. McMahon screamed, "Steamboat has swallowed his tongue! Steamboat can't breathe!" as the Dragon gasped for air. The hyperbole was balanced by Jesse "The Body" Ventura, who calmly corrected McMahon, telling him, "Steamboat's tongue is hanging out of his mouth." Still, as Steamboat was placed on a gurney, McMahon continued, "Steamboat's swallowed his tongue!"

The injury was made even more effective by Steamboat's amazing ability to sell. He continued grabbing his throat and writhing around the ring as medical personnel tried to place him on the stretcher, falling off not once, but twice. McMahon criticized the paramedics, pointing out that Steamboat couldn't breathe and he was merely trying to lift himself up to catch some air. It was a classic example of an announcer helping to put an angle (in this case, an injury) over.

Equally impressive was Ventura's subtle heel commentary. Ventura prided himself on being the man who "tells it like it is," but anyone who listened to him knew he favored the villains. Ventura was particularly good at calling the matches from a heel's point of view without being blatant about it. Like all good bad guys, Jesse could never admit to being wrong — and it was more obvious than when a video replay of Savage's flying axehandle to Steamboat was aired. While McMahon expressed disbelief at the heinous attack, Ventura matter-of-factly said, "Look at that move. I'll tell you what, McMahon, I've never seen this move done before — look at the length of that leap!" Ventura's praise continued as a replay of the timekeeper's bell being driven into Steamboat's throat was shown. McMahon wondered, "What's he trying to do?" and Ventura replied, "It's obvious what he's trying to do — he's eliminating Ricky "The Dragon" Steamboat as the number one contender.

As is often the result of sinister attacks in wrestling, Steamboat's injury was rumored to be career ending. (The diagnosis was a crushed larynx.) But in true wrestling tradition, he announced a comeback. Viewers watched Steamboat undergo exhaustive physical therapy, week after week, on WWF television — the Dragon promising revenge as he struggled to regain his voice. The two would settle the score at *WrestleMania III* in one of the most highly regarded wrestling matches of all time, with Steamboat pinning Savage to win the Intercontinental Championship.

RIC FLAIR REARRANGES RICKY MORTON'S FACE

Being the great ring operator he was, it wasn't surprising that "Nature Boy" Ric Flair decided to try his hand at plastic surgery. Perhaps it was his father the Doctor who inspired him. Or maybe it was being embarrassed on TV that drove him over the edge. Either way, the night Flair began practicing medicine was a moment Ricky Morton of the Rock and Roll Express would never forget.

In JCP, the Rock and Roll Express was an overnight sensation. To a legion of teen girls who followed their every move, the lightning-fast team were heart-throbs. And it wasn't long before they'd caught the attention of NWA world heavy-weight champion Ric Flair, who mocked them, calling their supporters "little girls in . . . training bras."

The Express confronted Flair during an episode of *World Championship Wrestling;* Ricky Morton took the lead and admonished Flair for turning his back on the fans. The "Nature Boy" brushed off Morton's comments, telling him that he didn't need anyone's help to succeed. Disgusted by Flair's contempt, Morton grabbed the champ's designer sunglasses and crushed them. Flair attacked, but soon found himself in the middle of the ring, at the mercy of the tag team specialist. By the end of the confrontation, Flair was on his back. Morton had embarrassed him on national television.

Enraged, Flair began stalking Morton, waiting for the right moment to get the receipt he felt was owed. Finally, he got his match. During the bout, Flair's allies Arn Anderson and Tully Blanchard jumped into the ring (along with manager James J. Dillon) and held Morton down. Flair then jumped off the second rope, driving his knee into the back of Morton's head and breaking his nose. It was meant as warning to Morton to back off — a warning that Morton chose to ignore.

As serious as his injury was, Morton came back and secured a non-title rematch. This time, Morton pinned Flair, furthering the champ's embarrassment. Flair went ballistic, and rallied his allies. They attacked the Rock and Roll Express in their dressing room. Joined once more by Anderson, Blanchard, and Dillon, Flair laid out Morton's tag team partner Robert Gibson before turning his attention to Morton.

In a move reminiscent of his attack on Ricky Steamboat years earlier, Flair took Morton's face and ground it into the dressing room floor. Only the timely intervention of Morton's friends prevented the Nature Boy from turning it into hamburger. Even so, Morton's face was a mess. Flair relished this, and exploited it in the promo he cut after the attack.

Flair talked about how he'd reduced Morton to nothing more than an itty-bitty "Ugly Duckling," and that there wasn't a woman in the United States who'd want to lay down with him now. The arrogant champ cut down the babyface, saying he'd found out what a cold place the world of professional wrestling could be. The promo was classic Flair, but it was answered by an equally effective rebuttal by Morton.

With the left side of his face heavily bandaged, Ricky appeared, promising that every dog has his day. After this, the two men would battle across the South as Morton challenged Flair for both revenge and the NWA championship. They put on some very entertaining matches in the process, but Morton would come up short when it came to winning the ten pounds of gold. Nevertheless, Ric Flair learned the truth of the old adage, "Don't judge the fight by the size of the dog in the fight; judge the fight by the size of the fight in the dog."

TERRY FUNK BEATS UP MEL PHILLIPS

For years, Mel Phillips was a nameless figure — even though he was seen by millions of fans week after week on WWF TV. Phillips was the guy who took wrestlers'

A Triple H chairshot takes out Lita and Matt Hardy

robes and other attire back to the dressing room during their matches. In the summer of 1985, however, he achieved wrestling notoriety by falling prey to a vicious beating at the hands of Terry Funk.

The former NWA kingpin was wrestling his debut match in the WWF against perennial loser Aldo Montoya. Before the match started, Funk handed his cowboy hat to the ring attendant whose job it was to take care of the wrestlers' outfits during the matches (wrestlers robes could cost as much as thousands of dollars). Mel Phillips was just having some fun when he grabbed the wrestler's cowboy hat and put it on his own head. The mercurial Funk's eyes flashed with anger when he saw the ring lackey parading around in his hat and he attacked Phillips mercilessly.

After such a brutal beating, you'd expect Phillips to learn his lesson. Not so; Phillips repeated the same behavior weeks later. Funk hadn't learned anything either. (He had been fined for beating up Phillips the first time.) Fortunately for the hapless ring attendant, the Junkyard Dog saw what was going on and he rushed out to his aid. The rescue introduced a feud between JYD and Funk.

With manager Jimmy Hart at his side, Funk went on a rampage, branding his opponents with a cattle iron after defeating them (fortunately for Funk's opponents, the "brand" was chalk affixed to the iron). Funk and the JYD battled throughout the WWF, and the Dog slowly began to gain the upper hand. Just when it looked like JYD had the best of Funk and that the feud was over, things got even more heated: Dory Funk Jr. entered the Federation.

Now facing two Funks instead of one, the JYD enlisted the aid of Hulk Hogan (who had his own score to settle with Terry Funk after being branded by the wild Texan). The two teams met on *Saturday Night's Main Event,* with Hogan and the Dog enlisting the help of midget wrestler the Haiti Kid to counter the presence of the Funks' manager Jimmy Hart. Hogan and the Dog would triumph, but a post-match attack by the Funks would tarnish the victory.

CHAPTER 8

THE TURNS

Whether it's applause or heckling, the emotional energy invested by wrestling fans can be a powerful force, ripe for manipulation. One of the oldest ways of playing off this is "turning" a wrestler — changing them from a babyface into a heel or vice versa. By turning a wrestler, a promoter can freshen up an act, or create new matchups. Few things inspire so much emotion in wrestling fans as a turn.

More than a few observers have noticed how face turns seem inevitable when a heel wrestler is built up as a monster. The saying, "Everyone loves a winner" is especially true in pro wrestling — consider, for example, the face turns of wrestlers such as the Undertaker and Abyss. But it's an oversimplification to say wrestling has always been about clear-cut, black-and-white characters. Fans have been cheering unorthodox wrestlers for decades — the Crusher and Blackjack Mulligan are just two examples.

Nevertheless, the public's ever-changing sensibilities have caused a dramatic change in how faces and heels are perceived. One of the most striking examples can be seen in the career of Bob Backlund. Back in the '70s and early '80s, Backlund was the quintessential babyface, an athlete who played fair and encouraged his fans to do the same. However by the Rock and Wrestling Era, Backlund's comic-book all-American persona was beginning to wear thin. By the early 1990s, he'd become a hated heel — without changing any of the characteristics that had once made him a fan hero.

Heel and face turns can backfire if handled incorrectly. A promoter must be careful not to misjudge the public's emotions when turning a wrestler. Jim Crockett Promotions learned this the hard way when they turned the Road Warriors heel. Despite the promotion's best efforts, the fans continued to cheer them, forcing JCP to abandon the idea. A similar situation occurred in 2001 when "Stone Cold" Steve Austin was turned heel and WWE fans refused to boo him.

A promoter must also take care not to turn a wrestler too often, which is what happened to Lex Luger during the late 1980s. Promoters turned him so frequently that the fans simply stopped caring.

THE MAN THEY HATED FOR EIGHT YEARS (BUDDY ROSE TURNS FACE)

There's a thin line between love and hate. Never was that more clear than when Pacific Northwest Wrestling fans watched "Playboy" Buddy Rose run in to save Billy Jack Haynes and Curt Hennig from a beatdown at the hands of Rip Oliver and the Clan (Oliver's nickname for his henchmen, the Dynamite Kid and the Assassin). Even the announcers couldn't believe it: "This is a man the fans have hated for eight years." Rose was the wrestler who'd injured some of the promotion's most beloved babyfaces — now, children were running into the ring to congratulate him.

What an amazing turnaround for the villain who had terrorized PNW. In some respects, he was the heel version of "The American Dream" Dusty Rhodes. Like Rhodes, Rose was no paragon of physical fitness, but he *was* able to wrestle sixty-minute Broadways, selling for babyfaces as few others could. Rose had charisma too; but while Rhodes extolled the virtues of the American Dream, the Playboy extolled the virtues of winning at any cost. Anyone who underestimated him took his life into his own hands. He'd stolen many a victory during his PNW tenure, and popular babyfaces like Roddy Piper and Rick Martel had been sent packing when they put loser-leaves-town stipulations up against him.

Rose was so hated that fans actually chose to cheer some of the most despised men in wrestling rather than root for him. Men like Bull Ramos, and even the Kiwi Sheepherders (Butch Miller & Luke Williams) heard cheers after Rose had betrayed them: such was the hatred he generated with his biting promos and nefarious ring tactics.

As history has shown, the greater the fans' loathing, the greater the effect when a heel becomes a babyface. The fans' reaction to Rose's turn was a testament to both the way the turn was planned and Rose's effectiveness as a performer.

The Playboy had purchased the services of fellow heel the Dynamite Kid as part of his quest to capture the territory's tag team championship. Rose and Dynamite found themselves facing local heroes Billy Jack Haynes and Curt Hennig in a two-out-of-three falls match — with the winner to receive a title shot against Rip Oliver and the Assassin. Things soured for Rose during the last of the three falls. He looked to have things well in hand when he grabbed and held Haynes for the Dynamite Kid to hit him from off the top rope. But as Dynamite flew through the air, Haynes moved, and Rose was left in the line of fire. Haynes covered him for the pin, winning the match and the title shot. A frustrated Dynamite Kid punched Rose, but the Playboy quickly regained his composure and stunned Dynamite with a kick to the gut. When Oliver and the Assassin came in for an interview, things got ugly. They restrained Rose, while Dynamite laid into him. Hennig and Billy Jack weren't sure whether or not they should help, especially after all of the trouble he had put them through during their careers. The two babyfaces turned and walked away, but as they did, Oliver and the Assassin chose to attack them, no doubt trying to soften them up before their next title defense. Referee Sandy Barr went down when he tried to help Rose; and Rose himself was beaten further when the Dynamite Kid delivered a flying headbutt. Finally, Hennig and Haynes came in to clear the ring of the heels, saving Rose from further abuse.

Afterward, the Dynamite Kid told announcer Dutch Savage that Rose was finished. The Playboy had paid him to be on a winning team, only to lose two falls in the match.

Then, in a promo that seemed completely out of character, a bloody Rose apologized to Dutch Savage, Don Owens, and all the wrestlers he had wronged in the past. He said he wasn't going to change his style of wrestling but promised to change his attitude. Ultimately, Rose vowed revenge on Oliver and the Clan and acknowledged that the fans might not have a reason to believe him. Dutch Savage was dumbfounded.

Rose's face turn would be complete when he saved Billy Jack Haynes and Curt Hennig from Oliver and the Clan. Bloody and bandaged, he then told Haynes and Hennig he understood they might not trust him, but that he hoped they would give him a chance. Rose recalled how Hennig was the first wrestler to put him out of wrestling, then swore on his mother that he was being sincere in asking Curt to form a tag team with him. Rose then extended his hand, and Hennig accepted, telling Rose he would be an asset in his own campaign against Oliver and the Clan. Next, the Playboy turned to Haynes. Just a year earlier, Rose had spit in Billy Jack's face when he'd asked for a chance to break into wrestling. Now, he acknowledged Haynes' drive to become a wrestler. A gracious Haynes also agreed to team with Rose to settle their individual grudges against their collective opponents.

Although it lasted only a year, this turn is a powerful example of how effective a properly executed turn can be. Rose would eventually return to the dark side, feuding with the faces of PNW once more before leaving to work in the AWA as part of a tag team with Doug Sommers. It is still talked about to this day by fans of PNW.

MR. WONDERFUL TURNS ON HOGAN

> *A competent and self-confident person is incapable of jealousy in anything.*
> *Jealousy is invariably a symptom of neurotic insecurity.*
> —**Robert A. Heinlein**

There's always someone better than you . . . Paul Orndorff never subscribed to that theory, and yet reality was giving him a harsh lesson. No matter how hard he tried, he could not step out of the shadow of Hulk Hogan. After being blamed for his team's loss at the inaugural *WrestleMania*, Orndorff made it clear he wasn't going to be anyone's scapegoat and quickly severed ties with his former manager and tag team partner "Rowdy" Roddy Piper, earning the cheers of WWF fans in the process. Orndorff soon became one of the more popular wrestlers in the Federation — but he was clearly not the most popular.

With a nickname like "Mr. Wonderful," Paul Orndorff obviously was no stranger to pride. Factor in a hair-trigger temper and he was an explosion waiting to happen. A heelish "Adorable" Adrian Adonis recognized this and knew he had an excellent opportunity to capitalize on it.

When Orndorff appeared on an edition of Adorable Adrian's talk segment, "The Flower Shop," the ever-crafty Adonis stirred the pot, insinuating that Hogan didn't really have Orndorff's back. To make his point, Adonis asked

Orndorff to try phoning Hogan. Orndorff agreed, but soon had egg on his face when Hogan didn't answer his call. While he tried to ignore Adonis' gloating, it was clear Orndorff's ego had been bruised.

Adonis' taunting led to Hogan and Orndorff appearing on "The Flower Shop" together. Hogan addressed the phone call, letting Orndorff and Adonis know that he had been busy working out, and that by the time he got to the phone, Orndorff had hung up. Hogan warned Adonis not to get between friends, then responded to a challenge from Bobby "The Brain" Heenan, pitting his behemoths, King Kong Bundy and "Big" John Studd, against him and Orndorff. Heenan was so confident in his team that he had issued a $100,000 reward to anyone who slammed Studd or pinned Bundy. At that point, it remained uncollected.

To prepare for the match, Hogan and Orndorff squared off against the rough and tumble Moondogs. Watching, it was clear that Orndorff had something to prove. Rather than relying on Hogan as a partner, Mr. Wonderful turned the contest into a handicap bout, going out of his way to show he could handle the Moondogs by himself.

After the match, it was clear that Hogan understood what was happening. While it was one thing to showboat against the Moondogs, it was another to try the same thing against Bundy and Studd. This was a team that had injured Hillbilly Jim — and put Andre the Giant on the shelf. Going into the match unfocused was a sure way to the emergency room.

Unfortunately, Orndorff went into the match acting as if he could take on Bundy and Studd himself. Mr. Wonderful started off strong, manhandling "Big" John Studd and keeping the giant-like wrestler off balance. And his performance was equally impressive when King Kong Bundy tagged in; Orndorff used his speed to avoid Bundy and strike back when openings arose. He even held his own when Studd came back in, attempting, though failing, to bodyslam Big John. When Bundy re-entered for a double-team, Orndorff dropkicked both wrestling colossuses, sending them out of the ring to regroup with Heenan. Mr. Wonderful basked in the fans' cheers and pointed at himself while Hogan frantically motioned to tag in. His partner was doing well, but Hogan knew Orndorff couldn't maintain this pace forever. Orndorff finally gave the fans what they wanted, and tagged in the Hulkster.

Two of the wrestlers who rushed to Hogan's aid (Dan Spivey and Sivi Afi) were intended as replacements for wrestlers (Barry Windham and Jimmy Snuka respectively) who had just left the WWF.

The WWF champion continued the assault against Studd. Hogan unleashed a barrage of blows, wearing the big man down and making him furious. When Studd lost his cool and bounced off the ropes towards him, he gave the Hulkster the opening he needed. Using his momentum against him, Hogan lifted Studd up and bodyslammed him, delighting the crowd and enraging the heels. But they weren't the only ones enraged. Mr. Wonderful slammed the ropes as Hogan posed in the ring, celebrating his successful slam. It was clear Orndorff was jealous of Hogan succeeding where he'd had failed just moments earlier. The fragility of the Hogan/Orndorff team was showing.

Energized by his successful slam, Hogan continued his offense; but then Studd caught Hogan with a clothesline and the tide suddenly turned. King Kong Bundy came in and the two men began double-teaming the champ, using their size and power to quickly smash through him. A desperate Hogan raked Bundy's eyes and head-butted Studd, creating an opening to tag in the waiting Mr. Wonderful. But as Hogan backed into his corner, he accidentally knocked Orndorff off the apron. Any relief from his partner was now out of the question.

As Orndorff lay outside the ring, Bundy and Studd continued working over Hogan, beating him senseless. Vince McMahon and Bruno Sammartino wondered when referee Dick Wehrle was going to force one of the heels back to their corner — tag rules stated a team had only a five count before one member had to leave the ring. When it became clear that the gigantic duo was ignoring the ref, McMahon wondered why the referee didn't disqualify them. With Hogan still being pummeled, Orndorff finally got to his feet and made his way back into the ring. Though no bell had rung, McMahon noticed that the ref had signaled for a DQ. Bundy and Studd didn't seem to care.

With his partner down, Orndorff cleared the ring of the heels. As the two big men bailed, Orndorff helped the Hulkster to his feet, making the number-one sign as he raised the groggy Hulkster's arm. But what looked like a gesture of friendship was actually the set-up for one of the most memorable heel turns in history. Lifting Hogan's arm, Orndorff stunned the Hulkster with a clothesline. The already battered Hulk was no match for the devilish attack, which made Orndorff's subsequent piledriver even easier to hit. When Orndorff lifted Hogan's three-hundred-pound-plus frame into the air and drove his head into the mat he destroyed anything that remained of their friendship.

As Hogan lay helpless, Studd, Bundy, and Heenan returned to the ring, ready to finish him off for good. Fortunately for the champ, a contingent of babyfaces also rushed the ring, preventing any further damage. After the match, Orndorff found himself welcomed back into the fold of the Bobby Heenan Family as

Heenan, Studd, and Bundy praised his actions. Even "Adorable" Adrian Adonis (the man who had instigated everything) was there to congratulate him. Heenan and the other members of the Heenan family chanted, "Wonderful. Wonderful!" as Orndorff paraded triumphantly backstage.

The betrayal started one of the hottest feuds of the 1980s as Orndorff battled Hogan across the country. Orndorff added insult to injury by making Hogan's "Real American" his new entrance music. So hot was the feud that the two some-times battled in more than one arena on the same day. In his autobiography, Heenan recalled finishing a match in one city and then hopping a jet to another for yet another contest. The feud's success led to the epic card in Toronto known as *The Big Event*. It also included a memorable cage match on *Saturday Night's Main Event*.

Interestingly, there was no real blow off to the Hogan/Orndorff program. When Andre the Giant began feuding with Hogan, Orndorff's hatred for Hogan was as strong as ever. During a battle royal on *SNME*, Orndorff attacked Hogan as if nothing had been settled. But with the threat of Andre looming, there was no sense in continuing the hostilities.

Eventually, Orndorff's hot temper would see him leave the Heenan Family once more, this time after Bobby Heenan told Mr. Wonderful to acknowledge that "Ravishing" Rick Rude had the superior physique. Orndorff took exception and quickly fired Heenan. As often happens in wrestling, the fans were eager to welcome a babyface Orndorff back.

Orndorff eventually left the WWF and began working for WCW both in front of the camera and behind the scenes. In 2005, he was inducted into the WWE Hall of Fame.

MR. WRESTLING II TURNS HIS BACK ON MAGNUM T.A.

The time-tested teacher meets student angle took an interesting twist when Bill Watts pitted long-time hero Mr. Wrestling II against his protégé Magnum T.A. Traditionally, it is the protégé who turns on his mentor, but the Cowboy was never afraid to think outside the box. Mid-South Wrestling featured some of the most innovative angles in history of the business.

After minor successes in Florida Championship Wrestling, when Terry Allen came to MSW Bill Watts began to build him into a main-eventer. His belly-to-belly suplex was touted as a powerful finishing move, and Allen's good looks helped him get over with female fans. His resemblance to Tom Selleck's "Magnum P.I.," gave birth to the nickname of Magnum T.A. Slowly but surely Terry Allen was becoming a star.

His rise to the top in MSW was helped along by a mentor: Mr. Wrestling II, a popular masked wrestler who unlike most hooded grapplers, wrestled a clean scientific style. Magnum learnt much from the popular veteran, and it wasn't long before the two formed a successful team, chasing the region's tag championship.

Things were looking good, but they got even better when Magnum was awarded an unexpected shot at Butch Reed's North American heavyweight championship (the territory's most prestigious title). Reed wanted to defend his belt against the up-and-coming star, apparently feeling that the less-experienced Allen would be easy to turn back. Reed couldn't have been more wrong. Allen fought with a skill and intensity that overwhelmed the champion. When the final bell rang, Magnum T.A. was the new North American champion.

Allen's reign was short-lived (since the title match was unsanctioned, Allen's title was not official), but a new title shot was on the horizon. On December 25, 1983, Magnum and Mr. Wrestling II defeated Jim Neidhart and Butch Reed to capture the Mid-South tag team championship. The win was the culmination of Magnum's hard work and the training he'd received from Mr. Wrestling II.

Magnum's good fortune continued when he was named the number one contender for the North American title. His luck ran out, however, when his mentor lashed out during the contract signing between Magnum and the latest champ, the Junkyard Dog. During the ceremony, the masked man made it clear he felt Magnum was too green to have a chance. He then criticized JYD (a fellow babyface), accusing him of cowardice in wrestling someone who was obviously going to be an easy opponent. When Magnum tried to calm Mr. Wrestling II down, he was slapped in the face.

Seeing what his title opportunity was doing to his friend, Magnum offered to hand the title contract to him. Mr. Wrestling II responded with more anger, slapping Magnum again. Despite this treatment, Magnum continued to support his mentor, tearing the contract up and refusing to let it ruin their friendship.

Over the next few weeks, Magnum's relationship with Mr. Wrestling II continued to deteriorate. Things came to a head during a tag team title defense against the Midnight Express (Dennis Condrey and Bobby Eaton). The Midnights had quickly worked their way into contention for the Mid-South tag championship and they were hot on the heels of the titleholders. On March 13, 1984, the Midnights faced the champions, and a match stipulation meant that the losing team would receive ten lashes from a belt. When Mr. Wrestling II walked out on him during the match, Magnum learned just how much his mentor had changed. Despite a brave battle,

Magnum fell to the challengers, losing the tag team titles in the process. He prepared to accept his stipulated punishment, the only bright spot being that fellow babyface Terry Taylor manned up and offered to take five of the ten lashes.

At this point, Allen had to accept that despite his best efforts, he and Mr. Wrestling II were through. His mentor had become a full-fledged heel; he cheated his way to victory over the Junkyard Dog for the North American title, and began breaking in a new protégé, Mr. Wrestling III. Betrayed, T.A. engaged Mr. Wrestling II in a series of matches. In the end, Mr. Wrestling II would discover just how good his teaching was when Magnum defeated him to become the new North American champion. The lessons Magnum learned would come in handy when he left MSW to work for Jim Crockett Promotions, where his star would rise to even greater heights.

THE END OF THE ROCKERS

No matter how successful a tag team is, it's only a matter of time before they split. Anyone who's watched professional wrestling for a while knows that it's one of the sport's conventions. There are always exceptions, but for every team that's stayed together, ten have broken up. Smart promoters know that there are very few things as exciting as two former teammates trying to rip out each other's throats. But to get the fans to really care you need that all-important breakup angle — and it's never been done better than when Shawn Michaels called it quits on the Rockers. It was so successful that to many WWF fans, the Rockers are as well known for their breakup as they are for anything they achieved during their partnership.

When Shawn Michaels and Marty Jannetty got together in the American Wrestling Association (AWA), many fans wrote them off as one of many poor imitators of the Rock and Roll Express. Known as the Midnight Rockers, Jannetty and Michaels quickly proved they were second to none, lighting up the dim tag landscape of the AWA, and recapturing fans for a promotion that was dying a slow death. During their run, they captured the AWA world tag team championship on two separate occasions: observers could see this was only the beginning.

Of course, it wasn't long before Vince McMahon signed the Midnight Rockers for his WWF. Unfortunately, in short order the duo's notorious partying allegedly got them booted out. They returned to the AWA, to rebuild and wait for a second chance.

When they finally rejoined the WWF, Michaels and Jannetty became known simply as the Rockers. Their lightning fast double-team moves quickly won over fans who hadn't seen such fast-paced action since the British Bulldogs. To many, the Rockers seemed destined for at least one run with the WWF tag championship.

But despite their ability and popularity, Michaels and Jannetty were never more than a mid-level tag team. They had their share of victories, but they were never quite able to establish themselves as a dominant force. Why they stalled is a topic of debate. Some blame a match in which the Rockers accidentally injured a novice wrestler, costing the WWF (as well as Michaels and Jannetty personally) a large sum of money. Others have pointed to a rumored dispute between the Rockers and the WWF over their payoffs.

Whatever the reason, Shawn Michaels came to the realization that his career as a tag specialist had gone as far as it could. As 1992 dawned, Michaels convinced WWF officials to split up the team. On January 11, the Rockers appeared on "The Barber Shop," a notoriously lame talk segment hosted by Brutus "The Barber" Beefcake.

Beefcake introduced his guests for the week, calling them a tag team rumored to be on the verge of splitting up. Out came the Rockers, and Beefcake asked them to comment. Michaels quickly spoke up, referring to himself as the team captain as an incredulous Marty Jannetty looked on, and said the rumors of a split were unfounded. The Rockers, he said, were as strong as ever.

But the look on Jannetty's face said different — the Rockers were definitely in trouble. Marty spoke then, bringing up recent matches the team had lost, a missed championship opportunity against the Legion of Doom, as well as another match they'd nearly lost because of Michaels spending more time flirting with female fans than focusing on wrestling. Shawn Michaels fired back, noting a recent match in which Jannetty had "helped" him into losing to Ric Flair.

Things came to a head as Jannetty delivered an ultimatum. He told his partner he was going to turn his back, and that when he turned back around, Michaels could forget about their problems and work on making the Rockers tag team champions, or he could simply walk away.

Unfortunately for Jannetty, Michaels came up with a third option. When Jannetty turned back around around to face him, Michaels shook his hand and hugged him. The Rockers looked to be back together as HBK lifted his partner's arm in victory. Then, in a flash, he delivered a superkick to Jannetty's jaw, knocking him senseless. As he watched Jannetty on the floor of the Barber Shop set, he eyed a window. He then grabbed his dazed ex-teammate and threw him headfirst through the "plate glass." Blood poured from Jannetty's head as Brutus Beefcake came to his aid, preventing any further assault.

Shawn Michaels would go on to incredible success as a singles wrestler, while

Jannetty faded from the wwf save for a brief feud with Michaels after this incident and a short-lived run with Al Snow as the New Rockers.

THE MEGA POWERS EXPLODE!

They were two of the greatest World Wrestling Federation superstars of all time. Individually, both men had attained the pinnacle of success: the wwf championship. They were unstoppable, until they met the foe that no team can overcome — jealousy. The night Hulk Hogan and Randy Savage went from teammates to mortal enemies still stands as one of the greatest heel turns in history.

In 1985, Randy "Macho Man" Savage finally hit the big time after years of stealing the show in territories like the Championship Wrestling Association. Savage possessed the muscular look the wwf looked for, along with incredible charisma, and the combination made him a natural during the Rock and Wrestling Era. Given his abilities, it wasn't long before he battled Hogan for the wwf title, putting on memorable matches in Madison Square Garden and across the country. Little did fans know that was just the appetizer to an even bigger feud.

Savage's abilities made him incredibly popular and a babyface turn was inevitable. After his turn, only one goal remained — the wwf title, which Savage won in a tournament held to crown a new champion (the previous champion Andre the Giant, had been stripped of the belt after he tried to hand it over to the Million Dollar Man). Savage's opponent was Ted DiBiase, the man who had just tried to buy the title. He was facing more than just one opponent, however. DiBiase had stacked the deck by buying the aid of the Giant. Fortunately, the Macho Man wasn't without his own backup. Hulk Hogan (who had been eliminated earlier in the tournament) came to Savage's aid when both Andre and DiBiase's bodyguard Virgil interfered in the match, and Savage was eventually able to score the pin.

This unlikely alliance of former foes became known as the MegaPowers; the dream team was accompanied by Savage's manager, Miss Elizabeth. When DiBiase stepped up his efforts to wrest away the title, Hogan teamed with the Macho Man, at *Summer Slam,* against DiBiase and Andre the Giant. From then on the MegaPowers became an unstoppable force that demolished any and all competition.

Like many of the great tag teams in wrestling history, the duo's greatest enemy turned out to be themselves. As time passed, fans saw that the Macho Man was becoming jealous of the time Elizabeth was giving to Hogan. Savage was used to being the sole object of her attention and fans could tell that he was beginning to grow tired of the arrangement. Matters escalated when Hogan accidentally eliminated Savage from the *Royal Rumble*. Only the intervention of Miss Elizabeth prevented the two partners from fighting each other then and there.

During an episode of *The Main Event* (a prime-time wrestling special on NBC), Hogan and Savage squared off against the team of Akeem and the Big Bossman. The Twin Towers (as the heel team was known) had met the MegaPowers before in an elimination match at *Survivor Series*. Now, the two top teams in the WWF would go head to head. The size and power of the Twin Towers made them formidable foes. Both teams would have to be at the top of their game.

Things were going well for the MegaPowers until Savage was thrown out of the ring by Akeem. The Macho Man accidentally collided with Elizabeth, knocking her out cold. An anxious Hulk Hogan raced her back to the dressing room for medical treatment, leaving the Macho Man to fend for himself. Hogan remained with Elizabeth until she regained consciousness and told him to return to Savage — in an acting performance that foreshadowed Hogan's tour de force in *Mr. Nanny*, the Hulkster prayed Elizabeth would survive and told her, "Randy didn't mean to hit you."

Back in the ring, Savage fought on, no doubt wondering where Hogan was. Amazingly, he managed to survive until his partner returned, mounting a comeback against both Akeem and the Bossman. Savage was none too pleased with Hogan's absence and he paid him back in kind by leaving him on his own in the ring. To make it clear how upset he was, Savage tagged the Hulkster in by slapping him in the face.

Savage raced back to the dressing room, where in one of the all-time great Macho Man moments, he gave Elizabeth a verbal beatdown as she lay helpless on the gurney. Savage told her he was the star of the show and that she had forgotten that. Thanks to her and Hogan, he'd been relegated to a back seat in the team.

After defeating the Twin Towers, Hogan returned to the dressing room where he and Savage began to argue. Savage accused Hogan of lusting after both the title and Elizabeth. He berated his partner for being a jealous ex-champion. All the while, Elizabeth pleaded with the two to stop fighting. Finally Savage exploded, smashing Hogan over the head with the WWF title belt. As Hogan lay helpless on the floor, Savage went at him with his fists. The lovely Elizabeth tried to intervene but Savage tossed her aside.

Then, in one of wrestling's greatest live bloopers, Brutus Beefcake rushed into the room before he was supposed to, inexplicably said "Sorry," and walked off.

Savage continued his attack and went to hit Hogan with the belt again but was stopped by Beefcake (hitting his cue this time), who received a beating from Savage for his efforts. Finally, WWF officials arrived to stop further carnage, but not before Pat Patterson got pummelled as well.

The fuse had been lit and at *WrestleMania V*, the MegaPowers exploded. Hogan and Savage squared off in one of their best matches ever. The two would meet again several times over their careers but nothing compared to the hype built by this incredible angle.

AUSTIN/HART DOUBLE TURN

If turning one wrestler heel or babyface is tricky business, imagine the complexity a promoter faces when trying to turn two wrestlers at the same time. Such a move is rare in the history of the sport, and for a good reason — it's like playing with dynamite. Still, when done correctly, it is a thing of beauty.

Bret "The Hitman" Hart and "Stone Cold" Steve Austin had been feuding for months when Vince McMahon decided to make Austin a babyface. Few were surprised: Austin's redneck character had become too popular. Ever since "Austin 3:16," a Stone Cold face turn seemed plausible. The WWF's new philosophy, WWF Attitude, made it inevitable.

At that time, McMahon believed wrestling fans had become more sophisticated; they no longer wanted absolutes, and black and white characters were being replaced by shades of grey. The new WWF superstars would no longer be superheroes or supervillains. Yes, there would still be those that fans cheered and others they booed, but in the Attitude era wrestlers would be more realistic, involved in situations that mirrored life in the real world.

Bret Hart epitomized the traditional babyface. He wasn't as one-dimensional as Bob Backlund or Hulk Hogan, but he portrayed someone who children could look up to. In Hart's mind, it was what his fans expected. When McMahon suggested he switch from hero to heel, Hart wasn't so sure.

McMahon convinced him that he could continue to be a babyface while performing in his native Canada and abroad. But when he wrestled in the U.S., he would be seen as self-righteous, someone who extolled the Canadian way of life and looked down on what he perceived as the questionable morality of America.

Hart had taken some time off after dropping the WWF championship to Shawn Michaels at *WrestleMania XII*. During that time, Austin established himself. After defeating opponent after opponent, Austin began to call out Hart.

"The Excellence of Execution" (a nickname given to Hart by WWF announcer Gorilla Monsoon) answered Stone Cold's challenge, defeating him by pinfall at the *Survivor Series* pay-per-view. But Austin continued to plague Hart, cheating him out of a *Royal Rumble* victory in 1997. The two fought again at the *In Your House: Final Four* pay-per-view where Hart won the WWF championship. The next night, on *Raw*, Austin continued to make the Hitman's life miserable, this time costing him the title during his match with "Psycho" Sid.

While Hart was still wildly popular, Austin's fanbase exploded during their battles. The two continued feuding, and eventually faced each other in a submission match at *WrestleMania 13,* with former Ultimate Fighting Championship star Ken Shamrock serving as special referee. The match stipulation called for victory only when an opponent submitted. The match went back and forth with both men refusing to surrender. Finally, Hart locked Austin in his finisher, the sharpshooter. Despite a dogged effort, Austin could not escape the hold. Still, he refused to quit. Shamrock finally called for the bell after Austin passed out from an apparent combination of pain and blood loss.

After winning the bout, an angry Bret Hart refused to let go. He had experienced enough of Austin's taunts and attacks to last a lifetime. Several moments passed before Shamrock intervened and Hart broke the hold. The fans cheered for Austin, despite the fact he'd lost.

The story behind the match went like this: Austin's refusal to quit would be the turning point in the fans accepting him as a babyface, while Hart's poor sportsmanship would cost him his once loyal followers. The reality was that Austin was already over. The bout at *WrestleMania* was simply the WWF's way of officially recognizing Austin as a babyface. Hart's actions at *WrestleMania* would be used to help explain his heel turn when he cut scathing interviews about the fans in the U.S.

NOBODY MAKES FUN OF ME (VALENTINE BREAKS FLAIR'S NOSE)

Greg "The Hammer" Valentine and "Nature Boy" Ric Flair: the blonde bombers were arguably the toughest team in Jim Crockett Promotions. They not only battled the promotion's top babyface teams but actually managed to hospitalize the feared heel duo of Gene and Ole Anderson. Their NWA world tag team championship reigns further solidified their reputation as the best in the area. Valentine and Flair ruled the roost as partners, but their destinies eventually took them separate ways. When Valentine left JCP to pursue the World Wide Wrestling Federation title in New York, Flair turned babyface and began hearing cheers.

But when Flair began having problems with heel manager Gene Anderson and his charge Jimmy "Superfly" Snuka, opportunity seemed to knock. Valentine returned to JCP, and acknowledged that while he and Flair had different philosophies, he wanted to reunite their legendary team one last time. Valentine told Flair he had seen the light and was a changed man. No doubt aware of Valentine's past, Flair nonetheless agreed to the partnership and they teamed against Jimmy Snuka and the Iron Sheik. Flair would soon get a refresher course in what Valentine was capable of.

The match was a brutal bout; Flair absorbed endless punishment from Anderson's team but the resilient Nature Boy held on. If he could just make the tag, everything would be fine. He struggled on, but as he reached his corner, everything became clear: he'd been betrayed. Valentine jumped from the mat apron, hanging Flair out to dry.

Flair was eventually pinned, but his troubles were just beginning. Valentine entered the ring and a four-on-one beatdown began. A nearly lifeless Flair was held; Valentine took Gene Anderson's cane and smashed it across his face. As the cane broke, so did Flair's nose. Flair was old school, and believed injuries had to look legit. This time would be no exception.

Flair appeared on television with his nose in a protective brace. As videotape of the attack aired, he painfully recalled each moment leading to Valentine's betrayal. The Hammer had taken liberties, and he would pay.

It was the start of a war that saw the two men trade Flair's United States heavyweight championship in brutal matches night after night. Eventually, the Nature Boy would triumph and get the revenge he had been seeking.

USA! USA! USA!

Heroes may not be braver than anyone else. They're just braver five minutes longer.
—**Ronald Reagan**

In 1983, a simple walk back to the dressing room turned into one of the bloodiest feuds in WWF history. Sgt. Slaughter had earned a reputation as one of the toughest men in the sqaured circle. His former Marine drill sergeant character exercised brutality in the ring and earned him the hatred of wrestling fans. Slaughter disdained those who he saw as weak and undisciplined. Whether it was whipping Bob Backlund with a swagger stick or blind-siding Pat Patterson after an interview, Slaughter had a way of throwing his weight around and riling up the fans.

Despite the widespread hatred for Sarge, all it took was a confrontation with the even-more hated Iron Sheik for him to earn the love of fans everywhere. After winning a match, Slaughter left the ring and was on his way back to the dressing room when he ran into the Iron Sheik. Neither man would move. Both men had tremendous pride and for Slaughter, there was the undeniable element of patriotism.

Although it had been two years since the resolution of the Iranian hostage crisis, memories of that dark time in American history were fresh. The Iron Sheik proudly proclaimed his heritage as an Iranian at every opportunity, infuriating fans (although at the height of the hostage crisis, the Iron Sheik's Iranian heritage was downplayed over concerns for his safety).

After this run-in, Slaughter led the crowd in the Pledge of Allegiance, sealing his turn. All of his past sins were forgiven, as he led the WWF's fight against the hated Sheik. Slaughter was suddenly the patriotic babyface, battling the forces of evil that sought to defame the good name of the United States.

Slaughter's turn came at a time when patriotism was on the rise. President Ronald Reagan presented a very black-and-white picture of the world which many citizens found refreshing in a post-Vietnam era. After the Soviet invasion of Afghanistan, the Cold War threatened to go hot. Americans realized that war was once again a possibility and foreign heels were suddenly once again something for promoters to exploit. Russians began appearing in every promotion, as did Russian sympathizers such as Jim Neidhart and Krusher Krushchev.

Of course there were always old standbys like the Sheik. Unlike many American-born wrestlers who claimed to be from abroad (Fritz Von Erich and Baron Von Raschke are just two examples), the Iron Sheik was the real deal. He had competed in the Olympics for Iran and was rumored to be a former bodyguard of the late Shah. Early in his career, the Sheik worked for Verne Gagne as a trainer for hopeful wrestlers.

Bob "Sgt. Slaughter" Remus first got into wrestling when a reporter friend told him about a story he was doing on Verne Gagne's wrestling camp. After a grueling tryout, Remus was told he was welcome to come back. Bitten by the wrestling bug, he ended up working for Gagne in the American Wrestling Association (AWA), initially as Bob Remus, and later under a mask as Super Destroyer Mark II. Super Destroyer II was managed by Lord Alfred Hayes until Bobby Heenan returned to the AWA and Destroyer turned on Hayes to join Heenan.

In 1980, Remus entered the World Wrestling Federation as Sgt. Slaughter. He battled some of the WWF's top babyfaces, including Andre the Giant, Bob Backlund, and Pat Patterson. After a successful tour of duty in Jim Crockett Promotions, Slaughter returned to the WWF, where he challenged Backlund again for the WWF heavyweight championship. Slaughter continued to brutalize WWF babyfaces until January 1984, when he confronted the Iron Sheik about his anti-American comments. The former Marine had heard enough from the heel bashing the United States and he soon found himself in a brutal feud with the one-time WWF champion.

The feud with the Iron Sheik catapulted Slaughter to the top, and his popularity rivaled that of Hulk Hogan. Slaughter's program with the Sheik allowed him to main-event WWF house shows in one area while Hogan worked in another. As Slaughter commented in *Raging '80s*, "We really had it going on, Hogan sold out the West, I sold out the East. Then, Hogan would sell out the East and I'd sell out the West. We were a powerhouse."

The matches between the two men were bloody. The fans wouldn't have wanted it any other way. Neither man could get a conclusive victory until Slaughter challenged his Iranian foe to a Boot Camp match, Slaughter's version of a Texas death match. Madison Square Garden hosted the event and it's still remembered as one of the all-time brawls. Naturally, Slaughter won, ending the feud.

After his program with Slaughter, the Iron Sheik continued with his anti-American ways, this time teaming with "Russian" wrestler Nikolai Volkoff. The two would go on to feud with the popular team of Mike Rotunda and Barry Windham (better known as the U.S. Express), winning the WWF tag team titles at *WrestleMania.*

Despite his immense popularity, Slaughter's WWF career seemed to stagnate after facing off with the Sheik. A feud with Niklolai Volkoff seemed repetitive, as did Slaughter's taking a young wrestler under his wing ("Private" Terry Daniels). Eventually, the Sarge butted heads with WWF owner Vince McMahon over merchandise revenue. He went to work for Verne Gagne's AWA, continuing as a patriotic babyface.

In 1991, Slaughter proved that anything can happen in the WWF. The Sarge returned during the U.S. confrontation with Iraq over its invasion of Kuwait. Rather than storming in as a patriotic babyface, Slaughter turned his back on the United States, siding with "Iraqi" wrestlers General Adnan and Col. Mustafa (Sarge's old sparring partner, the Iron Sheik). Slaughter's anti-American crusade saw him capture the WWF championship from the Ultimate Warrior, holding the belt hostage until Hulk Hogan liberated it at *WrestleMania.* The controversial program saw Slaughter put his family into protective custody after repeated death threats.

CHAPTER 9

WE CAN'T HAVE ANYTHING NICE AROUND HERE! (CELEBRATIONS GONE WRONG)

In the often-melodramatic world of professional wrestling, it just doesn't make sense to keep heroes happy. For sheer drama, pulling the rug out from under your protagonists ranks high. Promoters have made it an art-form, with long-time fans secure in the knowledge that no wedding will go without rain and no trophy will be presented without it being smashed over the winner's head. The few exceptions to this only prove the rule, and fans can rest assured that whereever there's a moment of happiness, disaster is lurking in the wings.

UNDERTAKER CRASHES MACHO MAN & LIZ'S WEDDING RECEPTION

"Macho Man" Randy Savage and Miss Elizabeth captured the hearts of WWF fans ever since Elizabeth was unveiled as Savage's manager in 1985. It was a curious relationship; in the beginning Savage wrestled as a heel, while Miss Elizabeth was always seen as a paragon of virtue. Unlike other heel valets or managers, she never interfered on Randy's behalf, which was made even more curious because Savage browbeat her. Fans were puzzled — why would she remain with Savage? It would be years before Elizabeth left the Macho Man's side (not until Savage accused his tag team partner, Hulk Hogan, of "lusting after" her).

But after losing a retirement match to the Ultimate Warrior at *WrestleMania VII*, Savage and his former manager were reunited when Elizabeth ran in and beat up Savage's latest valet, Sensational Sherri. Sherri had been with Savage for some time, but when the Macho Man lost the match, she lost it and attacked him. With Randy in trouble, Elizabeth sent Sherri packing.

As often happens in wrestling, a simple act of kindness was all it took to reconcile two estranged parties. Before long, it was as if the two had never split. Soon, wedding bells were in the air and wrestling fans couldn't have been happier. The ceremony was incorporated into the 1991 *Summer Slam* pay-per-view.

Given wrestling's history, fans were wondering what disaster would befall Savage and Elizabeth at *Summer Slam*. Fans were no doubt delighted and surprised when their nuptials went without a hitch. "The Match Made in Heaven" was a tremendous celebration, recognizing not only Savage's face turn, but the fans delight with wrestling's favorite couple.

While the wedding went smoothly, the happy couple didn't fare so well at the reception. At first, everything seemed fine; the happy couple greeted guests, drank a toast made in their honor by "Mean" Gene Okerlund, and then opened the dance floor with the traditional first dance. After the ceremonial cake cutting, Elizabeth tossed the bridal bouquet and the couple proceeded to open their gifts. Elizabeth tried to get the Macho Man to wait, but an eager Savage would have nothing of it. Had he known what gift awaited him and his wife, he would have listened. But realizing that there was no persuading her new husband, Elizabeth gave in and began opening gifts herself. As she opened a box, her smiling face transformed into a look of terror. First, a snake jumped out at her. Then, the Macho Man was blindsided. The Undertaker bludgeoned him with an urn, knocking him unconscious. The couple's happy day had suddenly turned black — Jake "The Snake" Roberts and the Undertaker (accompanied by manager Paul Bearer) hovered menacingly. Roberts taunted Elizabeth with his snake. Fortunately, WWF newcomer Sid Justice (a.k.a. Sid Vicious) prevented further carnage by grabbing a chair and chasing the wedding crashers away.

In the crazy world of professional wrestling, things would have been easily settled with Savage meeting Roberts in the ring. Savage could do no such thing though, as he had been retired from wrestling by the Ultimate Warrior. The diabolical Roberts gloated over his actions, doubtless relishing the fact Savage was unable to exact payback.

Fans were furious. They demanded that Savage be reinstated, but WWF president Jack Tunney refused to bow to the pressure. Even when the WWF was flooded with letters of protest, he stood firm. Savage had agreed to the retirement match, and he would have to deal with the consequences.

Things changed when Jake the Snake took things too far. During an episode of *WWF Superstars*, Roberts taunted Randy, who was working in the announcers booth. Finally, Savage could stand no more and charged the ring. The Macho Man's ring rust was apparent as Roberts was able to trap him by tying his arms up in the ropes. Things got worse when Jake unleashed a cobra. The snake danced around Savage before striking him in the arm. Announcer Vince McMahon went beserk, screaming, "That snake better be devenomized." As he did, his broadcast colleague "Rowdy" Roddy Piper was able to run Roberts off. Savage writhed in agony as the snake's venom poured through his veins.

The attack caused Tunney to lift Savage's ban. A match was signed for the *Tuesday in Texas* pay-per-view. Savage beat Roberts brutally and won, but afterwards, Roberts attacked and slapped Miss Elizabeth. Nothing had been settled.

The drama continued on the February 8, 1992, edition of *Saturday Night's Main Event* when Savage brutally beat down Roberts after a match, seemingly intent on ending his career. Savage delivered his finishing move, the flying elbow smash, several times before WWF officials finally intervened. After dishing out as much punishment as he could, Savage returned to the dressing room area with Elizabeth. Roberts, apparently a glutton for punishment, wasn't done. He waited there for Savage and Elizabeth. The diabolical heel grabbed a steel chair and prepared to strike the next person who walked through the curtain. Before Roberts could swing, however, an unlikely savior emerged. The Undertaker grabbed the weapon, giving Savage time to strike Roberts down with his own steel chair.

The fued was finally over but the Snake wasted no time beginning a new battle — this time against the man who had stopped him from attacking Elizabeth. Roberts would lose to the Undertaker at *WrestleMania VIII* in an extremely lopsided match.

WHAT HAPPENS IN VEGAS STAYS IN VEGAS

After a bloody battle with both the Mean Street Posse and Shane McMahon, it looked like Andrew "Test" Martin had finally won the heart and hand of Stephanie McMahon. The rookie wrestler began as a member of McMahon's heel faction, the Corporation, after first appearing on *Monday Night Raw* as a bodyguard for the rock band Mötley Crüe. Test would soon leave McMahon's group, turning babyface in the process.

Around this time there was a mysterious person or organization called "GTV" which would air hidden-camera video footage of wrestlers in compromising situations. No one knew who or what was behind "GTV," but when the footage aired, it was usually something the stars would have preferred to remain secret. When GTV revealed Test having a hotel rendezvous with Vince McMahon's daughter, their secret romance became public information.

Stephanie McMahon was the latest member of WWF mogul Vince McMahon's family to appear on WWF TV. Just months earlier, the Undertaker began stalking Stephanie as part of an apparent plan to take over the WWF. The sequence led to her eventual kidnapping.

After the Test/Stephanie relationship became public, a whirlwind romance was documented. Stephanie's brother Shane, however, objected. He enlisted the help of his friends, the Mean Street Posse. Shane and his three childhood friends attacked Test and told him to back off or face permanent injury. But Test proved his mettle and eventually earned Shane's respect and approval.

Not long afterwards, a wedding was announced for *Monday Night Raw*. Forces beyond Test's control would eventually lead to Stephanie being wed to one of the most hated men in the WWF. Hunter Hearst Helmsley (a.k.a. Triple H) had been having problems with WWF owner Vince McMahon. Hunter manipulated the bad blood to obtain a restraining order against McMahon, further angering the WWF boss.

For a short time, it looked like the wedding might not happen at all. Stephanie was injured by the British Bulldog, and after the shot to the head from Davey Boy Smith, she developed amnesia. Fortunately for her and for Test, her memory was restored; the wedding was back on. The couple could not wait, and just days before the wedding, Stephanie was fêted by some of the ladies of the WWF on an episode of the WWF's new Friday night show, *Smackdown!*

The night of the wedding saw the entire McMahon family gathered. Before the pair could be joined in holy matrimony, Triple H appeared, taunting both the McMahons and the bridegroom, and said he was already Stephanie's husband . . .

Hunter and Steph

Video footage revealed that Triple H had taken a drugged and unconscious Stephanie to a drive-through wedding chapel in Las Vegas. Once again, Triple H had broken the rules, this time defying the one that said, "What happens in Vegas stays in Vegas." Stephanie was Triple H's bride. Hunter taunted Vince McMahon further, telling him, "I know you can only have one question on your mind, Dad, and that is not did we, but how many times did we, consummate the wedding."

McMahon challenged Triple H to a match with the stipulation that if he won, Stephanie could obtain a divorce (the WWF ignored the obvious plot holes). Although Mr. McMahon was no wrestler, his determination to save his daughter gave him the edge he needed. Victory seemed to be McMahon's until he was betrayed by the unlikeliest of people — his daughter. Vince was ready to defeat his new son-in-law, when Stephanie stopped him and suggested instead that Vince use a sledgehammer on Triple H. Before Vince could grab the weapon, Triple H took it and used it on his father-in-law to win the match.

Stephanie congratulated him, shocking fans as well as her father. Stephanie hugged the man she claimed she hated as the pay-per-view ended. The next night, on *Raw*, Stephanie explained why she'd betrayed her own father. She recalled how Vince had her abducted by the Undertaker as part of an elaborate plan to get revenge on "Stone Cold" Steve Austin. Stephanie didn't forget the suffering her father put her through, and it was time for revenge. She was no longer "daddy's little girl," she was Mrs. Hunter Hearst Helmsley. The marriage ushered in the "McMahon/Helmsley Era."

Behind the scenes, the onscreen romance mirrored real-life. The storyline marriage between Triple H and Stephanie ended onscreen in 2002, but their real-life marriage continues to this day. The two were officially married in 2003, and on July 27, 2006, they celebrated the birth of their first daughter, Aurora Rose.

CHAPTER 10

THE INDUSTRY STAGGERS (1990–1994)

The early 1990s were difficult for professional wrestling. The boom of the 1980s fueled the national expansion of both the WWF and WCW, but the competition also eliminated most of the regional promotions that had dotted the North American landscape. Then, the industry stumbled as the big two tried to replicate the success of the Rock and Wrestling Era, with dismal results. Small independent shows would try to capitalize on fan resentment, but most would fail, lacking the resources to compete. One small Philadelphia company would succeed, however, by mixing traditional wrestling with a new "hardcore" style, revolutionizing the industry and guiding the big companies into the most successful period in history. . . .

After running many of his competitors out of business and establishing the WWF as the number one force in sports entertainment, life should have been good for Vince McMahon. Despite his tremendous success, the future seemed uncertain. The federal government had filed criminal charges against him, responding to allegations that he had distributed steroids. Years earlier McMahon had gambled his company on the success of *WrestleMania;* now, in characteristic style, he would gamble not only the WWF, but his personal freedom as well.

At WCW, things weren't quite as grim, but they were bad enough. After Jim Crockett Promotions had been sold to Turner Broadcasting, the company was renamed World Championship Wrestling, with Ted Turner providing the financial security. Despite the corporate patronage, WCW was losing money hand over fist. Various executives had tried to right the ship, but the only real result was the kind of changes in creative direction that hurt the product. At first, the company promoted itself like a traditional southern outfit (similar to JCP). When that didn't work, it began to copy the WWF — only to find that most WCW fans weren't interested in seeing cartoonish characters in their ring.

But as history has shown, wrestling is a hardy sport. Long-time fans were disappointed with the product but they hadn't given up on the industry. Instead, they turned to smaller promotions like the Global Wrestling Federation and Smokey Mountain Wrestling, which featured a more traditional style. While these companies lacked the star-studded roster and high production values of the WWF and WCW, they were able to stay in business with a fan-friendly product.

While the GWF and SMW were unable to break out, they proved that fans wanted something different. Soon a new promotion, Eastern Championship Wrestling, began running shows in the northeast. ECW (which later changed its name to Extreme Championship Wrestling) would lead the industry into its next boom, incorporating elements of traditional wrestling with things most fans had never seen before.

In the 1990s, technological advances would affect wrestling again. The Internet meant fans could meet and discuss the good, the bad, and the ugly in real time. It also "smartened up" people to the inner workings of the business. Once upon a time, it was only an elite inner circle who followed not only what happened on stage, but offstage as well. These fans communicated with each other through the mail and by newsletters, exchanging insider information. With the Web, that information was quickly passed on to larger and larger numbers.

During this time, the WWF suffered a tremendous blow: Hulk Hogan left the company to work for arch-rival WCW. This forced Vince McMahon to create new stars, and his company began to focus on younger talent like Bret "The Hitman"

Hart and Shawn Michaels. In an interesting twist, the wwf adopted a more athletic approach, while wcw adopted the sports entertainment style the wwf had developed during the 1980s. The mass exodus of wwf wrestlers to wcw not only changed that company's style, it led to several wrestlers being knocked down in the promotion's pecking order. High-level players like "Stunning" Steve Austin and "Big" Van Vader soon found themselves doing jobs for the boys from the wwf.

By 1995, the industry began to show signs of a turnaround. After beating the government's steroid charges, Vince McMahon was able to focus his energies and the wwf found some success with the New Generation. Under the leadership of Eric Bischoff, wcw would turn itself around financially and use the wwf superstars of the 1980s to establish itself as not only a legitimate competitor but a real rival. Meanwhile, ecw would continue to delight its small but loyal fan base with innovations that would eventually lead to changes in both wcw and the wwf.

THE DEBUT OF THE UNDERTAKER

Wrestling fans have seen their fare share of monsters, but nothing could have prepared them for the Undertaker's 1990 *Survivor Series* debut. "The Million Dollar Man" Ted DiBiase had promised the Dream Team he'd bring a surprise partner. As the Dead Man made his way ringside a hush fell over the crowd. His size and ghastly appearance even stunned announcers Gorilla Monsoon and Roddy Piper. It didn't take long before everyone realized that the Undertaker was as fearsome as he appeared to be. Bret Hart charged into the ring but was chokeslammed for his trouble. When Jim "The Anvil" Neidhart tried a shoulderblock, he bounced off like a pinball. Teammate Koko B. Ware tried utilizing his speed, but the big man effortlessly dodged the Bird Man's attack and bounced his neck off the ring rope — finishing him with a tombstone piledriver. When team captain Dusty Rhodes entered the fray, he too went down as the Undertaker clobbered him with a flying axe handle from the top rope. It is unlikely anyone on Rhodes' team could have prevailed, but the newcomer was eliminated when he went out of the ring to defend his manager from Rhodes and was counted out. 'Taker seemed impervious to pain but more than capable of dishing it out.

The man behind the gimmick was Mark Callaway. He had just come from a stint in wcw as one half of the Skyscrapers, and where he was later known as the Master of the Heart Punch. Callaway had worked in the territories before hitting the big-time in wcw, but he'd never reached the level of success he would find in the wwf.

To some, the character seemed like yet another crazy WWF gimmick. In the hands of other wrestlers it might not have worked, but Callaway played the part to perfection. His stature and look made him larger than life. Equally helpful was the management of Paul Bearer, once better known to fans as Percy Pringle. At first, the Undertaker had been managed by Brother Love, the WWF's answer to the TV evangelists who peppered Sunday morning television. But soon Love's preaching duties would prevent him from continuing in that role. He knew someone up to the task, however, and introduced "Brother Bearer" (first name "Paul"). Fans might have laughed — but they didn't. Instead, they became fascinated by the way Bearer guided the Undertaker's career.

Part of the Undertaker's phenomenal success came from the way he was booked — as unstoppable. He almost never lost, and just as the Road Warriors had been booked to the top via a string of major wins (some might even say squashes), so too did the Undertaker plow over foe after foe. It wasn't long before the Dead Man was working programs against top stars, including the Ultimate Warrior and Hulk Hogan. A year after his debut at the *Survivor Series*, the Undertaker reached the top of the mountain when he defeated Hulk Hogan for the WWF championship — quite the accomplishment for someone just one year into his WWF career.

McMEMPHIS: THE SHAPE OF THINGS TO COME

Wrestling fans in the famous Mid-South Coliseum couldn't believe their eyes. They knew it was Vince McMahon, but they had never seen him like this before. The Vince they knew sat behind an announcer's table and called matches. He didn't go after wrestlers or taunt their fans. . . .

By 1992, the old territories were all but gone; they'd either morphed into national promotions, or fallen by the wayside. The United States Wrestling Association (USWA), which evolved from Memphis wrestling's CWA, was one of the few survivors. USWA had been formed initially as a national promotion attempting to compete against the big two. The new promotion was an amalgam of the CWA, WCCW, and the AWA. Unfortunately, the AWA and WCCW did not last, leaving the Memphis territory to stand on its own.

Standing in the large shadows of WCW and WWF, USWA pressed on. The promotion survived with a mix of veteran superstars like Jerry "The King" Lawler and up-and-coming talent. The promotion also got a shot in the arm after Lawler went to work for the WWF and Vince McMahon agreed to a talent exchange with the small promotion. WWF stars would make appearances for the USWA while Lawler continued to work in both promotions. Interestingly, Lawler was a heel in the wwf while remaining a babyface in Memphis.

The talent exchange led to one of the most talked-about angles of the time — the heel debut of Vince McMahon. Like many of the well-crafted storylines in Memphis, this one was carefully built. Lawler and Jeff Jarrett had finished battling with Bret and Owen Hart with the resulting story being the wwf wrestlers had no respect for the smaller Memphis promotion, its fans, or wrestlers. Eventually, the name of wwf owner Vince McMahon began to come up.

During a promo for an ambulance match against crooked referee Paul Neighbors, Lawler dropped McMahon's name and told the Memphis fans that Vince considered them hillbillies and yokels. During another promo, Neighbors dropped a bombshell by announcing that McMahon would soon be in his corner. The announcement was confirmed on "The King's Court," when McMahon told the King he'd be there after he'd learned of Lawler's promise to refund the fans' money if he lost. Lawler promised McMahon a "whopper."

True to his word, McMahon appeared in Memphis, along with the wwf's Pat Patterson. McMahon told the fans he didn't like Lawler, and that he didn't like anyone who liked Lawler. During the match, Vince tripped the King as he chased Neighbors outside the ring. Before Lawler could confront McMahon, Patterson intervened. Lawler threw Patterson into the corner and then focused his attention on McMahon, daring Vince to strike him. McMahon stalled, but finally took his suit coat off and stood next to the King. It was a trap, as Patterson had regained his bearings and crept up behind Lawler he held the Memphis legend, allowing McMahon to haul off and punch him. The two threw Lawler into the ring. Despite the help from McMahon and Patterson, Neighbors was no match for Lawler and soon fell to two piledrivers. As Neighbors was stretchered out, Lawler delivered a parting gift as he threw fire in Neighbors' face.

Neighbors was finished, but a new war loomed. Lawler was set to face Bret Hart in a cage match and McMahon made his feelings known, deriding those who considered Lawler their king. McMahon invited Lawler to put his money down, promising him a big surprise. Lawler agreed and promised to refund the fans their tickets if he lost to Hart.

The surprise was big — the "8-foot-tall, Giant Gonzales" broke into the cage and attacked the King. In the end, Lawler was able to steal a win after Gonzales accidentally struck Hart, but after the match, Lawler was beat down.

Lawler was still happy with his victory. McMahon sent in a video promo, denying any complicity in Gonzales' appearance. He said Gonzales had obviously gotten wise to Lawler, as perhaps some of the Memphis fans were doing. He quoted Jim Nabors, hoping the fans would relate. "Surprise, surprise, surprise!" Lawler no longer had a surprise — he had a big problem in the form of the giant. Lawler acknowledged the fans' viewed him differently, especially in the "Rotten Apple" of New York City. The King said he'd earned his nickname by putting many wrestlers on the shelf. If Vince McMahon wanted to interfere, he'd be happy to add the names of WWF superstars to his list.

After defeating Gonzales with some fire, Lawler was pitted against the undefeated Tatanka in an "end of the trail" match. Lawler put his unified belt up against Tatanka's undefeated streak. McMahon cut another promo calling Lawler the "King of Cheaters" and promising that Tatanka would show him fire.

Lawler cut his own promo. He acknowledged his commentary job in the WWF and told the Memphis fans he went there to show the WWF they weren't everything they thought they were. McMahon's WWF snubbed their noses at anything not affiliated with them. He talked of how he wanted to silence the voice of the WWF, but McMahon hid behind his bodyguards. Lawler challenged Vince to return to Memphis.

When Vince did return, it was on a video promo where he wore the USWA belt Tatanka had won from Lawler. Lawler had a rematch booked, but Vince reminded him of "Custer's Last Stand."

A cocky Tatanka then appeared on Memphis TV and ran down both Lawler and Memphis, praising himself and the WWF. Lawler challenged Tatanka to a *Survivor Series* match in Memphis, with the Moondogs and Jeff Jarrett on his team against Tommy Rich, the Dogcatchers, and Tatanka. The catch? The USWA title, tag titles, and unified world title were all on the line.

Lawler prevailed, recapturing the belt from Tatanka after Tommy Rich's interference backfired. McMahon wasn't through, however, and sent "Macho Man" Randy Savage down to Memphis for a "fire on the mountain" match. Lawler promised he'd ignite the match and did, throwing fire at Savage after a ref bump. But the fire didn't hit its mark and Savage was able to land a punch powered by a chain. Savage covered Lawler for the pin but the decision was reversed after Jeff Jarrett informed the ref of Savage's chicanery.

A rematch was signed and Savage promised to slap Lawler and everyone in the Mid-South Coliseum. He also promised McMahon would be in his corner. The matchup saw Lawler fall to Savage, losing his unified title.

Regrettably, the USWA/WWF angle came to an abrupt halt after the WWF pulled out of the talent exchange. Around that time, Jerry Lawler had become embroiled in a criminal case (the charges were eventually dropped) and was let go from the WWF. Randy Savage was stripped of the unified title and the angle was quietly dropped.

While the ending of the feud was anticlimactic, it would be remembered by wrestling fans as the moment Vince McMahon began exploring his evil "Mr. McMahon" character. From that point on, whenever Vince did anything even slightly out of character, the Internet would buzz with speculation about whether the McMemphis version of Vince was on his way. It finally happened when McMahon confronted "Stone Cold" Steve Austin to ignite one of the biggest angles in wrestling history.

THE NWA IS DEAD (SHANE DOUGLAS THROWS DOWN THE TITLE)

The NWA had seen better days. The once-proud organization that controlled much of wrestling in the United States and Canada was now a shell of its former self. The general public was now more familiar with the rap group N.W.A. than they were with the National Wrestling Alliance.

When WCW left the organization in 1993, the NWA lost its last major promotion. But the remaining members refused to quit, and a tournament to crown a new champion was announced by a new NWA affiliate known as Eastern Championship Wrestling.

After playing an old school babyface in WCW, Shane Douglas was frustrated with the state of wrestling. Following his father's advice — that those who made it took chances — he decided to try something different and began working in ECW. He created a realistic character nicknamed the Franchise, who evoked old school wrestling with a pull-no-punches style of interview and attacked everything he felt was wrong with the mainstream.

ECW had been formed out of the ashes of Tri-State Wrestling, a short-lived promotion run by Joel Goodhart. Although the WWF and WCW still dominated the scene, independent shows continued to provide fans with solid action. Promoter Tod Gordon (the former ring announcer for Tri-State) knew that he couldn't offer the same star-studded shows as his predecessor, yet he understood there was a demand for something different.

By 1993, a former manager named Paul E. Dangerously (Heyman) had joined ECW, and he helped shape its direction. In Paul Heyman's mind, wrestling had to get with the times. He compared wrestling's old ways to the "hair bands" of the '80s that had been replaced by grunge rockers like Nirvana. Wrestling needed to appeal to a younger, cooler audience.

Heyman's vision for wrestling would have little to do with the NWA of the time. In fact, what he wanted to see was almost diametrically opposed. From the beginning, Heyman decided to show the world just how little the NWA meant to him: "We knew that the NWA was everything we wanted to get away from. Old school, old mentality, and we wanted to shake everything and everybody up."

ECW's Shane Douglas was booked to win the NWA world title in a tournament. The prestigious belt had been worn by such legends as Lou Thesz, Harley Race, and Ric Flair. After winning the belt, Douglas cut a promo celebrating his win. He then changed his tune. Douglas threw the belt down and introduced his ECW title, proclaiming himself the ECW champion of the world: "From the Harley Races to the Barry Windhams to the . . . Ric Flairs . . . I accept this heavyweight title. Wait a second. Wait a second. On Kerry Von Erich, on the fat man himself, Dusty Rhodes. This is it tonight, Dad. God, that's beautiful . . . and Rick Steamboat . . . And they can all kiss my ass. Because I am not the man who accepts the torch . . . from an organization that died, R.I.P., seven years ago. 'The Franchise' Shane Douglas is the man who ignites the new flame of the sport of professional wrestling."

Brandishing the ECW title, he continued, "Tonight, before God and my father as my witness . . . tonight, I declare myself, the Franchise, the new ECW champion of the world. We have set out to change the face of professional wrestling. So tonight, let the new era begin. The era of the sport of professional wrestling. The era of the Franchise. The era of the E-C-W."

It was a bold move by Heyman and Douglas, setting ECW apart from the others. Not everyone was happy. Dennis Corraluzzo of the NWA board decried the move, saying, "What happened tonight was a disgrace. I'm disappointed."

Corraluzzo had every reason to be disappointed. His goal had been to crown a new NWA champion, with Eastern Championship Wrestling as just one of several promotions under the NWA banner. The reality was that he had been used by Tod Gordon and ECW to help them make a name for themselves.

In the documentary *Forever Hardcore*, Tod Gordon talks about how he sat with Corraluzzo during Shane Douglas' controversial night and assured him it was all an angle. According to Gordon, he even suggested to Corraluzzo that he threaten to suspend ECW from the NWA (knowing full well this was what he wanted). Shane Douglas recalls that Corraluzzo was so convinced that it was all a swerve that he agreed to cut promos where he threatened to take the NWA title from Douglas. Naturally, this only added to the heat generated by Douglas' move, giving more momentum to the budding promotion.

Tod Gordon quickly announced that he was folding NWA Eastern Championship Wrestling. In its place, Extreme Championship Wrestling, with Shane Douglas as its champion, was born. The move sent shockwaves through the independent scene.

TOMMY DREAMER DEFEATS RAVEN

ECW wasn't about wrestlers fighting over a stolen dog or a shampoo commercial, it featured realistic situations that struck a chord with people tired of the cartoonish WWF and WCW of the time. When Paul Heyman decided to pit Tommy Dreamer against Raven, the feud was based on a dynamic anyone could relate to: Tommy Dreamer had been the high school jock who tormented the outsider Raven. Now, years later, Raven had come to ECW seeking revenge.

The Raven character was one of many transformations for Scott Levy. He began wrestling in Memphis as Scotty the Body, then worked other territories such as the Pacific Northwest, All-Star Wrestling, and the Global Wrestling Federation (GWF), before hitting the majors as Scotty Flamingo in WCW. After some success, he entered the WWF as manager Johnny Polo. While his wrestling was satisfactory, his work behind the scenes in production and in the announcer's booth was what caught Vince McMahon's eye. McMahon encouraged Levy to focus on that side of the business and began grooming him for the job.

In 1995, Levy came to work for Paul Heyman's ECW. The grunge movement was at its height at the time and Levy adopted a persona to match that mindset and look. He called himself Raven (after the poem by Edgar Allan Poe); it was a character like none before.

Raven got off on the wrong foot when Heyman first called to discuss his plans. As soon as he hung up, there was a problem — Raven had been so strung out from a night of partying that he'd forgotten the entire conversation, including his start date. Fortunately the Mensa member figured a way out. Raven stopped by the next ECW show — when Paul Heyman riminded him he wasn't starting until the following week, his problem was solved.

While he could be eccentric, Raven quickly impressed those around him with his knowledge of the business. Heyman once bragged that Raven could do anything he wanted, and do so with passion he'd never seen before and that might never be seen again.

The feud with Dreamer would go on for years. It was particularly unique in that Dreamer wrestled for three years before finally winning a match. It sustained itself through the tremendous creativity of Heyman, Raven, and Dreamer. Like several other ECW programs, the Raven/Dreamer feud brought in other wrestlers as well, transferring some of the heat to them in the process.

Dreamer would finally taste victory on Raven's last night in ECW, pinning him after scoring a DDT. Dreamer didn't have to wait long for his next program to begin. Jerry Lawler rushed the ring and attacked him . . .

SABU VS. TAZZ

It was a year in the making. As is often the case, Tazz and Sabu had once worked together as tag partners. That all changed when a match in Japan conflicted with a match in ECW — and Sabu was promptly fired by Paul Heyman.

In the documentary *Forever Hardcore*, Sabu recalls double-booking himself and choosing Japan over ECW. At the time, ECW was a once-a-month job while Japan was his meal ticket. Sometimes the burgeoning star would get paid for a week there, even for working just one show.

Peter "Tazz" Senerchia began working in Eastern Championship Wrestling as one half of the the Tazmaniacs. After the team split, he worked with a variety of partners, including ring veteran Kevin Sullivan. Although he had a one-night reign as ECW television champion, the focus of his ECW career was in the tag ranks. Sabu was another partner; the two would go on to share the ECW tag team championship.

In 1995, Tazz suffered a severe neck injury when a spike piledriver went awry. The tough-as-nails Tazz actually walked into the hospital under his own steam. The doctors were astounded, hardly believing he was still on his feet. The injury would put him out of action for the next year. Despite the layoff, Paul Heyman continued to pay him, an act of kindness that would earn Tazz's respect and loyalty.

Unable to wrestle, Tazz decided to repackage himself. When he returned to ECW, it was with a new look and gimmick. With the rise of mixed martial arts (the UFC in particular), Tazz would go with the gimmick of being a legitimate shoot fighter. Upon his return, it worked to perfection — he was preseted as an "unstoppable force."

If you're familiar with Sabu's uncle then it's easy to understand the character that Terry Michael Brunk would play in wrestling. The nephew of legendary wildman the Sheik, Brunk became Sabu, a man crazy in his own right. After training with his uncle (along with Rob Van Dam), Sabu worked in the Sheik's outfit before going to the wild Japanese promotion Frontier Martial-Arts Wrestling (FMW). FMW was known for its extremely hardcore matches and Sabu picked up a number of scars during his time there.

After Dennis Corraluzzo referred him to Tod Gordon, Sabu began working for ECW. His image as a wildman didn't take long to catch on, as he was brought out to the ring in restraints and attached to a gurney (a nod to the evil Hannibal Lecter character from *Silence of the Lambs*). Sabu wasn't thrilled with the idea, but went with it after being offered $500. When released, Sabu went after his opponents with an animalistic fury, using a combination of high flying moves and brawling to secure victory.

In addition to his entrance, Sabu became known for putting his opponents (and sometimes himself) through tables. Word of Sabu's antics quickly spread through fandom and he became a darling of the hardcore faithful.

After returning from a neck injury, Tazz began calling Sabu out, demanding a match. Tazz would even beat up other opponents and call them Sabu. Sabu wasn't even working for ECW at the time — but that didn't stop Tazz from whetting the appetite of Philadelphia fans.

The match finally occured at ECW's *Barely Legal*, and it lived up to its billing as the grudge match of the century. The buildup had been perfect and anticipation ran high — a good thing considering it was the company's first PPV. Tazz would win in the end with the Tazzmission. After the match, Sabu raised his former partner's arm, acknowledging his respect.

Sabu and Tazz would go on to have many classic match-ups with both men fighting over Tazz's "FTW" (Fuck the World) title.

SANDMAN AND SON

Wrestling has seen its share of heinous acts, but few compare to the sheer wickedness of Raven using Sandman's own son against him.

Fans unfamiliar with Sandman's early ECW days might be surprised to find out that his original gimmick was that of a surfer. Needless to say, he wasn't getting over. When he began incorporating more of himself into the act, however, his popularity soared. At first, he would come to the ring smoking a cigarette. Later on, he added beer-drinking to the entrance. Another trademark became entering the ring from the stands. The "beer-drinkingest, cigarette-smokingest, cane–wieldingest" wrestler was soon beloved.

Sandman became embroiled in a feud with Raven. With no regards for family ties, Raven set out to hurt Sandman in every way possible. Sandman could absorb tremendous amounts of punishment in the ring, but Raven found a different way to hurt him. Raven discovered that Sandman was divorced and that he had an eight-year-old son named Tyler. With this information in hand, he quickly went to work arranging one of the most despicable angles in wrestling history.

Raven's ruthlessness was demonstrated by a series of vignettes he cut with Tyler and his mother Lori. Tyler seemed to take an immediate liking to Raven, telling him, "I love you more than my own daddy," and blaming Sandman for his parents' divorce. As if that wasn't bad enough, Tyler set Sandman up, coming into the ring wearing a Sandman shirt in an apparent attempt to make peace with his father.

When Sandman went to hug his him, he was attacked from behind by Raven with a Singapore cane. Emotional, controversial, and highly effective — it had everything you need for a great angle.

The feud was no-holds-barred, as both men seemed hellbent on destroying each other. But even the hardcore fans of ECW had their limits — and on this night, ECW crossed the line. A Raven piledriver had just put Sandman through a table. Then, he was tied to a makeshift cross and hung up in the ring — with a "crown" of barbed wire placed around his head. If that wasn't bad enough, Raven lorded over him, with his ex-wife and son by his side.

Backstage, Olympic wrestling gold medalist and future WWF star Kurt Angle expressed his disgust. He had been brought in by Tazz and was considering working for the company. When he saw Sandman "crucified," he warned Heyman that if he was shown on TV, or in any way connected to the angle, his attorney would be calling. Heyman assured Angle he'd had no idea that this would happen. Angle didn't know who to believe. Tod Gordon and Heyman later made Raven apologize to the fans present — an almost unprecedented move — and the angle was never aired on television.

HULK HOGAN'S WCW DEBUT

By 1992, Hulk Hogan and the WWF were like America and apple pie — linked together, seemingly, forever.

When Eric Bischoff began running WCW, he'd inherited a company that had not only bled cash, but was also burdened with a serious image problem. WCW had survived many management regimes, with new bookers coming in through a revolving door. The company lacked a sense of direction; Bischoff resolved to change that.

To stem the red ink, Bischoff cut costs. Whether it was dropping house shows (which were poorly attended) or counting pencils, Bischoff tried his best to steer WCW into the black. But in the end, he knew he needed asses in seats and PPV buys if it was going to thrive. To achieve this, he needed wrestlers people wanted to see.

Despite all the upside to signing Hogan, there was also the potential for trouble. At the time, the Hulkster was still plauged by the steroid scandal that had rocked the WWF. Vince McMahon was defending himself against the federal government and Hogan had been subpoenaed to testify. If McMahon was convicted, there was no telling what the fallout might be. Hogan made it clear to Bischoff that while he wasn't yet damaged, he might be once he started working for WCW.

Sandman in ECW

Signing Hogan was treated with much fanfare. Bischoff used the relationship he'd built with Disney World to arrange for a ticker-tape parade celebrating Hulk's arrival. Given Hogan's contributions during the 1980s, the parade wasn't unwarranted. Still, the move was questioned by many.

Hogan was immediately put into a main-event program with WCW champion Ric Flair. Although the two had met in the WWF, the Hogan/Flair dream match had been nothing more than a skirmish. After Flair had won the WWF championship at the *Royal Rumble*, most fans expected a *Wrestle-Mania* spectacular. But other than some house shows, the two had no real feud to speak of. As a result, there was still an aura of anticipation surrounding the Hogan/Flair WCW encounter.

The two began fighting after Flair won the WCW title from Sting. Flair cheated during the match and Hogan intervened to protest Flair's tactics. The resulting chaos led to their first bout. In that match, Hogan defeated Flair for the WCW title. Their next enounter saw Hogan waylaid by a mystery man in black. A lead pipe did the bulk of the damage. Despite being injured Hogan continued, but he eventually lost by count out. This lead to a rubber match, with an added stipulation: Flair would retire should he lose.

CHAPTER 11

THE PIER SIX BRAWLS

Donnybrooks, slobberknockers, or pier six brawls: whatever they're called, fans know they will be wild and exciting.

The origins of the term "pier six brawl" remain in doubt, but announcer Gordon Solie is widely acknowledged as the man who made the phrase synonymous with professional wrestling.

Pull-apart battles are a great way to show just how much two men hate each other — wrestlers begin brawling and continue until referees and/or other officials try to break up the action. Usually, someone will break free and attack again, restarting the whole process.

Wrestling has had so many wild brawls it's difficult to choose the best. What follows are some of the most memorable from the last thirty years — brawls that are still talked about by grapplers and fans alike.

THE TUPELO CONCESSION STAND BRAWL

Mention the Tupelo Concession Stand Brawl and people are probably going to give you several different accounts. It's not a case of fuzzy memory syndrome — it's just that people are prone to remember variations on the angle they've seen over the years. The Tupelo Concession Stand Brawl has become almost mythical, and promoters have revisited it on countless occassions.

The event occured after a match between the team of Jerry Lawler and "Superstar" Bill Dundee and the Blonde Bombers (Wayne Ferris and Larry Latham). The Bombers upset the veterans for the tag team championship. A post-match donnybrook spilled into the back of the arena near a concession stand, and history was made.

It didn't take long for it to become the stuff of legend. In 1981, Eddie Gilbert wanted to recreate the brawl during a run in CWA. The 1981 encounter saw Masa Fuchi and Mr. Onita battle Gilbert and Ricky Morton. This brawl was equally memorable, and some fans even prefer it to the original. Even the promoter became involved.

Many wrestling historians cite the Concession Brawl as the origin of hardcore style. The truth is, wrestling had always had its share of moments that would later be called "hardcore." The difference is that earlier generations of promoters used these things sparingly to preserve their novelty — and to cut down on injuries, too.

The angle would be revisited many times over the next three decades, including a 1995 pay-per-view match between Harlem Heat and Nasty Boys. Other favorite versions of the match include the 1992 USWA bout between the Moondogs and the team of Jerry Lawler and Jeff Jarrett.

"GET HIS FACE!" (THE MIDNIGHT RIDER VS. EVERYBODY)

As exciting as Barry Windham's heel turn was, it paled compared to what happened next. The not-so-mysterious Midnight Rider confronted Windham after he'd betrayed "The Total Package" Lex Lugar against Arn Anderson and Tully Blanchard. But there was one small problem: the masked man had done it in the heel locker room. An army of bad guys pounced, grabbing at the Rider's mask.

The scene ended with J.J. Dillon admonishing a cameraman, telling him to chase after the hooded wrestler as he was spirited out of the dressing room by his baby-face allies. . . .

The story actually began much earlier, when fans welcomed Magnum T.A. back to JCP. After months spent recovering from a terrible automobile accident, Terry Allen was once again in front of the camera (albeit not as a wrestler). When the Four Horsemen's Tully Blanchard put his hands on Magnum, Dusty Rhodes went berserk and attacked. In the mêlée, the American Dream assaulted an NWA official, and for that, he was promptly banned from wrestling.

When the hooded Midnight Rider soon emerged, the Horsemen cried foul. Earlier in his career Rhodes had been accused of using this persona when a similar similar situation in CWF also resulted in a ban. The heels of JCP were certain Rhodes had returned to an old identity to get around his latest suspension.

Around the same time, James J. Dillon warned a babyface Barry Windham that Lex Luger would leave him hanging one day. Windham took the words to heart, and ultimately decided to strike first. During a tag team title defense against Arn Anderson and Tully Blanchard, Windham found himself wrestling most of the match alone while Luger lay incapacitated outside the ring. Eventually, Lex crawled back in, barely conscious. When a frustrated Windham finally reached him for a tag, a confused Lex promptly powerslammed his partner. In retaliation, Windham gave the Total Package a lariat. Windham's attack flattened Luger, leaving him at the mercy of Anderson and Blanchard. The Horsemen capitalized, and Arn Anderson scored the pinfall regain the NWA world tag team championship.

As Sting, Steve Williams, and Nikita Koloff checked on Lex, the Midnight Rider stormed into the dressing room area. He confronted Windham, asking him to account for himself, but he was ignored. The newest member of the Horsemen told Rhodes — I mean, the Rider — that he had nothing to say to him and turned to leave.

As Windham walked away, reality dawned. The Midnight Rider was sur-rounded by over a dozen heels, many of whom held deep-seated grudges against the man they believed was underneath the hood. For a moment time stood still, then the Rider began throwing punches. The odds, however, were just too over-whelming. The Rider quickly went down as Ric Flair screamed, "Get the hood." The wrestlers ripped at the mask and in seconds it was off. Now, they just had to get a cameraman to show the Rider's face to the world . . .

Before that could happen, however, Williams, Sting, and Koloff raced in, attacking the heels, and more importantly, covering their friend from view. The three wrestlers formed a human cocoon around the Rider, ushering him out of the dressing room as J.J. Dillon howled. All the cameras managed to catch was a swirl of blond hair.

MURACO VS. SNUKA

Don Muraco is best known as "Magnificent Muraco," but his self-proclaimed title, "The Prince of Darkness," was a far more appropriate monicker: it described the dark heart at his core. This became clear when Muraco appeared on "Buddy Rogers Corner" and began spewing venom about opponents such as Tito Santana, Rocky Johnson, and WWF champion Bob Backlund. Muraco boasted that he was the first man to reverse the figure-four leglock and praised his own defense of the Intercontinental Championship. He continued ranting until the fans erupted. They were cheering, but not for Muraco (who the fans loved to deride as "Beach Bum"). It was the arrival of Jimmy "Superfly" Snuka that caused the stir.

Snuka had become one of the hottest stars in the WWF after turning babyface when Buddy Rogers uncovered the fact that Snuka's manager Lou Albano had been robbing him blind. When Snuka confronted Albano, he was waylaid by Ray "The Crippler" Stevens and piledrived two times onto the concrete floor. By the time Snuka returned from his storyline injury, fans were solidly behind him.

An insulted and enraged Muraco approached the ring and glared at Snuka, whose only reply was a smile. WWF announcer Vince McMahon confidently predicted Snuka would not lose his cool, but he was soon proven wrong when Muraco walked up to the mat apron and spit at the Superfly. Muraco jumped off the mat apron and celebrated his misdeed. Snuka dove over the top rope onto Muraco, flattening him. Then, the Superfly tore off Muraco's sports coat and pounded him in the face.

Clearly, Snuka *had* lost his cool. He continued tearing into Muraco, tearing off his shirt and eventually ripping his pants to reveal his wrestling trunks. As Muraco flailed around on the arena floor, several preliminary wrestlers ran out to try and restrain Snuka. As they did, Muraco rolled into the ring and grabbed a microphone. When he rolled back out, he swung it at Snuka (who was still being held by the other wrestlers).

After taking his cheap shot, Muraco continued to rain down blows, his tattered clothes flying about him. More wrestlers emerged and attempted to restrain both men, but the task seemed impossible. They were that determined to get at each other, one way or another. Snuka broke free momentarily, getting a few blows in on Muraco before the swarm of wrestlers finally managed to separate the combatants.

The incident launched a red-hot feud, with Snuka battling Muraco both for revenge and the Intercontinental belt. The two would meet in several inconclusive bouts until a cage match was signed for Madison Square Garden. Just as he had done during his earlier match against Bob Backlund, Snuka performed his Superfly death dive off the top of the cage.

"The Prince of Darkness" Don Muraco

CHAPTER 12

THE MONDAY NIGHT WAR (1995–2001)

The Monday Night War saw the wrestling business soar towards new heights even as both WCW and the WWF risked losing it all. It resulted in some outrageous angles and some damned fine wrestling.

Irony was at a premium as Vince McMahon saw the tactics he'd used during the national expansion of the Rock and Wrestling Era turned against him. Long-time fans couldn't help but cry foul when McMahon lambasted Eric Bischoff for "stealing" talent from the WWF. While the big two battled each other, ECW seemed to fly under the radar, promoting small shows to its diehard fanbase. In reality, it did not go unnoticed by either WCW or the WWF. Bischoff eventually signed some of ECW's top stars and the WWF eventually emulated much of the ECW style.

After years of dominance in the wrestling industry, the WWF was close to the edge. WCW could seemingly do no wrong, and *Nitro* expanded from one to two hours, then three. The success of the nWo angle carried WCW to new heights, but it too eventually wore out its welcome. The first sign of this was the nWo themed pay-per-view *Souled Out,* which drew significant criticism. WCW was reportedly planning on making *Nitro* an exclusive nWo show but dismal ratings during an nWo takeover led WCW to scrap the idea. Still, WCW revisited the nWo time after time with angles such as the Latino World Order and the nWo splitting into two versions: nWo Wolfpac and nWo Hollywood.

While WCW regurgitated its biggest success, the WWF abandoned its family-friendly approach. (Curiously, wrestling has long been seen as family entertainment, despite the violence and mayhem long associated with the sport.) With stars like "Stone Cold" Steve Austin and Degeneration X pushing the envelope, the WWF attracted new fans in droves. By 1997, the WWF was gaining ground in the ratings war, but the controversial content shift caused a stir about the use of profanity and sexual innuendo. Vince McMahon defended his company, suggesting the changes in his product reflected changes in society. An interview he did with America Online makes this clear:

> **Question:** Vince, You must realize that many young children idolize the wrestlers of the WWF. I was wondering if you were at all concerned what the kids were picking up from the middle fingers and sex references from the wrestlers?

> **McMahon:** It's the 90s! The WWF is only reflecting what is contemporary in today's society. I dare say there are a great deal more middle fingers and sexual references in everyone's life than are portrayed in the WWF. Nonetheless, it is every parent's discretion as to whether people watch the WWF or any other TV program on the air.

Despite the criticism (or perhaps because of it), the WWF became wildly successful and would eventually overtake WCW on all levels. Just as he had done when defending himself against the federal government, Vince McMahon had come back from what looked like certain defeat, stronger than ever. The success would lead to McMahon, in 1999, taking the WWF public, making him (for a short time) a billionaire.

By 2001, wrestling's Monday Night War was history, and the WWF was victorious. In terms of success and creativity, it proved once again that customers are the winners when there's competition.

AUSTIN STUNNERS MCMAHON

A "Stone Cold" Steve Austin stunner became wrestling's equivalent of Caesar crossing the Rubicon. An imaginary line had existed for years, and Austin erased it. Nothing would ever be the same. Vince McMahon went from a guy at ringside calling matches to someone at the center of the action — becoming, at times, the federation's number one heel.

The evolution of the Mr. McMahon character can be traced back to the USWA angle discussed earlier, but the first rumblings in the WWF proper began at the time of Bret Hart's transformation into a heel. While most fans remember Austin's stunner (and subsequent attacks), they often ignore the time Hart shoved McMahon, or the time Hart slapped him. These incidents would break the ice for Stone Cold.

A storm was on the horizon and everyone but the man who had brought "Stone Cold" Steve Austin into the business saw it coming. Austin had suffered a career-threatening injury at the hands of Owen Hart, and had been sidelined since the WWF refused to clear him to wrestle. Austin didn't care about the injury and wanted to get back into the ring to do what he did best — open a can of whup-ass. When the WWF refused to budge, Austin took matters into his own hands.

September 22, 1997, was historic in more ways than one. *Monday Night Raw* was in Madison Square Garden for the first time, with an enthusiastic crowd waiting to see the next chapter in the Austin story. Owen Hart was in the ring, congratulating himself for putting Austin out, when Stone Cold appeared and promptly threw him out. New York's finest arrived, cornering Austin and trying to keep the situation from getting out of control.

At ringside, WWF owner Vince McMahon had been calling the action. He asked the police to give him a minute with Steve. McMahon kept asking Austin, "What's the matter with you?" He acknowleged that he had every reason to be upset, after all, he'd been forced to forfeit the Intercontinental and the WWF tag team championships. Still, there was no need to break the law. As McMahon tried to reason with Austin, Stone Cold egged the police on, daring them to hit him.

McMahon continued trying to talk sense: "Don't you know you're not physically ready to compete?"

Austin's doctors had told him he'd risk permanent paralysis if he wrestled in his current condition, something the WWF didn't want on its conscience. McMahon said Austin's fans didn't want to see him in a wheelchair. Finally,

McMahon told Austin that people cared about him — people in the WWF also cared about him, and Austin simply had to work with the system. After McMahon's speech, Stone Cold reminded the boss that wrestling was what he did for a living and nobody did it like him. It was easy enough for McMahon to tell him to take his time, but he wasn't the one stuck at home. Still, McMahon's words seemed to strike a chord. "If that's what it takes to make you and the WWF happy," he said, then he would work within the system. Austin said he appreciated the fact that people in the WWF cared — then he changed his tune. He told McMahon, "I appreciate the fact that you can kiss my ass!"

Austin had had enough. He kicked McMahon in the gut. Everyone in the building knew what was coming — still few could believe it when he delivered a Stone Cold stunner to the owner of the WWF!

New York's finest wasted no time cuffing Austin. His work done, Austin did not resist. He did get one last shot at McMahon though. As the police hauled him away, Stone Cold flipped the boss the bird.

The Austin/McMahon rivalry would go on for over a year, catapulting *Monday Night Raw* to the top of the ratings in the Monday Night War. Austin's portrayal of the rebel redneck defying his boss struck a chord. WWF fans loved the weekly exchanges, delighting in Vince getting his comeuppance after trying to force Austin to fit into his mold of corporate correctness. The program between was fresh and fun, and resulted in great business.

Austin played the antihero to perfection, refusing to give in to McMahon no matter what. His portrayal of the Stone Cold character would make him arguably the most successful performer in the history of the business. Just as important, however, was McMahon's portrayal of the evil corporate head. A hero is only as good as his villain, and Vince played the overbearing, arrogant boss very well. McMahon's effectiveness as a villain might have been best captured by Jim Ross: "If you're a bad guy, if you're a villain, if you're an antagonist worth your salt, then the yardstick is, they pay money to see you get your ass whipped. And people to this very day will still pay money to see Vince McMahon get his ass whipped."

An entire book could be written about the great matches and angles that came out of the Austin/McMahon war. Whether it was Stone Cold driving a beer truck to the ring and spraying McMahon with beer, or battling McMahon with one arm tied behind his back, or storming the arena in a Zamboni, Stone Cold and McMahon always entertained. Although the feud has run its course, the two still draw loud reactions whenever they interact, a testament to the talent of both men as well as the timelessness of the feud.

PAGING DOCTOR AUSTIN (MR. SOCKO IS BORN)

It's the rare wrestling feud that works its way into the collective consciousness, becoming the stuff of legend.

There were several factors that made Austin and McMahon so special. First was its novelty. While authority figures have long played an important part in establishing storylines, none became the focus of the program, nor played the role as well as McMahon. The evil owner would become a staple of professional wrestling (and sadly, eventually a cliché), but in 1998, it was still fresh. Then there was the incredible charisma of both men, with Austin's rowdy, hard-drinking personality providing the perfect foil for McMahon's corporate conformist. Finally, well-crafted angles sustained the feud's fever pitch for over a year.

One of the best parts of the storyline involved Vince being paid a visit by Stone Cold while he was recuperating from injuries suffered at the hands of Kane and the Undertaker. The owner of the WWF had been incapacitated after giving the brothers the finger — definitely not one of his brightest moves. WWF fans learned McMahon was at an "undisclosed" medical facility. But the location was no real secret — at least not to two WWF superstars.

The first man in the know was Mankind (Mick Foley). The always-odd wrestler had developed a bizarre fixation with Vince, treating him like a kind of father figure. When he arrived at the medical center to try to cheer up his moody boss, he told McMahon he had brought someone who would amaze him with what she could do to a dog . . .

McMahon wanted nothing to do with this, but he was in no position to do anything other than ask the nurse to send Foley away. Foley proved stubborn, and quickly introduced Vince to a female clown who said she would help cheer him up. She handed the WWF kingpin a bouquet of balloon animals. McMahon was definitely not amused.

When Foley realized his boss was not impressed, he introduced his *pièce de résistance*: a new friend, named Mr. Socko. When a sock puppet failed to cheer Vince an unsuccessful Foley departed.

With Mankind gone, McMahon reminded the nurse that no one but family was allowed access. The nurse then left when a doctor emerged and told her he would take over. McMahon's face twisted with recognition — the doctor was none other than "Stone Cold" Steve Austin, there to make sure he got the "treatment" he deserved.

A horrified McMahon screamed while Austin dispensed a prescription of whup-ass. After slugging him with a bedpan, Austin grabbed a defibrillator —

and used it. He wasn't through, though, an I.V. needle was injected where the sun never shines. The attack would undoubtedly add extra days to McMahon's hospital stay; even worse was the public humiliation: Austin's attack aired to millions on *Monday Night Raw*.

The incident furthered an already white-hot feud, but it was also important for the creation of Mr. Socko. Even though Mankind was only indirectly involved, his role helped him get over and made the Mankind character more fan-friendly. Mr. Socko introduced fans to Mick Foley's sense of humor, something that would help him become one of the most beloved stars in WWF history.

GOLDBERG BEATS HOGAN

The nWo juggernaut seemed unstoppable. Hulk Hogan maintained a stranglehold on the WCW world heavyweight championship. WCW had sent in countless challengers and come up short, with the exception of brief title reigns by Lex Luger and Sting. But a new star was on the rise and his name would soon haunt "Hollywood" Hogan.

Since exploding onto the WCW scene, rookie Bill Goldberg had built an unprecedented winning streak. He'd had victories over a who's-who of wrestling. Before long, championship gold found its way around his waist, when he defeated Raven to become the United States champion. His streak continued, and the WCW world heavyweight championship became his next target. (Goldberg's string of victories would eventually be inflated to nearly 200 wins in a row.)

To the surprise (and delight) of many, the match wasn't a pay-per-view event — it aired for free on an edition of *Nitro*. While Hogan/Goldberg would likely have earned an impressive buy rate, WCW was starting to feel the heat of the WWF's comeback. With ratings beginning to falter, the freebie seemed like a good way to re-establish dominance.

On July 6, 1998, Goldberg met Hogan — roughly ten months after his official debut. He began the match with a side headlock, pushing Hogan down to one knee. Hogan was renowned for his strength but his opponent seemed even more powerful. After the headlock, Goldberg shoulderblocked Hogan, sending him crashing to the mat. Hulk backed up and stared into the crowd. His look of astonishment betrayed his nervousness: he could be Goldberg's next victim.

After Hogan was unsuccessful in a double finger-lock, it was clear that Goldberg was the stronger man. The champ was brought to his knees and forced to grab the ropes to break the hold. Sensing the trouble he was in, Hogan resorted to questionable tactics. He raked Goldberg's eyes, then punched him. With the challenger momentarily stunned, Hogan grabbed his weight-lifting belt and began whipping him with it. Goldberg shrugged off the attack and took the belt from Hogan. Then, in a bold display of confidence, Goldberg threw the belt away.

Hogan's desperation mounted. Goldberg quickly escaped from a hammerlock and countered with a full nelson. Hogan's neck buckled under the pressure and he wasted no time in snapping his leg back, delivering a low blow that brought Goldberg to his knees. He followed up with stomps, punches, and a clothesline. Goldberg's amazing endurance gave him the strength to dodge out of the way as Hogan dropped elbowsmash after elbowsmash. The challenger then rose to his feet and sent Hogan over the ropes — the leader of the New World Order quickly rallied outside to catch a breather.

Goldberg made the mistake of following Hogan outside the ring. Ever the brawler, Hulk showed Goldberg just how dangerous he could be. He slammed Goldberg's head into the guardrail, then followed up with several chair shots. Referee Charles Robinson tried to bring the two back into the ring but Hogan was in his element and he would not let up until he was ready. When he was, he continued his offensive in the ring, dropping two legdrops on his opponent. Normally, one legdrop was enough for Hogan to win a match — but he wasn't taking any chances.

Just then, the nWo's Curt Hennig walked towards the ring, ready to lend a hand if needed. Right behind him was "Diamond" Dallas Page and basketball star Karl Malone. Page and Malone had crossed paths with the nWo before and there was no doubt why they appeared. After hitting the second legdrop, Hogan covered Goldberg for the pin. Shockingly, Goldberg kicked out. Hogan looked outside, only to see Hennig taken down by Malone. He then made a key mistake: he turned his back on Goldberg. The challenger took the opportunity to catch the Hulkster with one of his finishers, "the spear." Hogan was knocked senseless. Goldberg then hit his other signature move, "the jackhammer," driving Hulk hard into the mat. Seconds later, Goldberg was the new wcw champion.

While Goldberg was already a bona fide star, his live television win over Hogan cemented his status as a true main event player. It was a mixed blessing, however; Goldberg had no place to go but down. He lost his first match in an anticlimactic battle with Kevin Nash at the end of the year pay-per-view, *Starrcade.*

After Hogan lost the title to Goldberg, the nWo would splinter and undergo several reformations over the next few years, each less successful than the previous.

FEAR THE SPEAR: GOLDBERG AND BRET HART

After a year with wcw, Bret Hart was tired of hearing people go on about how Bill Goldberg was the man to beat. The success of Goldberg's finisher, the spear, had launched its own catchphrase, "fear the spear." But the "excellence of execution" would prove that fear can be overcome with a little forethought.

With *Nitro* broadcasting from Toronto, Ontario, Hart came out to a hearty welcome. Color commentator Bobby "The Brain" Heenan noted Hart's popularity, likening him to former NWA world champ Gene Kiniski, whose nickname was "Canada's Greatest Athlete." In Heenan's estimation, Hart had surpassed him.

The Hitman's jump from the World Wrestling Federation to wcw was met with much fanfare. Hart was the latest WWF star to be signed away and wcw fans could not wait to see him compete. But oddly, Hart's wcw run had misfired. After showing up at wcw's *Starrcade* pay-per-view in 1997, the Hitman seemed to languish. And after joining the nWo, he was booked more like a mid-carder star than a main-event attraction.

Behind the scenes, Hart's disappointment was exacerbated by a nagging groin injury and a painful divorce. Wondering where his career was headed he met with Eric Bischoff to discuss his future. Hart explained that it didn't make sense for him to lose so many matches given what wcw was paying him. The discussion ended with Bischoff agreeing to start a Hart and Hogan program, a surefire moneymaker.

Before that would begin, Hart was scheduled to work with Goldberg. The two met and devised an angle they believed would work. After several false starts, Hart was finally given the go-ahead.

Wearing the jersey of the Calgary Hitmen, Hart took the Toronto ring and talked about his year in wcw, about how no one had the guts to face him. He blasted legends like Hogan, accusing them of hiding. Hart told the fans Eric Bischoff had signed him promising to build on his reputation, not destroy it. The Canadian fans refused to boo Hart, despite the fact he'd been booked as a heel — they ate up every word. Hart then turned his attention to wcw's franchise player — Bill Goldberg. He mocked the champ, calling him a chicken and ridiculing a Goldberg challenge to the wwf's "Stone Cold" Steve Austin (Goldberg had put up money challenging Austin to a match). Hart reminded Goldberg that he had beaten Austin, then rallied the Canadian fans by mocking the champ's football background, telling him, "This is hockey country." As he did this, Hart took off his Hitmen jersey to reveal a hometown Maple Leafs sweater. Toronto went wild.

The taunting produced results: Goldberg's music played as the big man came into the ring. Hart motioned for Goldberg to come after him — and he got his wish. Goldberg charged, hitting Hart with the spear. Hart crumbled, but he wasn't the only one down on the canvas. For some reason, Goldberg had been knocked silly as well. *Nitro* announcers Tony Schiavone, Mike Tenay, and Bobby Heenan wondered if Goldberg had hit the move wrong. After several moments, the cause of Goldberg's problem was revealed as Bret Hart got up and took off his hockey jersey to reveal a steel plate.

It was a great setup, but unfortunately wcw was spiraling out of control. The program failed to live up to expectations, and Hart suffered a career-ending concussion after a poorly thrown Goldberg kick. Goldberg would continue working in wcw until it went out of business. Later, he would spend a year in the wwe and eventually defeat Triple H for the world heavyweight championship.

AUSTIN/TYSON SHOWDOWN

> *Mad, bad, and dangerous to know.*
> **—Lady Caroline Lamb, describing Lord Byron**

"Stone Cold" Steve Austin had never been much for decorum. The beer-drinking redneck's hair-trigger temper had earned him the nickname the Texas Rattlesnake, and tonight he was in rare form. What wwf promoter Vince McMahon had planned as a simple meet-and-greet quickly escalated into World War III.

On January 19, 1998, McMahon proclaimed he was about to make the biggest announcement in wwf history. But before he did, he wanted to introduce the fans to "the baddest man on the planet." Boxer Mike Tyson came to the ring with an entourage and shook his hand, leading the fans to wonder what their relationship might be. Then, the sound of breaking glass was heard: "Stone Cold" Steve Austin was on his way.

No sooner had Austin entered the ring when he was joined by a small army of wwf officials — referees, agents, and Vince's son Shane. Ignoring the throng, Austin went to each and greeted his fans. As the wwf officials buzzed, Vince announced that Mike Tyson would serve as special enforcer for the Shawn Michaels/Steve Austin main event at *WrestleMania XIV*. When he'd finished, McMahon confronted Austin. The wrestler told McMahon he was sick and tired of all the hand-shaking. Tyson extended his hand to Austin, only to be warned by Stone Cold that he wasn't here to make friends. Austin said he respected what Tyson had done in boxing, but his wrestling ring was a totally different world.

Stone Cold made it clear that he wanted a piece of Tyson, questioning his reputation as "the baddest man on the planet." Calling himself the "toughest S.O.B. on the planet," Austin boasted that he could beat Tyson any day of the week — and twice on Sunday. And if "Iron Mike" had trouble hearing, then he'd use some sign language: he gave Tyson the finger with both hands. Tyson had had enough and he shoved Austin to the mat. All hell broke loose and WWF officials tried to restrain Austin. At the same time, Tyson's crew kept him from doing something he might regret.

Eventually, the combatants were separated and a full-scale riot was averted. As Austin was taken out of the ring, Vince McMahon screamed that he'd ruined everything.

The confrontation had the world talking for weeks. The buzz augmented *WrestleMania XIV* buyrates, as fans wondered what kind of chance Austin had with an angry Tyson officiating his match.

Austin would ultimately defeat Shawn Michaels to become the new WWF champion. Despite fears about Tyson's willingness to call the match squarely, "Iron" Mike took no sides in his role as special enforcer. When the referee was incapacitated during the contest, Tyson's true allegiance was revealed. He made the three-count against a just-stunned Shawn Michaels. After being defeated, an angry HBK would confront Tyson — only to get knocked out by "Iron" Mike. With the match over and Austin the new WWF champion, Tyson took off the DX T-shirt he was wearing to reveal an Austin 3:16 shirt. DX had been fooled by both men, and the era of "Stone Cold" Steve Austin was headed for new heights.

WHERE TO STEPHANIE?

"The Undertaker has become his character," Vince McMahon said, worrying about his family, particularly his daughter Stephanie. As the Monday Night War raged in 1998, storylines that blurred fantasy and reality were commonplace, but none were as chilling as this.

Something in the Undertaker had snapped and he now believed he was the creature of darkness he'd personified for so many years. To make matters worse, he had recruited several of his fellow wrestlers and created a Ministry of Darkness, terrorizing the WWF as he demanded total control of the federation. When he began stalking Stephanie, Vince McMahon found himself fighting to protect both his family and the company he had spent decades building.

The Undertaker's initial attempts to capture Vince's little girl were unsuccessful, but on the night of a WWF pay-per-view, Stephanie finally fell into his clutches. Entering a limousine that was supposed to spirit her to safety, she soon realized the Undertaker was the driver. The Undertaker's last words, "Where to Stephanie?" sent chills up the spines of wrestling fans. What sinister plan did the Dead Man have for the apple of Vince's eye?

The next night Vince McMahon was given an ultimatum — sign over control of the WWF or Stephanie would be gone, forever.

The usually indomitable McMahon was reduced to a quivering lump. The cold reality, that Stephanie was in the clutches of a madman, had set in. There was no hesitation on McMahon's part. The McMahon patriarch would deliver the papers transferring control of his company at a remote location, and he would do so alone. Any attempts at a double-cross would lead to a price too high for Vince to contemplate paying. He left the arena, briefcase in hand.

What came next was even more surprising than the ease with which the Undertaker had coerced McMahon into doing his bidding. 'Taker's demands had been a ruse designed to send the bewildered daddy on a wild goose chase. With McMahon waiting elsewhere, the leader of the Ministry of Darkness unveiled his true plan — a black wedding between himself and young Stephanie. The Ministry assembled in the ring, with Stephanie affixed to the Undertaker's symbol. Backstage, Stephanie's brother Shane kept a member of the Corporation from making a rescue attempt.

While Stephanie's own flesh and blood denied her help, there were plenty of wrestlers willing to step into the lion's den. The first was Ken Shamrock, who ran to the ring wielding a two-by-four. Unfortunately, the World's Most Dangerous Man didn't get far, as he was gang-tackled and subdued by members of the Ministry. Next came the Big Show, who looked for a while like he might succeed where Shamrock had failed. The massive superstar battled his way through the Ministry's minions, but he was waylaid by their leader when The Undertaker grabbed Shamrock's two-by-four and broke it over the Big Show's back.

With Shamrock and the Big Show out, things looked desperate. However, before the Undertaker and Stephanie could be joined in unholy matrimony, help came from the unlikeliest of sources. The familiar sound of breaking glass filled the arena and fans went crazy. "Stone Cold" Steve Austin, Vince McMahon's arch-rival tore through the members of the Ministry and dispatched of the Undertaker. When the smoke had cleared, Austin was standing in the ring with a grateful Stephanie McMahon. Despite the many injustices he had suffered at the hands of her father, Stone Cold's sense of decency had prevailed.

It was later revealed that Vince McMahon had orchestrated the abduction as part of an elaborate ruse to gain revenge on Austin. The angle would set a precedent, however: marriages and Stephanie McMahon do not mix (at least in the squared circle). McMahon's machinations would come back to haunt him, with his daughter citing this angle as her motive for aligning with Triple H against him.

YOU'LL BELIEVE A GLORIFIED STUNTMAN CAN FLY!

> *"I do not care how many thumbtacks Mick Foley has fallen on, how many ladders he's fallen off, how many continents he's supposedly bled on, he will always be known as a glorified stuntman."*
> **—Ric Flair commenting on Mick Foley in his autobiography *To Be The Man***

When Mick Foley first entered the WWE as Mankind, he received a stratospheric push by working a program with WWE icon the Undertaker. He also won his fair share of their encounters. As expected, they fought wild brawls, but nothing compared to their Hell in a Cell encounter at *King of the Ring*.

While the Mankind/Undertaker feud had run its course, no one had a problem watching them battle again, especially in a cell. Shawn Michaels and the Dead Man had staged a classic in the same environment, and the pressure was on to meet that standard. Little did the fans know they'd be treated to one of the most talked about matches in history.

Considering the bad blood, no one was shocked when a wild pre-match brawl broke out. The Undertaker and Mankind battled all around the cage and soon found themselves at war on top of the structure. They fought on, getting closer and closer to the edge. Once the Undertaker had Mankind in position he sent him crashing down sixteen feet. On his way down, Foley hit the Spanish announcers' table — it broke his fall and possibly saved his life.

With this, Jim Ross made one of the most historic calls in professional wrestling: "Good God almighty! They've killed him! As God is my witness, he is broken in half!"

J.R. was dead serious; there was real concern that Foley might have been seriously injured. Emergency medical personnel emerged. Foley was placed on a stretcher, and was legitimately going to be taken backstage. Amazingly, however, he rose from the stretcher and returned to the ring.

Fans could not believe what had just taken place — nor could they understand the ferocity of the Undertaker. Despite Foley's death-defying fall, 'Taker held nothing back in dishing out more punishment. Eventually, the two men returned to the top of the cage. This time, the Undertaker grabbed Foley and chokeslammed him. As Foley hit the roof of the structure, a portion collapsed. This time Foley was sent crashing to the mat. He lost consciousness. While Foley was down, Vince McMahon and Terry Funk came down to ringside to check on him. Announcer Jim Ross cried, "Will somebody stop the damn match?"

As Foley began to revive, the Undertaker killed time by attacking Funk. By then, Mankind had regained his bearings and went after the Dead Man. At one point, Mankind was able to apply his finishing hold, the mandible claw, but in the end, the Undertaker proved to be too strong and took the victory with his signature tombstone piledriver.

Following the match, Foley discovered just how much damage his body had sustained. The injury report read like one from a multiple car crash — only all the damage was sustained by just one man. Foley had suffered a dislocated jaw, a dislocated shoulder, two broken ribs, a bruised kidney, and a broken tooth (which had slammed up through the roof of his mouth and into his nose). Foley's wife was horrified and both she and McMahon begged him to never repeat this kind of performance.

IT'S A FAMILY AFFAIR (TEN MAN MATCH AT SADDLEDOME)

The Attitude Era saw many changes, but none more curious than Bret "The Hitman" Hart's bipolar adventure.

Hart had been a heel in America since the double-turn with "Stone Cold" Steve Austin at *WrestleMania*. His previous image, as a wholesome hero, just didn't seem to fit with the new WWF and the call to turn him was made by Vince McMahon. Hart's Canadian fans refused to boo him, however, and the WWF acknowledged this by allowing him to be a face north of the border.

The turn was well-played, with Hart denouncing crowds in United States. If they wanted to cheer the vile Stone Cold, that was fine — he still had his Canadian fans. Soon, the split became a simple case of U.S. vs. Canada. For years, the neighboring countries had enjoyed a healthy rivalry. Although it was nothing like the traditional wrestling battles between U.S. wrestlers and foreigners out to dominate the industry, there was a definite hint of nationalism in the storyline.

As part of his new attitude, the Hitman soon reformed his old partnership with Jim "The Anvil" Neidhart. The reformation of the Hart Foundation didn't end there. Bret bolstered its ranks, adding Brian Pillman, Davey Boy Smith, and his brother Owen. Together, they would wage war on the WWF.

Things came to a head at *In Your House 16: Canadian Stampede*. The July 1997 PPV saw all five Hart Foundation members face off against the team of Steve Austin, Goldust, The Road Warriors, and Ken Shamrock.

It was an all-out war. The hometown crowd cheered the Canucks and booed their foes mercilessly. (Had they been wrestling anyone but the Harts they might have been cheered.) Adding to the tension was the presence of the rest of the Hart family ringside — including legendary father Stu Hart. This would play an important part in the match, with Bruce Hart throwing a soda into the face of Stone Cold. At one point, Austin looked to be going after the elderly Hart patriarch.

With Austin distracted, baby brother Owen seized the moment and rolled him up for the pinfall. The entire Hart clan entered the ring in one of the biggest post-match celebrations ever seen. While the Harts' victory might have seemed controversial to many American fans, in Canada it was nothing less than a national celebration.

THE LOOSE CANNON

If controversy creates cash, then this incident should have made millions for the WWF. Instead, it nearly got *Raw* cancelled.

For years, wrestlers had been battered, bruised, and bloodied with all sorts of foreign objects. Wrestlers had thrown fire, been hung from nooses, and gouged with everything from forks to railroad spikes. But one unwritten rule always seemed to be followed: wrestlers never used guns or knives. (One noticeable exception occurred in Memphis, where Jerry "The King" Lawler pulled a gun that was later revealed to be a toy. The incident still drew criticism. A wrestler could run someone over with a car — but guns were a no-no.)

Brian Pillman had come to the WWF after a firestorm of controversy (much of it intentionally generated) in WCW and ECW earned him the nickname "The Loose Cannon." Pillman had earned a reputation as one of the finest wrestlers in the world — and one of the craziest. Whether it was his high-flying moves in the ring or his wild antics outside it, he lived life to its fullest.

He'd spent the first half of the 1990s working for WCW. Despite his talent, his career had more downs than ups. After forming a very popular tag team with "Stunning" Steve Austin, management pulled the plug. Pillman took a while to bounce back, then landed a lucrative role in wcw as part of the heel faction the Four Horsemen.

As Eric Bischoff went to war with Vince McMahon, Pillman saw an opportunity to strengthen his position. Bischoff had shown that he liked clever angles designed not only to fool the fans, but the wrestlers themselves. Knowing this, Pillman suggested an angle to Bischoff, where he would be fired from the company for being out of control and travel to other promotions like ECW to raise havoc before finally returning. Bischoff loved the idea and arranged for a Pillman-gets-fired scenario. To make things seem more realistic, Pillman arranged for Bischoff to give him his actual release from the company.

Pillman left wcw after a "respect" match with veteran Kevin Sullivan. Behind the scenes, Sullivan booked wcw; Pillman acknowledged this immediately, saying, "I respect you booker-man." In effect, he gave up before the match had even started. wcw treated the incident as if Pillman had deviated from the script and gone into business for himself. Suddenly, he was gone from the company.

Calling himself "The Rogue Horseman," Pillman arrived in ECW and cut a controversial promo that ended short when he unzipped his pants and threatened to urinate in the ring. He would appear several more times, but he never competed in an ECW ring. During this time, Pillman played the wwF off against wcw, bargaining with both companies for a new contract. In the end, he opted to work for the wwF. But shortly after signing he was involved in an auto accident that nearly ended his career. Despite the injury, the wwF had faith in Pillman, and they soon began using him on the air though he wasn't ready to wrestle. Pillman hosted an interview segment that the wwF hoped would get the charismatic wrestler over prior to his debut. During one of these segments, Pillman was attacked by his former tag team partner, Steve Austin. Austin focused on his ankle, and Pillman was taken out in an ambulance.

After turning Pillman's ankle into jelly, Austin vowed to finish the job. During the November 4, 1996, episode of *Raw*, Pillman was interviewed at his home; several of his friends had gathered in the area to protect him should Austin come calling (as threatened). When Austin was reported to be in the neighborhood, cameras cut back to Pillman's house. Over the next hour, Austin systematically attacked Pillman's allies, incapacitating them. Inside the house, wwF announcer Kevin Kelly was shocked to see Pillman draw a gun and swear that he'd deal with the situation should Stone Cold dare to enter. True to his word, Pillman later pulled the 9mm Glock on Austin. And then, at that moment, the remote feed was lost. What followed was intense speculation as to whether or not shots had been heard.

The incident brought the WWF under fire, not only for the use of the firearm but for Pillman dropping an F-bomb on live television. The WWF weathered the storm by promising executives from the USA Network that this kind of thing would never happen again.

But it also helped Austin and Pillman get over with the fans. Austin's character became even more of a fearless badass, while Pillman's reputation as a grade-A maniac was cemented by his defense of hearth and home. Pillman returned to action once his injury had healed, and worked matches with Austin before beginning a program with Goldust. His career would be cut short: he died, tragically, from an undiagnosed heart condition.

"Iron Mike" and HBK

CHAPTER 13

HE'S NOT SUPPOSED
TO BE HERE!

Given the serial nature of wrestling shows, it should come as no shock that one of a promoter's most effective tools is surprise. During the early days of *Nitro*, Eric Bischoff made a habit of shocking fans with unexpected appearances. In *Controversy Creates Cash,* he explains that his booking philosophy revolved around a formula he liked to call SARSA — Story, Action, Reality, Surprise, and Anticipation. The more elements of his formula a story had, the more likely it was to have staying power and make money.

Through the years, promoters have developed many successful angles by creating the illusion that a wrestler has no business appearing. The surprise can take many forms — a wrestler who was thought to have been permanently injured, the reemergence of someone who's been gone from the promotion for some time, or the arrival of a star from a rival promotion.

MIDNIGHT EXPRESS VS. MIDNIGHT EXPRESS

Wrestling has never been shy about ripping itself off. Anyone with doubts need look no further than the number of copy-cats that emulated the Rock and Roll Express in the 1980s: the Midnight Rockers, the Fantastics, and the Rock and Roll RPMS are just a few. Likewise, the incredible success of the Road Warriors led to a legion of wannabes, including Demolition and the Powers of Pain. In a similar vein, promoters and wrestlers have never been hesitant to exploit the name of a previous success. Ric Flair was just one of many (but by far the most successful) who used the nickname "The Nature Boy," and only the most ardent fan can name all of the teams over the years that called themselves the Hollywood Blondes or the Heavenly Bodies.

Before promoters and wrestlers began trademarking their names, it was not uncommon for more than one wrestler or tag team to use the same name and compete in different promotions. It was quite another thing, however, to see two identically named teams competing in the *same* promotion. Just imagine two versions of the rock group KISS being on tour — except here both bands were beating each other senseless for the rights to the name. Such a scenario materialized when Jim Crockett Promotions had not one, but two Midnight Expresses working for the company at the same time.

The original Midnight Express began working in Southeast Championship Wrestling when Dennis Condrey teamed with Randy Rose following the retirement of Condrey's previous partner, Don Carson. The addition of Norvell Austin saw the team adopt the nickname the Midnight Express, supposedly inspired by the team's black outfits, black cars, and late-night partying. The heel trio proved quite successful, often performing with the understanding that any combination of the three could work a match (a practice also adopted by the Fabulous Freebirds that later became known as the "Freebird Rule").

When Condrey, Rose, and Austin went their separate ways, the concept of the Midnight Express proved too good to keep on the shelf. A new Express was formed after Mid-South Wrestling promoter Bill Watts teamed Bobby Eaton with Condrey. Watts added a third member to this Express as well, but it was in the form of a manager rather than a wrestler. (From this point on, every version of the Midnight Express would be comprised of a tag team and a manager.)

Watts' new team proved successful, feuding against some of Mid-South's top babyfaces, including the duo that would become their arch-rivals: the Rock and Roll Express.

The Midnight Express proved an enduring team. When Dennis Condrey left, Eaton carried on with the help of Stan Lane (best known for his work with Steve Keirn in the Fabulous Ones), leading this version of the Midnight Express to new heights as JCP world tag team champs. Around this time, the founders of the Midnight Express also returned to action, with Randy Rose and Dennis Condrey reuniting in the American Wrestling Association as the Original Midnight Express. Under the guidance of manager Paul E. Dangerously, the duo took a back seat to no one and captured the AWA version of the tag title.

Two high-flying teams with crafty managers and two teams that had won gold: two Midnight Expresses. It was only natural that fans began to wonder which was the best. As long as they worked for rival promotions, it seemed unlikely they'd ever find out. But that was about to change.

In JCP, the Eaton/Lane version lost the NWA titles to the Road Warriors when Hawk and Animal turned heel and ambushed them. It was just the beginning of their problems. During an episode of *World Championship Wrestling*, Eaton and Lane were once again ambushed. Their assailants turned out to be Randy Rose and Dennis Condrey, the Original Midnight Express. Led by Paul E. Dangerously, the original Midnights delivered a brutal beating. Even manager Jim Cornette was left a bloodied mess.

It didn't take Cornette long to get his men ready for payback. The fans were behind Eaton and Lane, but that didn't stop Cornette from instructing his team to do whatever was necessary to gain the upper hand. Over the next few weeks, the four men battled to see who would lay final claim to the name. The feud came to a close with a loser-leaves-town match: the new Midnight Express defeated the Original. Dangerously would continue to seek revenge on Cornette by sending the Samoan Swat Team and other duos after his rivals.

THE REAL WORLD CHAMPION

The rivalry between promotions had fans asking: which champ was the best?

The two men symbolized everything that their respective promotions stood for. Hulk Hogan was the larger-than-life performer who used showmanship and charisma to achieve superstardom in a company that prized showmanship over athleticism. Ric Flair, on the other hand, possessed plenty of charisma, but he took pride in being a natural athlete perfectly suited to the NWA's old school, more realistic approach to wrestling.

The impossible became possible when WCW underwent one of its many changes in management. And when Ric Flair finally arrived in the WWF, it was clear who he was gunning for.

When Vince McMahon took the WWF national, he changed the business in many ways. In the not-so-distant past, it wasn't unusual to see wrestlers from one promotion mentioned or featured in another. That's not to say that promoters gathered around the campfire to sing "Kumbaya," but there was certainly cooperation. But it was like McMahon couldn't acknowledge the competition for fear that it would give them some type of credibility.

WWF fans, of course, knew there was another show. They may not have watched WCW, but they certainly read about it in wrestling magazines.

But Ric Flair and his NWA championship was something entirely different. While McMahon wouldn't come out and say Flair was from WCW, even in the WWF it was clear that this guy laid claim to being the real deal.

Flair jumped to the WWF after his frustration with WCW executive Jim Herd became unbearable. In his autobiography, Flair talks about how disorganized and undisciplined WCW had become under Herd. Big money contracts were handed to untalented workers, while dedicated veterans were treated with disdain. Threatened with a 50 percent pay cut, Flair left. As if that wasn't bad enough, he took the NWA belt with him, holding it as collateral for the bond he had posted as world champion.

Back when the NWA was a syndicate of territories, it was this bond that protected the NWA from a champion going into business for himself. As Jack Brisco explains: "The reason behind the bond was not hard to figure out. The world wrestling heavyweight championship is a valuable commodity. The governing body of the National Wrestling Alliance did not want any one individual controlling the title on his own or dropping the belt to anyone and winning it back the next night. It was done, foremost, to protect the integrity of the title. The bond also made sure the champion wouldn't sell off the title to a promoter or lose it to someone who hadn't been ordained by the board of directors of the NWA."

With the belt in his possession, Flair was even more valuable to the WWF. To many fans, Flair was the embodiment of the NWA style. Now, the WWF had both Flair and the oldest title in the business. Almost anyone familiar with wrestling recognized the belt, and once it began showing up on WWF television, curiosity peaked.

The WWF played their cards to perfection. When manager Bobby "The Brain" Heenan appeared on WWF television with the NWA belt in his hand, he didn't have to say a thing. Over the next few weeks, he would simply promise that he was bringing in the "real world's champion." That day finally came when Flair debuted against preliminary wrestler Jim Powers.

When Flair appeared on Brutus Beefcake's talk segment, "The Barber Shop," he quickly got down to business. With Heenan holding the microphone Flair said, "So this is the World Wrestling Federation, where Hulk Hogan claims to be the world champion." He told the fans how he'd challenged Hogan for eight years to meet him and determine who the best was. Now, he was standing on Hogan's doorstep. Ever the professional, Flair put Hogan over, acknowledging over 300 million fans thought the sun rose and set with the Hulkster. As far as Flair was concerned however, until Hogan beat him, he was still the man.

Naturally, WCW was furious. By the time their lawyers were able to do anything about it, Flair had paraded around WWF television with the belt, establishing his credentials. When WCW was legally able to bar the WWF from using the title, the WWF shrewdly digitized a different belt, making it appear as if Flair still had it, but that the WWF couldn't show it.

The confrontation with Hulk Hogan finally occurred on another talk segment, Paul Bearer's "Funeral Parlor." Bearer brought in Hogan, the man who would soon face his charge the Undertaker. Hogan examined the set warily — the WWF champion knew that the Undertaker wasn't above lying in wait to ambush an opponent while Bearer conducted his interviews. As Hogan searched, Ric Flair made his way in.

Flair looked into Hogan's face and told him how long he'd been waiting to confront him. The "real world's champion" said he'd heard about Hogan's twenty-four-inch pythons for far too long. He also told Hulk not to fear the butterflies fluttering in his stomach. Flair was here to burst Hogan's bubble — knocking on his doorstep with the real world title. Whatcha gonna do, Hogan, when Ric Flair runs wild on you?

Hulk had had enough of Flair's posturing. He warned Flair that when he put the so-called real world's title up against the real WWF champion, he'd find out about Hulkamania. Before Hogan could finish, the Undertaker attacked, clubbing Hogan with an urn. As Hogan fell, Flair joined in. The Undertaker and Hogan continued to brawl until WWF color commentators Randy "Macho Man" Savage and "Rowdy" Roddy Piper came to the Hulkster's rescue, brandishing steel chairs. Savage struck the Undertaker with the chair but the big man shrugged it off. Savage and Piper shielded Hogan, threatening to strike Flair and the Dead Man should they cross the invisible line they'd drawn.

Flair then inserted himself into Hogan's title defense against the Undertaker. He aided the Dead Man in winning the WWF title by throwing a chair into the ring, which the Undertaker used to piledrive the champ onto. Hogan got his revenge in a rematch, but the WWF championship was held up after a controversial finish which saw Hogan use the Undertaker's urn to secure his victory.

With the WWF title in limbo and Hogan's program with the Undertaker concluded, fans waited for the WWF to pull the trigger on the first Hogan/Flair match (the two had already met at house shows). Sadly, the anticipation went unanswered as Hogan was put into a program with Sid Justice while Flair feuded with Randy Savage.

Despite a fantastic buildup, the WWF left a fortune on the table when they walked away from a Hogan/Flair series. The two legends would eventually feud in WCW years later, doing tremendous business and showing the WWF what could have been. To this day, no one knows for certain why the two never squared off in the WWF.

SCOTT HALL INVADES NITRO

> *By the rude bridge that arched the flood,*
> *Their flag to April's breeze unfurled,*
> *Here once the embattled farmers stood,*
> *And fired the shot heard round the world.*
> **—"Concord Hymn," Ralph Waldo Emerson**

At the time, in the WWF there was no guaranteed salary. Wrestlers were typically paid a negotiated percentage of house show attendance, PPV buys, and merchandise revenue. WCW, on the other hand, offered contracts with a guaranteed salary, which (along with WCW's lighter schedule) many wrestlers found tempting.

Fans have always longed for interpromotional dream matches. But given the highly competitive nature of the wrestling business, they've been few and far between and often unsatisfactory — no promotion wanted their wrestler seen as second-best. By the time Vince McMahon and Eric Bischoff were battling over Monday night, an interpromotional match was as likely as Barack Obama picking John McCain as his running mate.

While the wwf and wcw wouldn't collaborate, that didn't stop Eric Bischoff from making things happen. He had established himself as an executive who thought outside the box and he would demonstrate this once more when he created an illusory interpromotional war. All he needed were some top names from the wwf to get things started. Bischoff's boss Ted Turner had shown before that he was willing to dig deep into his pockets to make wcw competitive. When Bischoff learned that two of the wwf's top stars had contracts that were about to expire, he made his move.

Although he'd worked in wrestling since 1984, Scott Hall had bounced from promotion to promotion until he reinvented himself in 1992 as "Razor Ramon," a character based on Tony Montana from *Scarface*. The persona took off immediately, and Hall was soon a top wwf star, becoming the first wrestler to win the promotion's Intercontinental Championship three times. Backstage, he became close with fellow wrestlers Shawn Michaels, Kevin Nash, Sean Waltman, and Triple H, forming a real-life alliance known as "The Kliq." The men looked out for one another and quickly developed a reputation as both power brokers and troublemakers.

Bischoff began negotiating with Hall after his neighbor "Diamond" Dallas Page confided that both Hall and Kevin Nash had expressed interest in coming to work for wcw. Each man had worked for wcw before heading on to success in the Federation. According to Page, both Ramon and Diesel were miserable. Bischoff used DDP as his intermediary, sending word that if they jumped to wcw they'd get both guaranteed contracts and lighter work schedules.

Before long both men had signed, leading to intense speculation as to how they would be used. After speaking with Hall and Nash, Bischoff decided to rely on their history with both companies as part of the storyline behind their debut. Neither wrestler's careers had amounted to much in wcw, with Hall working as the "Diamond Studd," while Nash worked unforgettably bad gimmicks such as "Oz" and "Vinnie Vegas."

On May 27, 1996, Scott Hall showed up on *Nitro* in street clothes, by coming through the audience and claiming to be an outsider. Anyone not watching the show soon was — people grabbed their phones to call friends about the incredible appearance. While Hall's debut wasn't a surprise on the level of Lex Luger's, it was shocking nonetheless. He climbed the guardrail and made his way into the

"The Loose Cannon" Brian Pillman

ring. He grabbed a microphone and told fans that while they knew who he was, they didn't know why he was there. Hall then ran down Eric Bischoff, calling him a Ken doll and weatherman-wannabe, referring to a series of WWF parodies which portrayed WCW as a haven for washed-up wrestlers such as the "Huckster" (Hulk Hogan), the "Nacho Man" (Randy "Macho Man" Savage), and "Scheme Gene" ("Mean" Gene Okerlund). He said he had a challenge for anyone in the WCW: if you want a war, you're gonna get one. Not only was Scott Hall in WCW, talking about taking over — but he promised he wasn't alone.

The next day the Internet was abuzz with wrestling fans talking about *Nitro* — exactly the reaction Bischoff had envisioned. Even the "smart" fans were confused. Hall had supposedly left the WWF for WCW, but was this part of something bigger? Speculation ran rampant — so rampant, in fact, that the WWF's lawyers began investigating whether WCW had crossed the line from spirited competition to restraint of trade. Bill Watts claims he advised Vince McMahon to pursue action against WCW, and ultimately the WWF would launch a lawsuit that was eventually settled out of court.

As the weeks passed by, Hall would introduce his fellow outsider: Kevin Nash. The two would launch a campaign of terror, ambushing WCW's wrestlers and threatening to take over the company.

CHAPTER 14

CONTEMPORARY
(2001–PRESENT)

The problems of victory are more agreeable than those of defeat,
but they are no less difficult.
—Winston Churchill

When the Monday Night War concluded in 2001 there was no question who
ruled professional wrestling. Not only had Vince McMahon put his competition
out of business, he'd bought them outright, for a song. As part of the settlement
with WCW over its lawsuit concerning WCW's use of Scott Hall and Kevin Nash,
the WWF had acquired the right to purchase WCW should it ever come up for sale.

And when Paul Heyman folded ECW and filed for bankruptcy, the WWF bought them out as well. On paper, things were looking very good.

Whether it was promoting bodybuilding or boxing, Vince McMahon wasn't afraid to try his hand at something new. On February 3, 2000, McMahon announced the formation of the XFL (which, contrary to popular belief, did not stand for Extreme Football League), a professional football league he promised would be a return to the days of "smash-mouth football." The bold venture attracted considerable media attention, leading to impressive ratings for its February 3, 2001, NBC premiere. Subsequent shows would plummet in the ratings, however, and NBC would cancel its broadcasts after just one season, despite previously pledging to stick with the venture for at least two.

The WWF's problems continued as a lawsuit by the World Wildlife Fund forced the company to change its name. Fans wondered if the company might revert to the old WWWF moniker. Instead, the company was rechristened World Wrestling Entertainment (WWE), reflecting Vince's belief that the product he offered was sports entertainment rather than "professional wrestling." McMahon launched a Get the "F" Out promotional campaign to help spread the new brand.

Despite the setbacks, expectations were high, with fans speculating about how high the WWE's ratings might go. Sensing WCW fans might not necessarily flock to the WWE, the WWE toyed with the idea of resurrecting their rival. The trial proved disastrous and the idea was quickly dumped. (Later, the WWE would try creating separate identities for its *Raw* and *SmackDown* shows, a move that has its proponents and critics to this day).

In a shocking turn of events, the WWE failed to capture a significant number of WCW's old viewers. Even more unbelievable was the general downturn in business, as ratings, buyrates, and ticket sales actually decreased. People will forever debate what triggered this, but the end result was clear: the WWE's core audience had shrunk.

Although WCW had proven that wrestling was not a guaranteed moneymaker, new wrestling organizations were launched. One newcomer was the X Wrestling Federation (XWF), which began operations in late 2001. The promotion gained attention with the impressive array of talent (both in and out of the ring) linked to the company. While there was skepticism about its viability, the XWF answered critics by taping ten hours of wrestling in November 2001, featuring appearances by established names like Hulk Hogan, the Road Warriors, Roddy Piper, Jerry Lawler, and Bobby Heenan as well as rising stars Christopher Daniels, A.J. Styles, and Carly Colon.

With an impressive roster and rumors of strong financial backing, the XWF appeared off to a good start; scheduled house shows added to the new organization's credibility. But despite the promotion's strength out of the gate, it quickly became clear the XWF was facing a giant obstacle — the same one that had contributed to the death of WCW and which would plague aspiring promoters from 2001 on.

For decades, television had been wrestling's lifeline. Without it, it was almost impossible succeed. Before WCW was purchased by the WWF, Eric Bischoff had organized a group of investors seeking to purchase the company — until they learned WCW was no longer welcome in its traditional network homes. Without TV, Bischoff knew WCW couldn't survive, and he backed out of the deal.

Despite the ratings of the Monday Night War, wrestling had a bad reputation with many TV execs, who viewed it as low-rent programming that failed to attract advertising revenue. No matter how good a show's ratings were, they were next to useless unless advertising dollars accompanied them.

The men and women behind the XWF quickly learned wrestling had worn out its welcome with the big cable networks. The promotion struggled. To make matters worse, the WWE signed away many of the promotion's top stars (a tactic it had perfected in the 1980s and was used against it by the WCW in the 1990s), decreasing the chance that a TV outlet would show interest. In the end, the XWF fell by the wayside.

The XWF's failure became a cautionary tale for would-be promoters, and it would lead to innovative ways of promoting that bypassed the need for traditional television. Although most of these new organizations would lack the size and scope of the WWE, they would contribute to the growth and evolution of the sport.

THE ERA OF HONOR

For years, ECW entertained its fans with innovative matchmaking and its focus on wrestling ability rather than gimmickry. In 2001, the company folded, leaving a hole in the hearts of its fans. They weren't the only ones who suffered from the promotion's demise. RF Video, a media outlet specializing in wrestling videos, had earned much of its profits from the sale of ECW shows. With ECW gone, Rob Feinstein sought to fill the gap by creating his own promotion. Feinstein would record the new promotion's live events, with the intent of profiting from tapes and DVDs, just as he had done with ECW. The result was Ring of Honor — a promotion as innovative as ECW had been, and one which proved to be as important to wrestling in the new millennium as ECW had been to the '90s. Ring of Honor would become a place for wrestlers to hone their craft where size didn't matter —

where what you did in the ring was more important than what happened on the other side of the ropes.

In addition to their talented workers, Ring of Honor distinguished itself with its Code of Honor, a set of rules all of the wrestlers were to abide by. Unlike most promotions, where the rules were regularly ignored, if enforced at all, the Code of Honor was not something imposed by ROH officials; it worked because the wrestlers governed themselves by it. When the code *was* broken, it meant more and helped get wrestlers who violated it over as heels. The code had five basic tenets:

(1) You must shake hands before and after every match.
(2) No outside interference — no interfering in others' matches or having others interfere on your behalf.
(3) No sneak attacks.
(4) No harming the officials.
(5) Do not get yourself disqualified.

Ring of Honor debuted with a show dubbed *The Era of Honor Begins,* on February 23, 2002. The card featured a match between Eddie Guerrero and Super Crazy for the IWA championship as well as a triple-threat match between Low Ki, Bryan Danielson, and Christopher Daniels.

The decision to go with the triple-threat match as the main event as opposed to the match with the more recognizable Guerrero would define the company.

Booker Gabe Sapolsky's thoughts on the subject were clear: "I still consider putting this on as the main event of the first show as the most important decision in ROH history. I was endlessly debating whether to go with this match or the obvious Eddie Guerrero vs. Super Crazy choice, since they were the two marquee names at the time. The idea of ROH was to push the new breed of talent and put all the emphasis on them. In order to do that, they needed the top spot on the card. Having this match as the main event sent a message to all the fans and critics that ROH was about featuring new stars like Low Ki, Bryan Danielson, and Christopher Daniels. Those three also came through with the match that put us on the map because they knew that they had to really do something special to follow Eddie Guerrero and Super Crazy. Would they have had the same kind of match as the semi-main event? I don't know. What I do know is that this match and the fact it was the main event set the whole tone for the promotion."

Ring of Honor quickly built a reputation as a showcase for realistic-looking technical masterpieces, and ROH would launch the careers of young stars such as Christopher Daniels, Bryan Danielson, Low Ki, Samoa Joe, and C.M. Punk.

TOTAL NONSTOP ACTION

After the demise of wcw and the failure of the xwf, when Jerry Jarrett announced he was starting a new national promotion, people were understandably skeptical.

Still, if anyone could make such an idea work, it had to be Jarrett. He'd run the Championship Wrestling Association on a shoestring for decades, keeping it afloat long after every other territory had fallen to the wwf and wcw. Jarrett knew how to recognize young talent and how to manage money. His ability to keep up with the times had gained him a reputation as one of the shrewdest men in the business. But Jerry Jarrett's keen wrestling mind would soon be put to the test.

The idea for the new promotion came after former wcw and wwf star Jeff Jarrett (Jerry's son) worked some shows overseas and began to dabble in promoting. Jeff worried about his uncertain future in the United States, and approached his father with the idea of starting a new company. The elder Jarrett had retired from wrestling and started a successful construction company. But the more he heard about Jeff's ideas, the more intrigued he became.

Ring of Honor had demonstrated that it was possible to promote without television, but could a similar business model work at the national level? It didn't matter, as the Jarretts had no intention of simply copying ROH. They *would* sell shows directly to fans, but not on DVDs or tapes. Instead, weekly pay-per-views would both promote the product and generat revenue. There would be no house shows, just the pay-per-views. The show and the promotion would be called *Total Nonstop Action* (TNA).

The question was: would fans be willing to order a weekly PPV from an unproven promotion?

With wcw and ecw out of the way, there was a good pool of talent to choose from. Anyone familiar with the Jarrett style of promoting knew TNA wouldn't be throwing big money around; however TNA had other things to offer. The pay-per-view business model meant wrestlers had to work just once every two weeks. Jarrett also made it known that TNA stars could work for other indie promotions to supplement their earnings. (The wwe did not allow its contracted talent to work elsewhere.)

As Eric Bischoff had done when he launched *Nitro*, Jarrett set out to make TNA stand apart. One of the ways he planned to do that was by introducing the X Division. Unlike what has become commonly known as the cruiserweight division, the X Division's focus was on its high-flying, high-risk style and not the size of the worker. The X Division became defined by the phrase, "It's not about weight limits, it's about no limits." It quickly became one of the highlights of every TNA show.

As a nod to its recognition of wrestling's rich history, TNA affiliated itself with the National Wrestling Alliance. While the NWA was now nothing more than a loose collective of independent groups, it still traced its championship lineage back to the early days of North American wrestling. The move was one way to bring in old school fans who didn't care for the WWE product. On the night of TNA's debut, several of the biggest names in NWA history, legends such as Ricky Steamboat, Harley Race, and Jackie Fargo, gathered as the new promotion set out to crown a new world heavyweight champion.

Despite the big plans, the company got off to a rocky start. False estimates inflated the early PPV buyrates, throwing the business model askew once the true figures came in. Jerry Jarrett quickly realized the company was losing money and scrambled to bring in new investors. He appeared to succeed when he secured financial backing from a company called Health South. But his bad luck continued when the outfit decided to pull its support without warning. With TNA's survival in doubt, Jarrett looked high and low for other backers. Fortunately, Panda Energy stepped in with financing.

Despite the rocky early days, TNA would thrive and expand over the next few years, eventually changing its business model in a move away from weekly pay-per-views to more traditional monthly features. TNA also began airing a weekly television show called *Impact*. The success of this program would eventually cause it to be picked up by Spike TV (a network which had previously aired *Monday Night Raw*). By 2007, the show expanded from one hour to two.

While it's unrealistic to call TNA a true national competitor, the existence of a second promotion has created opportunities for wrestlers tired of working for WWE. TNA has benefitted as well from the addition of former WWE superstars such as Christian, the Dudley Boyz, Kurt Angle, and Booker T. It has also become a place for new talents to establish themselves.

INVASION!

By 2001, Vince McMahon acquired WCW and ECW's assets for a fraction of their worth. The WWF's lucrative acquisition gave it access to both promotions' names as well as their tape libraries. The result was that the WWE now effectively controlled the history of contemporary wrestling.

When Shane McMahon appeared on the last *Nitro* to tell his father he'd "bought" WCW, the idea was that WWE would keep both promotions alive as competitors. But then a WCW test match (between Booker T and Buff Bagwell) proved disastrous and the idea was unceremoniously dropped.

Changing course, the WWE opted to use some former WCW stars as part of an "invasion." When Booker T interrupted a pay-per-view match between "Stone Cold" Steve Austin, Chris Benoit, and Chris Jericho, all hell broke loose. Over the next few weeks, WCW stars appeared on *Raw* and *Smackdown* and attacked their WWE counterparts. As things unfolded, it became clear they were out to destroy the WWE.

The angle was fascinating, but it didn't pick up steam until a match featuring Chris Jericho and Kane against Lance Storm and Mike Awesome degenerated into a wild brawl. Allies Rob Van Dam and Tommy Dreamer rushed the ring to bolster Storm and Awesome; Jericho and Kane were surrounded. Fortunately for the WWF stars, their colleagues Raven, the Dudley Boyz, Tazz, Justin Credible, and Rhyno ran in for the save. Or so it seemed until, without warning, the five attacked Jericho and Kane as well. What was going on?

The mystery was quickly solved when Paul Heyman entered the ring. ECW's mad scientist high-fived the men he'd known so well before cutting a promo running down the WWE. He let the fans know the "invasion" was about to get extreme.

With this, Vince and Shane McMahon decided to call a truce and team up the WCW and WWE stars to crush the upstarts from ECW. A match was made: five WCW and five WWE superstars would square off against ten ECW stars. But the main event never materialized: the WCW stars attacked the WWE wresters before the bell even rang. The ECW stars came into the ring to join the mugging. Shane McMahon hugged Paul Heyman and everything became clear. Vince McMahon stormed the ring. And Paul Heyman introduced him to the new owner of ECW — his daughter, Stephanie McMahon. Together, Shane, Stephanie, and Heyman were going to crush the WWE.

This provided the invasion with the zip it needed. Without ECW, it simply wasn't working. The problem was that when the WWE purchased WCW they decided not to take over the contracts of most of their competition's top stars — the terms the wrestlers negotiated with Eric Bischoff made them too expensive for WWE 's taste. Without ECW the invasion simply lacked the kind of star power to threaten WWE.

The stars from ECW and WCW formed a group known as the Alliance. Shane and Stephanie McMahon were tired of waiting for their father to die — this was their way of seizing control of their birthright immediately. Over the next several months, the Alliance would take the WWE to the edge, with the angle culminating in a "winner takes all" match at the 2001 *Survivor Series*. On that night, the WWE's team triumphed, forcing the Alliance to disband and guaranteeing the survival of the WWE.

HOGAN VS. THE ROCK

By 2002, *WrestleMania* had truly earned the nickname, the Showcase of the Immortals. The WWE's flagship PPV had featured many unforgettable moments, but one would have to look back fifteen years to find a confrontation as epic as the one scheduled for *WrestleMania X8*. On March 17, 2002, a true wrestling dream match would take place when one era's superstar faced annother's.

When Vince McMahon decided to bring the New World Order into WWE, he opened the door for a number of fascinating matchups. The nWo's Kevin Nash, Scott Hall, and Hulk Hogan had been gone from the WWE for several years and during their absence, new stars like "Stone Cold" Steve Austin, Triple H, and the Rock had emerged. With *WrestleMania X8* fast approaching, Vince McMahon decided to pull the trigger on a contest fans were dying to see — Hogan vs. the Rock.

The son of wrestling legend Rocky Johnson and the grandson of "Chief" Peter Maivia, the Rock (a.k.a. Dwayne Johnson) — "the most electrifying man in sports entertainment" — had become one of the company's top stars. His rise to the top, however, had not always been smooth. From the beginning, the WWE was convinced Johnson was going to be a big star and they gave him a strong push. But his original smiling, happy-go-lucky Rocky Maivia character was introduced at a time when the fans' tastes were changing and the "Attitude" era began to take hold. Soon "Die, Rocky, Die" signs and chants filled arenas. To counter this, he was turned heel and put into a faction known as the Nation of Domination. The transformation began: Maivia became cocky and more aggressive on the mic; his catchphrases caught on. When he shortened his name to the Rock and began referring to himself in the third person a superstar was born.

The Hogan/Rock angle was set up by the Hulkster being embarrassed by his younger rival. Hogan didn't take kindly to the treatment, and with the help of Kevin Nash and Scott Hall, he layed him out. The beatdown was so severe, the Rock had to be taken away in an ambulance. But his problems were only just beginning. Hogan set out to finish the job by getting behind the wheel of a tractor trailer — and ramming it into the ambulance, promising the Rock that he was going to "lay the smackdown on [his] crippled ass."

It had been ten years since Hulk Hogan left the WWF but you wouldn't know it from the thunderous ovation he received as he walked the aisle at Toronto's SkyDome for *WrestleMania X8*. Before the match began, Jim Ross likened the match to an encounter between Babe Ruth and Barry Bonds. Jerry Lawler talked of how a young lion challenges the leader of the pack for supremacy — sometimes the young lion wins, and sometimes the challenge is repelled.

It began with Hogan and Rock sizing each other up. Making the most of his signature facial expressions, the Rock raised an eyebrow when the fans' support for Hogan became evident. Hogan started strong, knocking the Rock down then putting him in a side headlock. The support for the heel ringing through the stadium was unmistakable.

Hogan dominated, but the "People's Champion" was far from done. Rock caught Hogan with a clothesline and knocked his bandana off. The Hulkster realized he was in for a long night. The Rock then beckoned with his "Just Bring It" gesture and soon began peppering Hogan with blows. Hogan opted for a breather outside of the ring but the Rock was quick to follow.

The two competitors seemed evenly matched. One would gain the advantage, only to see the other come back. As the bout progressed, Jim Ross reminded the fans of Hogan's success at *WrestleMania,* but he was also quick to point out his previous loss in the SkyDome — to the Ultimate Warrior — at *WrestleMania VI*. Realizing how good his opponent was, Hogan used moves not normally part of his arsenal, trying both an abdominal stretch and a rollup. He also brawled as if his life depended on it: raking his nails across the Rock's back, choking him with the tape around his wrist, and even biting him.

A ref bump knocked out the man in stripes before the Rock placed Hogan in a Boston crab. Hogan tapped, but there was no one to call for the bell. Rock checked on the referee, who was slowly recovering, but then he was hit with a low blow. Next, Hogan surprised the Rock by using his own finisher against him — the rock bottom. The referee crawled over to make the count but Rocky escaped. Hogan continued his offense, whipping the Rock with a weight-lifting belt. This came back to haunt him, however, when Rocky DDT'ed him and then gave him a taste of his own medicine.

Sensing victory was near, the Rock hit the rock bottom and covered Hogan. Hulk kicked out and then did what he had done for so many years — "Hulked up." It was a story he'd told so many times in the ring — he blocked a punch, dished out some punches of his own, and whipped Rocky into the ropes for a big boot. What came next was no surprise to anyone who'd followed Hogan's career — the legdrop. Hogan had won countless matches this way, but this was a different story.

Rocky kicked out.

Hogan went in for a second legdrop. This time, the Rock found the strength to roll out of the way.

A groggy Rock hit another rock bottom, shaking the mat with Hogan's large frame. Jim Ross and Jerry Lawler were shocked when he refused to go for the pin. Instead, he hit a second rock bottom, apparently wanting to make sure Hogan was out. The coup de grace came when the Rock finished Hogan with the people's elbow, the Rock's "electrifying" version of an elbowdrop. After three rock bottoms and a people's elbow, Hogan was finally beaten. The Rock covered him for the three-count.

The Hogan/Rock match lived up to its hype, and even surpassed it. What came after the match was nearly as special as the match itself. As Hogan rose to his feet, the Rock glared, not sure what to expect. A dejected Hulkster extended his hand. The Rock hesitated then gave Hogan the benefit of the doubt and shook hands, exciting the crowd. Hogan pointed at the Rock as he exited, signaling his respect. Things weren't over yet, though. Kevin Nash and Scott Hall emerged to confront him over the handshake. Hall threw a toothpick as Nash sucker-punched their nWo teammate. The two began stomping him, but the Rock was there to make the save and help Hogan clean house.

Whatever allegiance Hogan had to the nWo had been destroyed. A new page was turning in the legend of Hulkamania. The Hulkster was about to leave the ring when the Rock motioned for him remain. There was still business to be taken care of — posing. Back when he was a babyface, it was a Hogan tradition to pose in the ring for his fans after winning a match. The Rock cupped his ears and reminded Hogan of how he did things back in the day. Hogan found that you could go home again, cupping his hand and holding it to his ear as the fans cheered ever louder. It was a once-in-a-lifetime moment and the Toronto fans welcomed Hogan back with open arms.

With a return to his trademark yellow and red, Hogan enjoyed another run as a WWE babyface. Hulkamania ran wild once more. He even won the WWE championship, enjoying a short title run after defeating Triple H at the 2002 *Backlash* PPV.

The night WWE fans welcomed Hogan back is best described by Jim Ross: "It was Hogan and his fans and their emotions, and they embraced. On that night, he literally became a god."

Hogan himself was amazed by the reaction he received: "I was crying like a baby. I had done something that everybody said I couldn't do. I had showed everybody who doubted me that I was still the man and I could do this better than anybody. And as I walked up the ramp to leave the arena with this kid who used to hang around the wrestlers' dressing room, I said, 'Brother we knocked that out of the park.'"

NEVER SAY NEVER

Only in professional wrestling could two men who fought viciously to put each other out of business exchange hugs. That's precisely what happened when former WCW head honcho Eric Bischoff met the WWE chairman during *Raw*. Just a few years earlier, Bischoff was challenging McMahon to a real fight for a WCW pay-per-view. McMahon's famous retort? He'd fight, but in a parking lot.

Now, the rivals were doing business together. In the WWE *McMahon* DVD, Bischoff recalls a conversation he had with Vince about coming to work for him. He told him that were the situations reversed, he would have hoped the same offer would have been made to him.

As Vince McMahon was about to introduce *Raw's* new general manager, he told fans that "it takes a real S.O.B. to be successful in this business." He continued, "from one S.O.B. to another . . ." then said the name no one expected to hear him utter — Eric Bischoff. McMahon hugged him and shook his hand, and then Bischoff made his way to the ring to remind fans who he was. He'd taken Vince McMahon to the edge and revolutionized the business; he forced McMahon to change the way he operated. After patting himself on the back for his many accomplishments, he told the fans that he was going to revive a sagging brand, meaning *Raw*.

Bischoff made an immediate impact. He said his job was to make the show more enjoyable and he was deadly serious about it. WWE fans learned just how far he'd go during a match between Shawn Stasiak and D'Lo Brown. The match was curiously saddled with a time limit of three minutes. After time expired, both wrestlers were attacked by two behemoths (Rosey and Jamal) who appeared out of the audience. Bischoff introduced the attackers as "Three Minute Warning." Over the next few weeks, the duo would show up and lay out anyone who overstayed their welcome.

Three Minute Warning was just one of the new ideas Bischoff introduced. Another was the elimination chamber, a variation on steel cage and Hell in a Cell matches. The elimination chamber saw four wrestlers encased in glass chambers that opened randomly at specific intervals until they, and the two men who began the match in the ring, were all involved in competition. The first elimination chamber was held at the 2002 *Survivor Series* PPV and soon became a WWE staple.

Bischoff would also become involved in one of the more controversial angles in WWE history when he made a surprise appearance at the "commitment ceremony" of Billy and Chuck, a gay tag team who outed themselves on WWE TV. The event drew a great deal of mainstream publicity, including an endorsement from GLADD. When the minister interrupted the ceremony to unmask himself, he was revealed to be Eric Bischoff. Three Minute Warning then ran in and attacked.

Over the next three years, Bischoff would be a constant thorn in the side of *Raw* babyfaces. Eventually, he would wear out his welcome, and leave on an unceremonious note. When McMahon tired of Bischoff's reign, he then ordered the GM be put "on trial." Of course, Bischoff lost; he was physically, and some might say poetically, removed by John Cena, who threw him into the back of a garbage truck.

THUMBS DOWN!

> *All animals are equal but some animals are more equal than others.*
> —*Animal Farm*, **George Orwell**

When Ric Flair returned to the WWE in 2002, fans began to speculate whether a new incarnation of the Four Horsemen might be in the works. An alliance with Triple H was soon bolstered by the recruitment of Dave Batista and rookie sensation Randy Orton. Four heels, vying for all of the WWE's top prizes — were the Horsemen riding again?

In a word, no — the new group was something unique. They described themselves as "the evolution of wrestling," and with that, Evolution was born. Like the Horsemen, Evolution ran roughshod, capturing championships and stomping anyone who got in their way. At one point, they had all the gold — with Triple H holding the world championship, Orton wearing the Intercontinental belt, and the tag team titles wrapped around the waists of Batista and Flair.

This success, however, was short-lived. As wrestling history demonstrates, when jealousy raises its ugly head, the end results are never positive. The first sign of trouble came when Randy Orton defeated Chris Benoit to become world champion. Benoit had defeated Triple H at *WrestleMania* and the Cerebral Assassin had been unsuccessful in his quest to retake the belt. Enter Orton. When Triple H's Evolution stablemate upset Benoit at *Summer Slam*, he became the youngest champion in WWE history. The next night on *Raw*, an Evolution celebration turned into a beatdown when Triple H gave the "thumbs down" signal to his cronies, ordering them to take out the new champ. Triple H had made it clear who the group's alpha male was.

The lesson did not go unnoticed — by Batista. While he was the group's strongman, he was no simple-minded gorilla. He'd learned from two of the best in the business — when the time came to make his move, he would be well prepared.

Batista won the *Royal Rumble* in 2004, earning a *WrestleMania* title shot. The question was, who would he challenge? *Raw's* champion, Triple H, or the *SmackDown!* kingpin, John Bradshaw Layfield? His decision would have long-lasting ramifications for the WWE and, depending on his choice, for Evolution itself.

Ever crafty, Triple H intrigued Batista with the idea of taking JBL's title so Evolution could consolidate their power by controlling the championships of both WWE brands. Batista held his cards close, and refused to make his choice known. Then fate seemed to intervene, making the choice easier. JBL issued a challenge to Batista during *Raw*, and when the Animal decided to confront him, Triple H joined in. The encounter nearly turned deadly as Bradshaw's trademark white limousine tried to run Batista over. Given these actions, it was becoming easy to guess who Batista would challenge.

To add to the drama, a televised contract signing was scheduled. However before the match with JBL could be signed, Batista overheard Triple H telling Ric Flair that he had masterminded the limo attack, hoping to provoke him into challenging JBL. On the surface, Batista did nothing to suggest he knew of Triple H's treachery.

In the ring, *Raw* GM Eric Bischoff was joined by his *Smackdown!* counterpart, Theodore Long. Both men were eager for Batista to pick their champion, knowing the encounter would lend prestige to their brand. The three remaining members of Evolution joined them. Batista held their two contracts in his hands. Once more, Triple H encouraged Batista to challenge JBL, reminding him of how Evolution would rule the world. When Batista dropped the *Raw* contract, Eric Bischoff was deflated, but Triple H was delighted, looking on with a smile and giving Batista a big thumb's up.

In an instant, Triple H's world turned upside down — when *Batista's* thumb did. He had no doubt what the Animal meant. After all, he'd given the thumbs down to Batista himself once, signaling the beginning of the attack on Orton. Triple H charged, only to be floored by Batista. After tossing Ric Flair out of the ring, the Animal picked Triple H up and delivered his finisher, the Batista bomb, planting him through a table.

The thumb's down gesture was the beginning of the end of Triple H's WWE title reign. At *WrestleMania XX*, Batista would win the belt with another Batista bomb.

THE TERRIFIC TRILOGY: JOE VS. PUNK

By 2004, Ring of Honor had established itself as the place for fans of technical wrestling. While its roster boasted some amazing stars, no one personified ROH more than CM Punk and Samoa Joe. Their 2004 series of matches for the ROH world title would epitomize what the indie promotion was all about.

CM Punk (born Phil Brooks) espoused a straight-laced lifestyle. He began wrestling in the backyard Lunatic Wrestling Federation, and from there he went on to train under Ace Steel in Chicago's Steel Domain Wrestling School. After gaining experience in the Independent Wrestling Association (IWA), Punk went to Ring of Honor, distinguished himself by twice sharing (with Colt Cabana) the ROH tag team titles.

Samoa Joe (born Nuufolau Joel "Joe" Seanoa) grew up in California, where he kept busy working in his family's Polynesian dance company, studying judo (he won the California State junior judo championship), and playing high school football. Joe then began extensive training as a wrestler and shortly after his debut in 1999, was signed to one of the WWF's developmental territories, Ultimate Pro Wrestling. Joe's skills earned him a stint in Japan's Zero One promotion, a real vote of confidence in his abilities. Although his physique was reminiscent of an earlier generation, his skills and toughness won him praise wherever he worked.

On June 12, 2004, Punk challenged Joe in Dayton, Ohio, at ROH's *World Title Classic.* Their first bout saw Punk employ a rope-a-dope strategy. Punk had studied the ROH champion thoroughly and believed he needed to exhaust his opponent by taking him past the half-hour mark. (Punk realized that most of Joe's matches had gone no longer than twenty minutes.) He also believed Joe's opponents made a mistake in trying to go blow-for-blow with the champ, and that this usually made for an early exit.

The strategy saw Punk using simple but effective old school holds like the headlock to wear the big man down. When Joe launched into an offensive, Punk did everything possible to reduce the damage by covering himself up so his arms rather than his head and torso absorbed the punishment. Punk knew he couldn't avoid being hit — but he could reduce the damage and conserve energy.

To a degree, Punk's strategy worked. Unlike many previous title contenders, Punk was able to last a full hour with the champ. In the end, though, he was unable to score a pinfall or force a submission. The match ended in a draw and Joe retained his title.

The stalemate led to a rematch being scheduled for early December, but this was moved forward to October 11, 2004, in Punk's hometown of Chicago,

Illinois, when Steve Corino was pulled from the card. Like their previous encouter, it was another sixty-minute broadway. Despite coming up short yet again, Punk received another rematch; this time, however, there would be stipulations — there would be no time limit, and it would be Punk's final shot at Joe's title.

Joe/Punk III took place at *All-Star Extravaganza* on December 4, 2004. Punk started the match by taunting Joe into aggression, and then taking the champion down with a backslide for a surprise pin attempt. Unsuccessful, Punk focussed on his strategy of using submission moves to wear Joe down. Joe bloodied the challenger, however, busting him open and tearing him apart outside the ring. Punk's forehead was so bloody that, at one point, the champ had to grab his hair to control him: his face was too slick to hold. Punk persevered and hit a shining wizard, leading to a near fall. Finally, when Joe applied a rear naked choke, it looked like it was all over. Ringside guest Ricky Steamboat had to grab the timekeeper to prevent the bell from ringing while pointing out that Punk was still conscious. The match continued, pinfall attempt for pinfall attempt.

Joe's frustration (some would say desperation) was revealed when he tried to pin Punk with heel tactics, propping his legs on the ropes for leverage. In the end, a rollup led to Punk's downfall. Joe countered Punk's schoolboy and again applied his rear naked chokehold. When Punk maneuvered to escape, Joe hit Punk with first a German suplex, and then a dragon suplex. As the fans chanted, "Please don't tap," referee Mark Sinclair rang for the bell: Punk was unconscious. Samoa Joe had finally triumphed.

The series was a throwback to earlier world title classics, reminiscent of Brisco vs. Funk and Steamboat vs. Flair. Each encounter had a big match feel, and the whole thing peaked in the third and final encounter.

Samoa Joe's reign as champion would help elevate the ROH belt from a regional title to a true world title. While it might be easy to scoff at Ring of Honor's production values, it's almost impossible to criticize the quality of both the wrestling and booking.

Given the talent on display, it was inevitable that larger promotions would come calling. Eventually, Samoa Joe went to work for TNA, making a name for himself with an unbelievable eighteen-month undefeated streak that saw him demolish many of the stars of the X Division (and included two reigns as X Division champion). Joe's quest would culminate with triumph on April 13, 2008, when he defeated Kurt Angle in a steel cage to become the TNA world champion (he became the first man to hold both the ROH and TNA world championships). After a brief stint with TNA, Punk signed with the WWE, leading some to question his likelihood of getting over in the sports entertainment environment. Punk answered his critics, first by winning the ECW world title and then by becoming the 2008 winner of the Money in the Bank ladder match. In late June, 2008, he matched Joe's TNA success by taking the World Heavyweight Championship from Edge on *Raw*.

REY MYSTERIO WINS THE WORLD CHAMPIONSHIP

If you've watched wrestling in the past couple of decades, you've probably heard the phrase "It's not the size of the dog in the fight, but the size of the fight in the dog." At 5'6", no one epitomizes the notion better than Rey Mysterio. "Wrestling's biggest little man" has defied all odds and expectations, reaching the pinnacle of success. Few moments have been as impressive as the night Rey became world champion.

The nephew of luchador Rey Misterio ("King Mystery" in Spanish), Rey climbed into the ring at the age of fourteen. Eventually, his uncle allowed him to take the name Rey Misterio Jr. He quickly made a name for himself in the Mexican promotion Asistencia Asesoría y Administración (AAA) with his amazing high-flying abilities.

In 1994, Rey garnered some mainstream U.S. attention when WCW co-promoted the AAA pay-per-view *When Worlds Collide*. He made his U.S. debut the following year with ECW. A match with Psicosis drew rave reviews, and his star began to rise.

During the 1990s promoters finally began to pay attention to smaller wrestlers, after years of promoting tall, muscular men almost exclusively. They became known as light heavyweights or cruiserweights, but the WWF and WCW were inconsistent in how they pushed them. Fans seemed to enjoy their fast-paced and innovative matches, but inconsistent booking for the most part stalled any momentum they generated.

In 1996, things changed when WCW's Eric Bischoff decided to push his cruiserweights. *Nitro* had expanded to two hours and Bischoff needed more programming. He was well aware of the excitement generated by his smaller wrestlers, and believed they'd be a good way to fill *Nitro's* undercard. Bischoff soon signed a number of top cruiserweight stars from around the world and created a cruiserweight championship for them to compete for.

Rey Misterio was one of the new cruiserweights Bischoff brought in. He changed the spelling of Rey's name to Mysterio, but that would be the extent of the meddling. Mysterio was quickly pushed and soon became not only cruiserweight champion, but one of the division's most popular wrestlers, amazing fans with action-packed matches against stars like Eddie Guerrero, Ultimo Dragon, Psicosis, and Dean Malenko.

Over the next few years, Rey became one of the most popular stars in the entire promotion. He was put into matches with some of the company's top names, including Kevin Nash, and pushed as a "giant killer." Even when Rey lost his mask in a match against Kevin Nash and Scott Hall, he continued to be one of the promotion's bright lights, staying with wcw until its demise.

In 2003, Rey came to the wwf — and the circumstances were actually extremely controversial. It revolved around the fact that Mysterio arrived wearing his mask, despite losing it during his run in wcw. Vince McMahon wanted him to do it, but the act was taboo in the lucha libra community. In their tradition, once a wrestler is unmasked, he can never don it again.

The wwe is famous for being a big man's world. Naturally, Mysterio's fans wondered how far he could climb before hitting a glass ceiling. He accomplished much, winning the cruiserweight championship and the wwe tag team championship, but few imagined he could achieve more.

But Mysterio would astound everyone. In 2006 he was the shocking winner of the *Royal Rumble*, earning in the process an automatic title shot at *WrestleMania 22*. Rey was just the second man to enter the *Rumble* but he outlasted the other twenty-nine entrants (including Triple H, who entered the match first). Before the *Rumble*, Rey had dedicated his performance to his late friend and former wwe champ Eddie Guerrero. Rey's devotion to Guererro's memory would soon put his title shot in jeopardy.

During a match on *SmackDown* Rey was interrupted by Randy Orton. The Legend Killer had been the last man eliminated from the *Rumble*, but he felt the title shot should still be his. Orton challenged Rey to a match at *No Way Out*, baiting Mysterio by attacking Guerrero's legacy. Rey was so irate that he put his title shot on the line. Mysterio went on to lose that match when Orton, of course, cheated, using the ropes for extra leverage in a pin attempt.

But the dream wasn't over. *SmackDown's* Theodore Long had seen it all, and while he could not reverse the referee's decision, he could do something else . . . That night, Long announced that the title contest at *WrestleMania 22* would be a triple threat match, with champion Kurt Angle facing both Randy Orton and Rey Mysterio.

Revenge was sweet; Mysterio went on to win the world title, pinning Randy Orton after landing his finisher, the west coast pop. Mysterio's victory proved again that anything can happen in wwe.

VINCE GOES BOOM

For years, Monday night's *Raw* broadcast became Tuesday afternoon "water cooler talk." But after the death of WCW, some of the zing was gone. Sure, there were exciting moments, but they just didn't seem to stand up against the glory days of the Monday Night War. That all changed on June 11, 2007, when both wrestling fans and the mainstream public were left wondering: What had just happened to the Chairman of WWE?

Spring 2007 had not been good for Vincent Kennedy McMahon. After having his head shaved at *WrestleMania 23*, Vince's troubles mounted when he lost the ECW championship to Bobby Lashley. Was Father Time catching up? Whatever might have been at the root of Vince's recent problems, it was clear he was severely depressed. On the night of June 11, Vince moped around the arena, oblivious to everyone. As *Raw* wound down, a despondent McMahon was shown leaving the arena. He headed for his white stretch limo and stepped inside. Seconds later a powerful explosion ripped the vehicle apart.

What? The WWE's website reported McMahon was "presumed dead." In an instant, the head of the WWE had apparently been eliminated for good — under the most suspicious circumstances. While wrestling fans understood this was just another scripted plot development, they were still captivated by the story. Even people outside wrestling became curious.

Behind the scenes, the limousine explosion had actually been taped the previous night. The production team maintained the illusion of real-time by bringing the fire-ravaged husk to the arena while fans were inside watching *Raw* live. As people left, they saw the devastated shell of the limo — it was as if the events shown on television had just occurred.

RIC FLAIR'S FAREWELL ADDRESS

> *Space Mountain may be the oldest ride in the park,*
> *but it still has the longest line.*
> —**Ric Flair**

In an industry full of illusion and hyperbole, Ric Flair's legacy is one of the few documentable truths. His life story is defined by an all-consuming desire to be the best, and he dominated the wrestling landscape for thirty-five years. In the ring, he was the master of making his opponents look like world-class athletes, regardless of their true skills, and he held the world championship on sixteen different occasions. (It should also be noted that most of his title occurred when the world title was not passed around like a hot potato.)

Wrestling historians will forever debate whether Hulk Hogan or Ric Flair was the sport's biggest star. When it comes to mainstream publicity, few will deny that Hogan, a household name, eclipsed the Nature Boy. But within the industry itself Flair is recognized as simply the best. Never was that more apparent than the night Flair bid farewell to his fans. It was bittersweet episode of *Raw,* and it took many by surprise.

After *WrestleMania 23,* rumors circulated about Ric Flair being inducted into the 2008 Hall of Fame. A storyline had reportedly been presented to Vince McMahon by "Stone Cold" Steve Austin, who lobbied for Flair to have one last great run . . . But as 2007 progressed, things seemed stalled. Flair had been curiously absent from WWE Television (rumor had it he was angry with management for not finding a spot for him at *WrestleMania 23).*

Flair finally made an appearance on November 26, during an episode of *Raw,* vowing he would never retire. As he had done so many times in the past, Flair talked of his undying love of the game. His fans believed he could wrestle forever. Even WWE chairman of the board Vince McMahon seemed to agree.

McMahon appeared and told Flair he could wrestle as long as he wanted — as long as he didn't lose. The next match Flair lost would be his last.

Flair's retirement seemed imminent when he was booked against WWE champion Randy Orton. Flair's former Evolution teammate had built his reputation as the Legend Killer, tarnishing the legacy of other former superstars. Ending Flair's career would be biggest notch in Orton's belt, and as the contest progressed, it looked like Flair's return would be short-lived.

But the Nature Boy wasn't the only superstar to recently return. Chris Jericho had reappeared just a week earlier, after a two-year sabbatical. Jericho was gunning for Orton's championship and he interjected himself into the match with Flair. By distracting the champ he enabled Flair to steal a rollup pinsfall victory. Flair's career was still intact — at least for one more night.

He'd dodged a bullet, fans couldn't help but wonder if he could keep this up. But as 2007 drew to a close, Flair scored victory after victory. After defeating Umaga during *Raw's* fifteenth anniversary broadcast, he was congratulated by a McMahon announcement: he would have to face his best friend, Triple H, on New Year's Eve. And in an effort to make sure Hunter had no intention of throwing the match, McMahon stipulated that a Triple H loss would mean he was barred from participating in the 2008 *Royal Rumble.*

With a new year about to dawn, the fans in the Greensboro Coliseum wondered if Flair's career might not live to see it. When Flair locked Triple H in the figure-four, it looked like he might score a submission win. Hunter refused to give up, however, and he forced a break by reaching the ropes. The tide turned quickly, and Triple H hit the pedigree. Out of nowhere, *Raw* general manager William Regal showed up, brandishing his trademark brass knuckles. Earlier that night, Vince McMahon had insulted Regal, and this caused him to interfere in the match to spite the boss. Regal introduced Triple H's face to the brass knuckles, setting Flair up for another victory. Once again, an outsider had saved Naitch's career.

McMahon's edict seemed to invigorate Flair. Over the next three months, he fought off challenges from some of the WWE's best, including MVP, Ken Kennedy, and even Vince McMahon himself. Things were looking good for the sixteen-time world champion — and they became even better when his good friend Shawn Michaels announced he was indeed to be inducted into the Hall of Fame. Then, it happened: after hearing the news, Flair told Michaels that the only thing that would make *WrestleMania XXIV* better would be for them to wrestle each other at the WWE's biggest show of the year.

While Michaels was honored by the request, he didn't want to be known as the man who ended Ric Flair's storied career. The Nature Boy insisted — and Michaels riminded him there was a reason he was called "Mr. WrestleMania." If Flair faced him at *WrestleMania,* there'd be no quarter given. Flair expected no less and Michaels finally agreed. As the match got closer, things grew tense, especially after Michaels intervened in the match between McMahon and Flair. The next week, Flair blasted Michaels, accusing him of disrespecting him. Michaels apologized, but the fans couldn't help wonder how sincere he was when Michaels compared Flair to Old Yeller. Irate at being compared to a dog that needs to be put out of his misery, Flair slapped Michaels' face.

At *WrestleMania XXIV,* Flair's family watched from ringside as the Nature Boy wrestled his farewell. Both Flair and HBK came close to victory, but in the end, Michaels prevailed. Mr. WrestleMania found it difficult to finish. In a touching moment, Michaels apologized to Flair and said, "I love you," before ending his friend's career with his "Sweet Chin Music" superkick.

The next evening, Flair styled and profiled his way to the *Raw* ring. As "Thank you Flair" chants filled the arena, an emotional Nature Boy thanked the fans — for the memories, the support, and for making him who he was. Finally, Flair bid farewell and began his exit from the ring, but Triple H arrived and told him he couldn't leave — there were many people who wanted to say things to him. What followed next was magical.

Triple H was the first to speak, expressing his love and respect for the legend and thanking him for all he had done for him. Triple H then dropped to one knee and bowed before reuniting Flair with some old friends. . . . Wrestling's original gang returned to the ring as Tully Blanchard, J.J. Dillon, Arn Anderson, and Barry Windham joined the leader of the Four Horsemen. The Horsemen had inspired many supergroups, but only one other included Flair — Evolution. Dave Batista joined the celebration, followed by two of Flair's greatest opponents, Ricky "The Dragon" Steamboat and Greg "The Hammer" Valentine. More

Ric Flair

wrestlers filed in until finally, the entire WWE roster lined up to show their appreciation, chanting, "Thank you Ric," as Naitch bawled.

It was unforgettable, with Flair's peers truly honoring thirty-five years of sustained excellence. Unlike the many wrestling celebrations that have turned sour to further an angle, this one was both real and purely joyful as fans and wrestlers alike acknowledged perhaps the greatest grappler of all time.

PHOTO CREDITS

INTERIOR PHOTOS

Pages X, 1, 71, 81, 82, 137, 154, 158, 159, 201, 221: Globe Photos

Page 34: George Napolitano

Pages 35, 192: Archive Photos

Page 200: Howard Baum

All other photos from the ECW archives.

PHOTO SECTION

All uncredited photos are from the ECW archives.